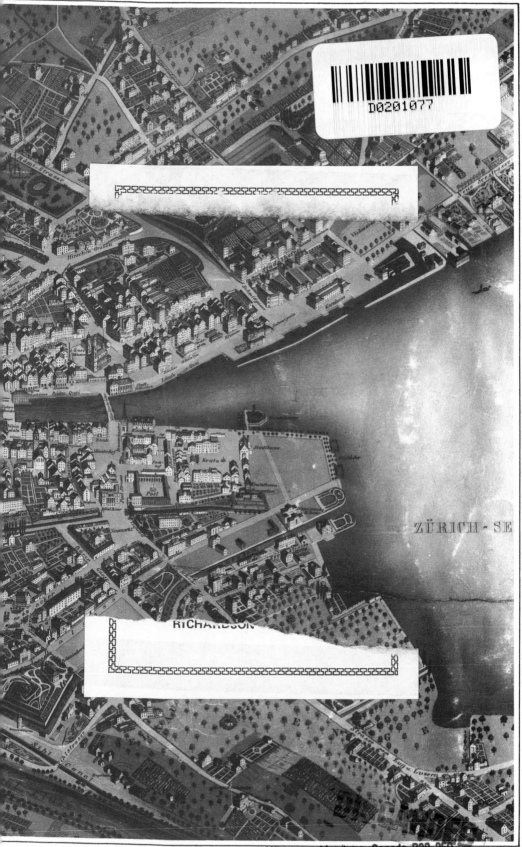

ZÜRICH - SE

RICHARDSON

The TRIUMPH of
LIBERALISM

Zürich 1849

OTHER BOOKS BY GORDON A. CRAIG

The Germans
From Bismarck to Adenauer: Aspects of German Statecraft
The Battle of Königgrätz
The Politics of the Prussian Army, 1640–1945
Europe Since 1815
Germany, 1866–1945
War, Politics and Diplomacy: Selected Essays
The End of Prussia
(with Alexander H. George) *Force and Statecraft:*
Diplomatic Problems of Our Time

The TRIUMPH of LIBERALISM

Zürich in the Golden Age, 1830–1869

◆

GORDON A. CRAIG

CHARLES SCRIBNER'S SONS   New York

Originally published as *Geld und Geist: Zürich im Zeitalter des Liberalismus, 1830–1869*
(c) C. H. Beck'sche Verlagsbuchhandlung (Oscar Beck), Munich 1988

Charles Scribner's Sons
Macmillan Publishing Company
866 Third Avenue, New York, NY 10022
Collier Macmillan Canada, Inc.

Chapter 8 of this work has appeared, under the title "Emma Herwegh," in *The American Scholar*, journal of the United Chapters of Phi Beta Kappa.
   Parts of Chapter 9 have appeared, under the title "A Swiss Passion," in *The New York Review of Books*.
   Parts of the Introduction and Chapter 10 have appeared in the "Magazin" of the *Tages-Anzeiger*, Zürich.
   Portrait of Emma Siegmund Herwegh, page 212, courtesy of Dietz Verlag, Berlin. All other illustrations and endpaper map, *Zürich 1850*, courtesy of Zentralbibliothek, Zürich.

Library of Congress Cataloging-in-Publication Data
Craig, Gordon Alexander, 1913–
   [Geld und Geist. English]
   The triumph of liberalism : Zürich in the golden age, 1830–1869 /
by Gordon A. Craig.
      p.   cm.
   Translation of: Geld und Geist.
   Bibliography: p.
   Includes index.
   ISBN 0-684-19062-1
   1. Zürich (Switzerland : Canton)—Politics and government.
2. Liberalism—Switzerland—Zürich (Canton)—History—19th century.
3. Zürich (Switzerland : Canton)—Social conditions.   I. Title.
JN9582.C7313   1989
320.5'12'094945—dc19   88-13929   CIP

For Felix Gilbert

◆

CONTENTS

◆

INTRODUCTION

◆

In the history of European liberalism in the nineteenth century, the Swiss experience was so important and served as a model for so many other peoples struggling to free themselves from the burdens of the past that it is surprising that it has attracted so little attention from non-Swiss historians. William L. Langer was a distinguished exception to the rule when he described Switzerland as the great testing ground of liberalism in the years before 1848, the country in which it proved itself capable of withstanding the seductions of utopian radicalism on the one hand and the impressive resources of reactionary conservatism on the other. "The victory of the Swiss liberals," he wrote, "had the effect of heartening the liberals everywhere. From Germany more than fifty addresses of congratulations were showered on the federal diet. Some were signed by prominent liberals and radicals, while others stemmed from . . . artisans, workers, even peasants. . . . People everywhere sensed that events in little Switzerland reflected larger European problems and that the victory of liberalism and nationalism in Switzerland presaged major changes in European life."

In the events that aroused this wonder and admiration, a leading role was played by the city and canton of Zürich. If the impulses that led, after some false starts, to the so-called Regeneration of the years after 1830 did not originate in the city on the Limmat, it was there that the movement for progressive change was strongest, most impressive in result, and, under persistent attack from the right, most resilient. Moreover, in the great crisis of federal affairs in 1846–47, Zürich's liberal leaders were the ones who saw most clearly that the consolidation of the reforms made since 1830 could only be assured by the solution of the national question and who forced the issue, as Huldrych Zwingli had done in 1531, although with more moderate aims than he and, because of that, with happier results. After the victory over the Sonderbund in 1847, Zürich's *Bürgermeister* Jonas Furrer was the architect of the new federal state, and its constitution was the result of his wise insistence upon a balance between the authority of the federal government and the autonomy of the individual cantons.

In the years that followed Zürich not only played a prominent role in federal affairs, strongly influencing the new Bund's foreign policy and its stance on such issues as neutrality and right of asylum but, in its own cantonal governance, gave Switzerland and its neighbors an impressive demonstration of liberalism in action, expressed in a program of ebullient economic growth, enlightened educational and social reform, and humanitarian sensitivity to the problems of people whom the turmoil of the mid-century had driven from their own countries. Thanks in part to this last aspect of Zürich's liberalism, the city enjoyed a cultural renaissance in the 1850s that was perhaps richer and more diverse than the one that took place during the eighteenth-century Enlightenment.

Writing about his city in the twentieth century, Adolf Muschg has commented ruefully upon its tendency toward materialism and stodgy solidity and its lack of excitement and has said that what most people perceive as characteristically Zürichean is the combination of "theology, financial expertise, civic propriety, and gray discretion." Whether that is true or not need not concern us here, although it might be suggested that a visitor to Zürich in the years from 1848 to 1867 would have received a radically different impression. These were years in which the liberal belief in progress through freedom was still unscarred by the disappointments of a later time, years in which anything and everything seemed possible, and in which Zürich under liberal leaders seemed to have cast off the constraints of its provincial past and to be developing, for the first time, a truly international character, so that Gottfried Keller, returning from a long absence in 1855, shook his head in consternation and wrote to his friend Ludmilla Assing, "It's frightful how the streets of Zürich pullulate with scholars and littérateurs, and one hears almost more High German, French, and Italian spoken than our old *Schwyzerdeutsch*, which earlier was not the case." Even the old native festivals were acquiring an international look. "Two weeks ago in Zürich," Keller wrote, "we had a big spring festival in the Old Town, in which all the nations in the world, wild and tame, with Lola Montez, the Tsar of Russia, Soulonque [the emperor of Haiti], New Zealanders, Greenlanders, Bedouins, Bashibazouks, in short, whatever you can think of, paraded through the streets in the richest and most delicately decorated costumes, on horseback, in carriages, and on foot."

In this society the materialism that was at the base of the liberal philosophy proved to be perfectly compatible with a high degree of cultural vitality and diversity. In it, indeed, there was a remarkable, because not later repeated, collaboration of *Geld* and *Geist* in which such diverse personalities as Alfred Escher and Jonas Furrer, Richard Wagner and Gottfried Semper, Friedrich Theodor Vischer and Georg Herwegh, Francesco De Sanctis and Gottfried Keller were, for a short time, partners in a common enterprise. This is the principal theme of this book, although it will be necessary, before it can be addressed, to say something about Zürich's early history and about its condition on the eve of the liberal era.

Charles the Great on the Münster Tower

Among the most beautiful of all the Swiss cities are those that lie both on a lake and on a river, in such a way that, like a broad gate at the lake's end, they receive the stream immediately, which then flows through them into the countryside beyond. It is impossible to imagine anything more pleasant than a voyage on one of those lakes, for example, on that of Zürich. One boards ship at Rapperswyl ... travels past the island where Hutten is buried, between the shores of the elongated lake, where the roofs of richly shimmering villages entwine themselves in a connected chain, until, after the country houses of Zürich merchants have become ever more numerous, at last the city itself rises like a dream from the blue water, and one finds that, without having noticed it, one has passed with increased speed under the bridges and on to the green Limmat.... From the scenes that flow by with the speed of arrows, two pictures of the past impress themselves most clearly on the mind: on the right, from the Münster tower, the great stone sculpture of the seated Charles the Great, a golden crown on his head, a golden sword on his knees, gazes over the stream and the lake; on the left, there rises on a steep hill, tower-high over the river, an ancient linden grove, like a floating garden ... green to the heavens.... The stream flows full and swift and, if one without thinking looks back for a moment, one sees in the south the broad, snow-pure Alpen range like a garland of lilies on a green rug.
—*Gottfried Keller,* Green Henry
(first version, Chapter 1)

Chapter 1

ZÜRICH AND THE ZÜRCHERS IN THEIR HISTORY

◆

Und, wie nach Emmäus, weiter ging's
Mit Sturm- und Feuerschritten:
Prophete rechts, Prophete links,
Das Weltkind in der Mitten.
—GOETHE (1803)

Huldrych Zwingli (by Heinrich Nather)

Because Zürich is small, compared with other major European cities, its public memorials are apt to be close to each other, a circumstance that sometimes has curious effects. From the Münsterhof on the right bank of the Limmat, which is dominated by the equestrian statue of the fifteenth-century *Bürgermeister* Hans Waldmann, a fascinating combination of soldier, statesman, speculator, and voluptuary, it is only a few steps across the bridge to the ancient Wasserkirche, where one will find Heinrich Nather's statue of the father of the Swiss Reformation, Huldrych Zwingli. Alternatively, if one remains on the right bank, one can walk from the shadow of Waldmann's *condottiere*-like figure in a northwesterly direction across the Münsterhof to the Storchengasse and then up the steep and narrow Schlüsselgasse, and in a few minutes one will be in the courtyard of the parish church of St. Peter. Here there is another kind of monument, the grave of Johann Caspar Lavater, in the eighteenth century Zürich's most eloquent preacher and, because of European interest in his work on physiognomy and human character, its most famous citizen.

If this juxtaposition of oddly assorted figures recalls the jesting verses of Goethe that are set at the head of this chapter, which refer to the poet's journey on the Lahn in 1794 with Lavater and Basedow, it should also remind us that Zürich's history was not infrequently characterized by such dissonant combinations of worldliness and spirituality. Some reflection on the lives and times of Waldmann, Zwingli, and Lavater will make this evident enough, while at the same time telling us something about the legacy of the past to Zürich and its people at the beginning of the modern period.

I

The career of Hans Waldmann can best be understood if seen in the context of the political demoralization and disunity that were the principal results of the almost continuous warfare that

3

involved the Swiss cantons from the middle of the fifteenth century until the brutal battles of Pavia and Marignano in 1510–15. The successful war of independence that the Forest Cantons (Uri, Schwyz, and Unterwalden) and their confederates Luzern, Zürich, Zug, Bern, and Solothurn had waged against the Habsburgs in the fourteenth century, far from laying the basis for national unity, merely encouraged separate cantons to seek special advantages at the expense of their allies, and the resultant territorial disputes soon led to open fighting, which gave foreign powers renewed incentive to intervene in Swiss affairs. The tendency was enhanced by the fact that the Swiss foot soldiers who defeated the Austrians at Morgarten and Sempach had revealed a new kind of warfare and demonstrated that disciplined pike-bearing infantry, standing and advancing in articulated columns (Gewalthaufen), were superior to the feudal array of mounted knights. As Hans Delbrück once pointed out, European rulers were suddenly confronted with the realization that a radical reordering of their armed forces was necessary. In the process Swiss mercenaries were eagerly sought after, and adventurous young men, especially from cantons where overpopulation and lack of economic development made their futures uncertain, responded just as eagerly to the call, going abroad in search of glory and booty—Reislaufen, as it was called—wherever there was fighting to be done. Thus we find Ariosto writing of

> Switzers [whom] hunger drives [on] to invade,
> Like famished animals, the Lombard plain,
> To beg among us for a crust of bread,
> Or end their poverty in battle slain.

At the same time cantonal officials and private entrepreneurs discovered the profits to be made from the raising of companies of Landsknechten, for foreign service or from making contracts with foreign governments for the regular supply of levies of their own subjects. This so-called Pensionenwesen became an established feature of the Swiss economy as foreign demand increased, particularly after the French King Louis XI used Swiss auxiliaries to break the power of Charles the Bold of Burgundy at Murten and Nancy in 1476 and 1477.

For all of Switzerland the moral and economic consequences of these developments were horrendous. Violence became the

Swiss way of life. Ernst Gagliardi has written that, by the middle of the fifteenth century, in addition to being involved through its mercenaries in a wide range of foreign quarrels, the Swiss Eidgenossenschaft had become a menace to all of its immediate neighbors, spontaneously organized bands of freebooters using any pretext or fancied slight to launch bloody forays across its borders. The prospect of plunder destroyed the incentive to work; the never-ending alarums and excursions stifled industrial development, interrupted trade, and ruined agriculture. In once-thriving towns extravagance and poverty lived cheek by jowl, and sensuality, disease, and crime were their companions. In some urban centers public order broke down completely, and there was no safety in the streets at night. Finally, there was growing tension between rural areas, where *Reisläufertum* flourished, and the towns, where there was a tendency to seek to control and limit it for reasons of local security or to organize it more efficiently for corporate profit.

In this sorry state of affairs Zürich was one of the notable casualties. As early as the ninth century the town on the Limmat—once the Roman strongpoint Turicum and then a settlement of Alemannic tribes until conquered by the Franks in the eighth century—had been an important and growing center, with a royal residence, two wealthy religious foundations (the Fraumünsterabtei and the Grossmünsterstift), one of the few Carolingian mints, and a thriving market. Under the German kings and the Zähringer dukes, it developed in the eleventh and twelfth centuries into the most important market town in central and eastern Switzerland, with trade links to northern Italy, the Rhine valley, and the Netherlands. In the thirteenth century, when its fortifications were completed, enclosing an area of forty hectares, Zürich's coinage and weights and measures regulated economic activity between the upper Rhine and the Alps and between Thurgau and the upper Aargau; it had become a flourishing textile center, exporting woolens and linens, and in the latter part of the century was importing raw silk from Italy and sending finished goods to markets in Poland and Hungary and perhaps to the fairs of Champagne. The increase in the number of Jewish residents testified to its increasing importance as an exchange. (There are no accurate statistics to help us here, but between 1378 and 1398 thirty Jewish families attained citizenship, and the Froschauergasse, where most Jewish residents lived, had long been popularly known as the Judengasse. A sign of their vital role in the economy was the Great Council's decision in 1345 to take them under its special care, protecting them against provocation and violence.) At the beginning of the fourteenth century Zürich was also assuming a not insignificant cultural importance, the patrician Rüdiger Manesse and his son acting as patrons and protectors of poets like Johannes Hadlaub and establishing an important archive of manuscripts of the courtly literature of the Hohenstaufen period, the so-called *Minnelieder*.

All of this promising growth, supplemented in the fourteenth century by a systematic policy of territorial growth by purchase in the lake area and the contiguous highlands, was checked by the internal disorders that resulted from the constitutional revolution effected by *Bürgermeister* Rudolf Brun at the end of that century—to which we shall have occasion to return—and destroyed by the long struggle with the Habsburgs and the falling out of the allies in its aftermath. In particular the Old Zürich War of 1442, caused by the city council's injudicious attempt to increase its territory and authority within the Eidgenossenschaft, had ruinous and protracted consequences. Zürich was isolated and besieged by the confederates; its garrison in Burg in Greifensee was ruthlessly slaughtered, and its other outlying possessions plundered and pillaged and left in a state of shock and rebellion. Saved from utter destruction only by French intervention, Zürich was slow to regain its reputation within the Eidgenossenschaft, and its economic recovery was even more belated. By 1470 its population, which had stood at 7,000 in the middle of the fourteenth century, had declined to less than 5,000; nearly 9 percent of its buildings were unoccupied, and one-fifth of its male population had been lost in the wars. The silk industry was long gone; the once strong linen and woolen guilds had been forced to merge, and the furriers and goldsmiths were in deep trouble. The glories of the medieval city had disappeared; Zürich was a small town again, with few public buildings, with swine roaming its largely unpaved streets and dung heaps contributing to its generally insalubrious atmosphere, with most of its citizens enduring the most meager of living conditions, and with a high rate of disease and a staggering infant mortality.

It was in the troubled years that followed the Old Zürich

War that Hans Waldmann made his way. From the beginning it was a violent one, for even as a youth he gave evidence of an unbridled temperament and a cold disregard for the rights and interests of others and was given to vandalism, brawling, whoring, incitation to riot, and violent attacks, sometimes with weapons, upon anyone who crossed him. Apprenticed first to a tailor and then to a tanner, he soon succumbed to the lure of foreign adventure and in 1458 took part in an ugly little attack upon Konstanz and was one of 350 mercenaries hired by a certain Jörg Beck in a private vendetta against the Abbot of Kempten, and two years later he played a prominent role in the Eidgenossenschaft's campaign in the Thurgau. In the pauses between these and other affrays, he rather surprisingly applied himself to his trade, and an uncommon financial shrewdness and his marriage in 1462 to a well-to-do widow facilitated his rise from the position of artisan to membership in the propertied middle class. The nature of his private life, however, which continued to be marked by breaches of the peace, summonses, court hearings, and fines, placed obstacles in the way of the career in city politics that would normally have followed from his economic position. His election as master of the tanners' guild was vetoed by the College of Guild Masters in 1466, and it was not for another seven years, and apparently in another guild, that he made good his claim as master and became a member of the city council.

By this time the negotiations of the Bernese *Schultheiß* Nicholas Diesbach with Louis XI and the judicious distribution of French subventions to the other cantons had maneuvered the Eidgenossenschaft into war with Charles the Bold of Burgundy, and Waldmann's great hour had come upon him. Whatever his fellow Zürchers might think of his behavior in quiet times, they respected his martial talents. In the Waldhuter War of 1468 he had served as captain of the Zürich pikemen, and when the new fighting began this commission was reaffirmed. Greater responsibility awaited him when the Burgundian War reached its critical stage in the spring of 1476 and Charles the Bold's regrouped forces were poised at Lausanne for an offensive plunge into the Bernese heartland. The Swiss diet hastened to send strong garrisons to Murten and Freiburg, which dominated the main routes, and Waldmann was placed in command at the latter strongpoint. At the beginning of June, when the Burgundians, contrary to general expectation,

chose Murten as their target and invested the town, Waldmann concentrated his forces in the vicinity of Bern, calmly
waited until a hastily mustered Zürich contingent joined him,
and then marched at the head of 2,500 men, by night and
through blinding rain, to Murten, arriving in time for the crucial
battle.

His precise role in the victory that followed, the greatest in
Switzerland's history, has never been clearly established. That
he was knighted on the eve of battle and given supreme command over all the Swiss *Gewalthaufen* is probably untrue. But
this became part of his legend, and hundreds of years later it was
repeated in the *Schweizerliedern* of Johann Caspar Lavater, who
gave Waldmann pride of place in his ballad of Murten, with the
perhaps not very felicitous lines:

> *Voll warmer Treu, voll Vaterland,*
>   *An Rath und Mut der Größt',*
> *Im Rauche, wie in Wolken stand,*
> *Gleich Felsen, Waldmann fest.*

> *Full of warm loyalty and patriotism,*
>   *Supreme in counsel and courage,*
> *Amid the clouds of battle smoke*
> *Waldmann stood firm as the rock.*

The fame that Waldmann won in the Burgundian War,
which was enhanced by his leadership of the Zürich contingent
in the Duke of Lorraine's mercenary army at Nancy, where
Charles the Bold fell amid the rout of his forces in December
1476, gave him an international reputation and a claim to the
highest political authority in his own city. His military exploits
had gone a long way toward rehabilitating Zürich's standing in
the Eidgenossenschaft, and in the years after the war he frequently acted as his canton's voice in negotiation with the confederates and with foreign princes. These activities seem,
however, to have been guided by no statesmanlike vision but to
have been motivated largely by the desire for pecuniary rewards
and pensions for services given or promised, and at times they
betrayed the worse characteristics of his private life, a tendency
to ruthlessness and unconditional violence that on one occasion,
in a badly managed dispute between Zürich and Straßburg,

threatened to embroil the whole Eidgenossenschaft in needless conflict.

Nor were his activities at home any more edifying. There were no effective barriers now to his political ambitions, and he advanced quickly, with the support of the guilds, to a position of considerable influence in the Great Council and, finally, in 1485, to the office of *Bürgermeister*. Here again he showed no truly creative gifts. Zürich, to be sure, showed signs during the 1480s of reviving economic growth: Kiburg, Winterthur, and Stammheim were added to its possessions, trade and handicrafts began to recover, and a new civic pride was manifest in the renovation of the Wasserkirche and the completion of the two towers of the Großmünster, which still dominate the city and serve as its symbol, in the building of new guild houses and ornate private residences, and in their decoration by a generation of gifted artists like the glass and portrait painter Lukas Zeiner. Waldmann had little to do with these things. In the early 1480s his energies seem to have been directed chiefly to undermining the position of his principal opponent, the *Bürgermeister* Hermann Göldli; once he had succeeded him, he was intent on making himself invulnerable to similar attack.

This he did by subverting the work of his predecessor Rudolf Brun. In the middle of the fourteenth century, Brun had unseated Zürich's old patriciate and created a new constitution in which there was a balance of power between the artisans' guilds and a body called the Constaffel (which represented those families capable of providing the state with mounted military service: nobility, great merchants, landed proprietors, bankers, and goldsmiths), in which government was exercised through a greater and a lesser council. Waldmann now sought to destroy the influence of the Constaffel and to diminish the authority of the councils by placing all effective power in the hands of the College of Guild Masters, which had become his instrument. This centralization of government, for that is what it amounted to, led, however, to nothing of permanent value, for Waldmann used it mainly to make military contracts with foreign powers and to manipulate the *Pensionenwesen* in ways that added to his already considerable wealth. Much of this he threw away in a life of conspicuous consumption and blatant sensuality that offended the taste of his fellow citizens.

There is little doubt that the growing criticism of Waldmann's immorality strongly influenced the chain of events that led to his fall, but two other factors were probably more crucial. In the first place his willingness to serve foreign princes for personal profit even when this conflicted with the interests of other Eidgenossen eroded the respect that he had enjoyed in the federation. Nothing contributed more to this than his maneuvers in the dispute between Wallis and the Bishop of Sitten on the one hand and the Duke of Milan on the other over territorial boundaries and legal rights in the valley of the Divedre and the Esch. Waldmann became an ardent and persuasive advocate for the Milanese cause, and under his influence a court of mediation meeting in Zürich decided in the Duke's favor. The impartiality of the judgment was thrown into doubt when it became known that Waldmann had demanded from Milan a payment of 3,000 ducats for himself and lesser amounts for the members of the court and the Zürich city clerk, and that he had then asked for an additional 3,000 ducats because his expenses and the necessary bribes amounted to more than he had expected.

Wallis, not surprisingly, refused to accept this judgment and in April 1487, supported by auxiliaries from Luzern and Unterwalden, sent an army over the Simplon into Milanese territory, where it sacked and pillaged the area around Domo d'Ossola. When part of this force became too intent upon booty to observe proper security, it was surprised and cut off by the Milanese at Crevola, with a loss of 300 Luzerner and about 800 Walliser, who were literally butchered, parts of their bodies being subsequently sold in public markets. The news caused an explosion of outrage in the Eidgenossenschaft, largely directed against Waldmann, who found himself accused of having incited the Milanese atrocities and now feared to leave the confines of his own canton, even for the periodic meetings of the Eidgenossenschaft's diet (Tagsatzung) when they were not held in Zürich.

Waldmann's reputation did not improve when it became known that he was playing an active part in the negotiations between the Habsburgs and the Eidgenossen for a guarantee of Archduke Maximilian's claims in Lower Austria and the Tirol after he succeeded to the imperial throne. As usual this was a simple matter of business to the Zürich Bürgermeister, but many perceived it to be an indication that he was working for an Austrian alliance, and this was deeply offensive to rural Switzerland, where hatred of the Habsburgs was handed on from generation to generation. This increased Waldmann's growing difficulties with Zürich's own rural dependencies.

Until well into the nineteenth century, as we shall see, the relationship between the city and the countryside was a troubled one. Zürich's role in the Eidgenossenschaft and in European affairs in general was to a large extent dependent upon the population and economic and military resources of the *Untertanengebiete*, but this did not make the city fathers conciliatory in dealing with the grievances of these areas, which were administered by governors (*Vögte*) appointed by the Great Council and had no share in decisions on matters of common interest. In some of them the feudal dues that had bound their inhabitants during the medieval period had been bought up by city merchants or guilds and were still enforced and had, in some cases, become more onerous; on all of them, the city—more for political and economic reasons than for moral ones—imposed elaborate police regulations that forbade gaming, dancing, excessive expenditure on dress and entertainment, the planting of new trees or vineyards without authorization, the pursuit of certain trades, service in foreign armies, and other activities. In general these rules were intended to bind the rural population to the soil and to make it a reliable market for city products and a dependable supplier of foodstuffs and, when needed, soldiers.

The villagers and farmers chafed under these restrictions, and Hans Waldmann's preeminence in Zürich and the rumors of the extravagance and debauchery of his life focused their resentment upon his person. Thus, in November 1488, when the Great Council issued a new *Sittenmandat*, placing limits on expenditure for baptismal and wedding feasts and renewing and sharpening existing decrees respecting luxury in dress, and when an order followed for the killing of dogs, in order to protect game for the upper classes, there was a spontaneous revolt that began in the communities around Zürich Lake with a series of feasts that openly violated the new regulations and ended with a siege of the city by the outraged countryside.

In this crisis all of the latent opposition to Waldmann inside the city—in the Constaffel, the councils, the clergy, and some of the guilds—came out into the open, and the country's greatest military hero was sacrificed in the interest of pacification. Arrested and imprisoned in the Wellenberg, the water-girt prison in the Limmat, not far from the place where his monument now stands, he suffered extensive torture, which he withstood manfully, without making any confession of guilt, before going to his death by the ax in April 1489 outside the city walls, bearing himself bravely, forgiving the executioner and the throngs who had come to see him die, and commending his soul to God.

II

If the life of Switzerland's nearest equivalent to a Renaissance despot was a reflection of the political disarray and the decline of public morals of his age, that condition was little relieved by his passing. The evils of the mercenary system continued to poison Swiss politics for another generation, and it took the enormous bloodletting of Marignano in 1518, when 10,000 Swiss mercenaries in the service of the papal curia were left dead on the field, to cause a public revulsion. It was the Swiss Reformation, coming on the heels of that tragedy, that effected a real change, and this became clear first and foremost in Zürich, where Huldrych Zwingli preached the cause of national regeneration.

Although he was not a native of Zürich, Zwingli is regarded by common consent as the greatest figure in its history, and we must try to understand why this is so. It does not help to compare him with the other great reformers, for on the whole his gifts were less than theirs. He lacked Calvin's logical mind and the powers of sustained systematic exposition that found expression in *The Institutes of the Christian Religion*, and he possessed neither Luther's almost electrical force of personality nor his creative use of the German language. Compared with the Wittenberger's translation of the Twenty-third Psalm, which has brought incalculable comfort and reassurance to people over the centuries, or his numerous and unforgettable contributions to the common speech (*Nächstenliebe, Sündenbock, Lückenbüßer, Machtwort, Fleischtöpfe Ägyptiens, himmelhoch jauchzend, angst und bange machen, Wolf im Schafspelz*), Zwingli's translations were wooden and his powers of invention meager.

On the other hand, he had none of Calvin's vanity, and he always showed more social conscience than Luther. Despite his undoubted learning, he remained closer to the common people than either of his fellow reformers. It is this above all that explains the uniqueness and power of his presence in Zürich's history. As the British historian G. R. Potter has written, "In his republicanism, in his belief in government by discussion in which the ignorant and illiterate would accept the leadership of the educated, all working toward the establishment of God's kingdom on earth, he was Swiss to the core." His deep love of his native land persuaded him that it was in this vineyard that God's work was to be done, and his unwavering conviction that God had chosen to speak through him gave him an inner strength that was so palpable that it induced his fellow citizens to place their confidence in him.

By instinct Zwingli was a man of action, but he was also a realist who knew that, in order to achieve the changes that his heart told him were necessary, he must work within the framework of local authority and the established political tradition of the community. In this respect it is worth noting the degree to which his circumstances were determined by the fate of his great secular predecessor, which had a permanent effect upon Zürich's attitude toward charismatic politics and whose legacy was a strong aversion to putting too much power in the hands of individuals. After Waldmann's execution Zürich returned to the constitution that he had tried to undermine, one in which government was exercised by councils that derived their authority from the guilds and the Constaffel, which meant, in effect, from the totality of the city's *Bürger*. There never was any question of Zwingli's superseding that arrangement, even if he had wanted to do so, and his tactics, as he pursued his mission, were shaped by his recognition of that fact.

With respect to the ending of the evils of military contracts and *Reisläufertum*, there was a pretty general correspondence of view between the city government and the reformer. At the meeting of the federal diet in 1508, Zürich's representatives had called for an agreement to forbid mercenary service by individuals and the negotiation of contracts for such service in any part of the Eidgenossenschaft. This proposal had failed of acceptance, but sentiment for such prohibition grew steadily in Zürich and its dependencies, particularly after the battle of Novara in 1513, where there were heavy losses among the Zürich contingent. Zwingli's experience as a field chaplain at Novara and Marignano clearly influenced his own feelings about the issue: after his return to his pastorate at Glarus, he underlined in his copy of Erasmus's sayings the words *Dulce bellum inexpertis* (War is sweet only to those who do not know it). But his position had moral and Christian roots as well, and by the time he had become parish priest at Zürich's Großmünster in 1518 he had come to the conclusion that the institutions that encouraged mercenary warfare must be destroyed. Hence his violent attacks upon military contractors, whom he likened to "the butchers who drive the cattle to Konstanz. They drive the beasts there and take the money for it and come back home again without them," and upon the cardinals who recruited for papal armies, from whose red caps and mantles, he said, "ducats and crowns fall out" when one shook them, and "if one twists them, then your son's blood, or your brother's, your father's, your friend's drips out." Zwingli probably had little direct influence upon the Great Council's decision in 1521 to stop supplying the French crown with troops, but his sermons on this and related subjects, by advancing the break with the Papacy, certainly helped make the ban on military contracts general and laid the basis for Zürich's modern policy of neutrality in foreign quarrels.

With respect to the reform of the church, there was a similar identity of view between Zwingli and the secular authorities. For some time the Great Council had, without challenging the spiritual authority of Pope and bishop, been concerning themselves with the administration of church properties and the competence and morals of the clergy and had gradually been taking over control of monasteries, prebends, and church courts and assuming the right to appoint the preachers in churches like the Großmünster. Zwingli not only welcomed this as a means of freeing the clergy from worldly concerns and enabling them to concentrate upon their religious functions but wished to have the council assume ultimate authority for changes in church dogma and ritual as well. Influenced by his belief that Zürich's corporate system of government resembled the polity of the early church, his goal was the creation of a Christian commonwealth in which there was no clear distinction between church and state but, in the words of Lewis W. Spitz, "both . . . under God, each in its own sphere, served Christian ends and the good of all members of the religiopolitical community." The first step toward this was to persuade the Great Council to accept his basic principle, which he derived from Erasmus, that the key to understanding God's will was to be found not in the traditions and authority of the Roman Church but in the Bible.

The council's mandate in the fall of 1520, instructing the canton's clergy to confine their preaching henceforth to the Scripture, was in some ways Zwingli's greatest achievement, for the rest of the Swiss Reformation followed from it: the purification of doctrine and cult, the abolition of the mass and the redefinition of the Sacraments, the expulsion of imagery from the church, the dissolution of religious orders, the ending of compulsory celibacy of the clergy, and all of the other changes that amounted to a total break with Rome. In all cases the changes were laid before assemblies in which the points at issue were debated by churchmen of different persuasions, and in which Zwingli's deep learning and piety overcame doctrinal opposition and won the hearts of his auditors; in all cases Zwingli deferred to the council's authority not only to make the final decisions but to determine the degree and timing of the changes made. This inevitably aroused the anger and, in the end, the violent opposition of more radical reformers, and in 1524 and 1525, Zürich was torn by the challenge of Anabaptism and the persecution and exile of those who professed it.

Meanwhile, the institutionalization of the Reformation went on apace. The council completed its absorption of the property and the external affairs of the church, encouraged the cloisters and foundations to close their doors (the Fraumünsterstift handed all of its property over to the city on 24 October 1524), dissolved the order of begging monks, and established the principle of public responsibility for feeding the poor and taking care of their medical needs. Of special importance as a contribution to Zürich's cultural rebirth was the transformation of the Großmünsterstift into a center of education, with special responsibility for improving Latin instruction in the schools, for training clergymen in biblical exegesis, and for providing instruction in Hebrew and Greek. Finally, the old Marriage Court, which had been under the jurisdiction of the Bishop of Konstanz, was turned into an agency that was charged with seeing that the spirit of the Reformation penetrated every aspect of cantonal life, an idea that soon commended itself to other Protestant communities and was imitated in Basel, Southern Germany, Straßburg, and Geneva. In practice the regulations of the *Ehegericht* did not differ substantially from the *Sittenmandate* of Hans Waldmann's time, although they were less arbitrary in application. Even so, they led inevitably to a high degree of interference in private life and an inordinate preoccupation with violent language, taking the Lord's name in vain, lechery, gambling, and other things that were offensive to the godly.

In all of these matters, and particularly in the elaboration of social policy and the transformation of the Großmünsterstift into Zürich's first theological seminary, Zwingli was the moving spirit, working in such close harmony with the *Bürgermeister* and leading members of the council that the citizen in him often seemed to take precedence over the preacher of the Word. In economic matters also his advice was sought, particularly after the unrest caused by the Peasants War in Germany in 1525 led to the refusal of some of Zürich's rural communities to pay tithes and to a general demand for such things as the abolition of the last vestiges of serfdom and the recognition of the right of congregations to elect their own preachers. Despite his frequent fulminations against great lords who enriched themselves by means of tithes, Zwingli believed that the Scriptures provided no justification for refusal to respect legal contracts, and he argued that, in any case, justice would be denied by the disruption caused by sudden changes in the existing, highly complicated web of obligations.

The council followed his advice by making only minor modification in existing tithes. It also abolished all forms of serfdom, another of his recommendations, but flatly refused to permit any change in the procedure followed in choosing clergymen, and it showed its utter opposition to local hopes of autonomy by a stern reference to the obligation of obedience to authority laid down in the thirteenth chapter of Paul's Epistle to the Romans. All things considered, Zwingli's Reformation effected no change in the economic and political relationship of town and country, and its principal social result was a widening of the Great Council's authority in areas of individual life formerly reserved to the church and less rigorously administered.

The influence of Zwingli's ideas spread rapidly in Switzerland, particularly in the cities. St. Gall, Glarus, Appenzell, the whole of the Thurgau joined the Reformation; so did Basel, the home of Zwingli's friend Oecolampadius, another of the great prophets of this age, and so did the powerful city of Bern, after the pressure of public opinion had overcome the political doubts of its leaders, and Schaffhausen and Mulhausen and Biel. But the

Forest Cantons and their allies Zug, Luzern, and Fribourg stood by the old faith. In his powerful short novel *Ursula*, which deals with these years, Gottfried Keller describes these cantons as "unchangeable, cunning, resolute, like an island in the middle of the tide ... relying upon well-tried and long-established strength, and egged on by the powers of the past that rule the world outside," hardly an objective judgment, although it was true enough that the Catholic cantons were counting on external aid to enable them to check the onward march of the Reformation.

As relations between the two confessional groupings deteriorated and open conflict began to seem unavoidable, the Reformation camp showed none of the solidarity of its antagonists, serious political and tactical cleavages appeared, and at the crucial moment, when Zwingli persuaded the council to force the issue, his strongest ally, Bern, deserted him, leaving him to meet the offensive of the Catholic cantons with an ill-equipped and outnumbered army. At Kappel, on 11 October 1531, the Zürchers were overwhelmed, and Zwingli died as a common soldier in the ranks, his body being quartered and burned after the battle as a heretic's. His long-harbored dream of uniting and renewing the whole of the Eidgenossenschaft died with him, and the confessional division of Switzerland remained the principal barrier to effective political union for the next three centuries.

III

Peter Stadler has written that what might be called the Zürich temperament or character grew out of the great crises of the fourteenth, fifteenth, and sixteenth centuries, the decision in 1351 to join the Eidgenossenschaft, with all the dangers and risks that that involved, the shattering setback in the Old Zürich War, and the even greater one at Kappel in 1531. The two defeats at the hands of the Eidgenossen did not in any serious way weaken Zürich's Swiss identity; three hundred years of experience had impressed upon the consciousness of all cantons the knowledge that they were nothing if they tried to stand alone. But the effect of the Kappel War and the memory of the disaster of 1442 were enough to induce a new political sobriety that became the hallmark of the Zürich style, a modesty in objectives, a willingness to focus on the near and the immediate and to foreswear distant goals and large ambitions.

After Zwingli's death the leadership of the Reformation passed from Zürich to Bern and eventually to Calvin's Geneva. This was accepted philosophically enough in the city on the Limmat, where primacy of internal policy became the order of the day. Other cantons continued to supply soldiers to French armies, and the Catholic ones often made military agreements with Spain and Austria and the Protestant ones with Holland. In contrast, Zürich permitted no recruitment on its soil, and its strict neutrality reflected a determination to concentrate upon its own affairs that in time gave it—in contrast with Bern or Geneva—a decidedly provincial air.

This was reinforced by the way of life professed by most of its citizens, which was bereft of color, ornament, style, or gaiety. Throughout the balance of the sixteenth century and all of the seventeenth, the government, with the strong support of the church, continued to issue directives concerning proper and improper behavior, motivated not only by concern for their fellow citizens' morals but also by a laudable desire to avoid the social consequences of extravagance and irresponsible husbandry; the *Sittenmandate* were, in this sense, the reverse side of the government's assumption of responsibility for the poor. Partly because of this pressure from above, but perhaps also because of their Alemannic heredity and a post-Zwinglian tendency toward puritanism, Zürchers were not only opposed to flamboyance of dress or behavior but even suspicious of what other people regarded as merely a mild exuberance of manner, and they extended this attitude to the objects around them. Unlike other major European cities, Zürich remained relatively free of imposing public buildings, and this was considered to be entirely appropriate, so that as late as August 1859, in an article on the city's appearance, a local newspaper (J. B. Spyri's *Eidgenössische Zeitung*) could write:

> One cannot demand of a republican community that it establish works of art that would be possible in different political and social circumstances, and it is a fortune beyond price for Zürich that in its community the building of unfruitful ornaments at the expense of the useful and the nec-

essary is impossible. We want no statues like those that decorate not only princely residences but also our sister cities of Bern and Geneva; we desire no heaven-thrusting fountains but are content with the little springs that play behind the fences in the Thalacker.

Even Zürich's churches were modest affairs, the Fraumünster and St. Peter's no larger than one would expect in a village square. The Großmünster, which Adolf Muschg has called "a monument in the diminutive," appears to have struck some Zürchers as excessive in its New Gothic style and, in the 1760s, narrowly escaped demolition. All of this explains why the baroque age left Zürich largely untouched, and its greatest achievement, the theater, found no reception there. The church was in any case opposed to playacting and was strong enough to ban it from the city even in the age of the Enlightenment.

The puritanical simplicity that marked Zürich life was accompanied by a dedication to work and a deep sense of civic responsibility that served the community well in its straitened circumstances after the Kappel War. Zwingli's work had put a definite end to what had once been a major source of income for the city, the business of supplying the sinews of war to other powers. It required a major effort to repair the deficit by expanding agriculture, the handicrafts, and trade, and the process was impeded by recurring visitations of plague in the sixteenth century (Zwingli almost died of it at the very beginning of his Zürich ministry) and in the first part of the seventeenth, with particularly severe outbreaks in 1611, the end of the 1620s, and 1635–36. The revival of trade and the beginnings of industry owed something to the asylum that Zürich gave to Protestant refugees from France and from the other cantons (about 20,000 between 1572 and 1720). Among those who came from Locarno in 1555 were the Muralto, Zanino, and Orelli families, whose services to what today would be called protoindustrial activities (textile spinning and weaving, the making of dyes, the introduction of charcoal burning in foundries) eventually secured them the right of citizenship. Local families who had made their money in small trades, like the miller's sons David and Heinrich Werdmüller, began to invest in new commercial enterprises or revive long defunct ones, like the spinning, weaving, dyeing, and exporting of raw silk, and by the end of the sixteenth century, trade and manufacturing began to experience an unexpected boom that continued through the following century, despite the unsettling effects of the Thirty Years War on prices and the security of trade routes. This was buoyed by a population that increased by 24 percent between 1634 and 1671, leveled off for the remainder of the century, and then increased by 35.7 percent between 1700 and 1762. At the end of the sixteenth century the population of the district of Zürich (that is, the city plus its suburbs and countryside) was less than 9,000; it doubled in the course of the seventeenth century and had reached 26,973 by 1792, less than half of whom lived in the city itself. The population of the connected territories—the districts of Andelfingen, Regensberg, Bülach, Winterthur, Pfäffikon, Hinwil, Uster, Meilen, Horgen, and Knonau—was much larger, 70,000 to 80,000 at the end of the sixteenth century, 95,000 in 1700, 150,000 in 1792.

As Zürich became a city of trade and industry, the number of wealthy families increased sharply, with notable political effects. At the beginning of the sixteenth century the upwardly mobile artisans had pushed the old Junker class aside; a century later their descendants, now the *nouveaux riches*, had checked new pressure from below. In the subsequent period this found its reflection in subtle changes in the city's social stratification—a new division between *Herren* and ordinary *Bürger*, for example—and in its politics, where there was a tendency toward concentration of power in the hands of certain families that was at variance with the democratic principles of the constitution. In the seventeenth and eighteenth centuries the government of the city became increasingly aristocratic, a tendency that an attack by the guilds upon the political influence of the rich merchants in 1713 did nothing to check. At the same time, in its relations with its rural communities and the *Untertanengebiete*, it became increasingly absolutist in style, demanding formal oaths of allegiance from all males, restricting the right of public assembly, governing by decrees that were enforced by local landvogts and bailiffs, and—a practice that can be explained in part by the fright induced in the upper classes by the hapless Swiss Peasants Revolt of 1653—punishing any signs of open hostility with the utmost severity, not stopping short of sentences to death by the rope or the ax.

IV

In the eighteenth century the Enlightenment came to Zürich, and the city of Huldrych Zwingli did not hesitate to open its doors to it. The seriousness, rationality, and materialism characteristic of the movement accorded well with the spirit of the great merchant families, who were now increasing their profits by exploiting the countryside by means of scientific agriculture and the encouragement of cottage industry, notably in textiles, and its emphasis upon critical inquiry and modernity stimulated a burst of literary activity, the founding of any number of historical and philosophical discussion groups, and the beginning of a newspaper press, although one that was held under very tight control. At the same time, since none of Zürich's *Aufklärer* were atheists, and since most of them had little practical interest in politics, there was, at least during the first half of the century, no conflict with church or government. Indeed, the attention that the Swiss Enlightenment received abroad, particularly in Germany, aroused considerable satisfaction. Local patriots began to talk about the Athens on the Limmat (an association not unique to Zürich, since Edinburgh claimed to be the Athens of the North, and it was not long before Berliners were vaunting the attractions of their Athens on the Spree), and Zürich historians are still apt to describe the eighteenth century as their city's cultural apogee.

There was no dearth of outstanding talents who could be named to justify such claims: Johann Jakob Scheuzer, naturalist and mathematician, Hans Caspar Hirzel, agrarian reformer, J. J. Breitinger, author of important works on the theory of poetry, Salomon Gessner, writer of idylls in poetic prose, to mention only a few. In terms of European influence, the most notable was Johann Jakob Bodmer, a parson's son who took up the mercantile profession and traveled widely in Italy before resolving to devote himself to literature. In 1721, in collaboration with Breitinger, he founded, under the name *Discourse der Mahlern*, the first critical literary journal in the German-speaking area of Europe. Sometime city clerk and teacher at the Carolinum, the city's school of theology, and city councillor after 1737, Bodmer wrote extensively in the field of aesthetics and literary theory; he was the founder of the Political-Historical Society at Gerwy (later called the Helvetisch-vaterländische Gesellschaft), which played a major role in the intellectual life of the city, and he had an extensive correspondence with writers in other countries, often encouraging them to come to Zürich and work on projects of common interest.

A sense of Bodmer's activity in this last respect emerges from a letter that he wrote to Friedrich Gottlieb Klopstock in April 1753, shortly after the poet's visit to Zürich. He wrote:

> Wieland [Christoph Martin Wieland, poet and protégé of Bodmer, later a novelist of stature] will stay with me for a long time yet, and I tremble at the thought of his return home. [Bodmer was encouraging him to translate Shakespeare.] Breitinger and Hess [Johann Kaspar Hess, Altstetten pastor and author of a book about Klopstock's *Messias*] are our daily fare. We hope that Breitinger will write a treatise on the sublime. This would do much for the biblical epic. Kynzli [Martin Künzli, director of the city school in Winterthur] and Waser [Johann Heinrich Waser, author of the satire *Letters of Two County Pastors*] have visited us. Wieland has won their hearts completely. Dr. Hirzel [Hans Kaspar Hirzel, later councillor and Chief City Physician in Zürich] and his companions have withdrawn their hearts from me. This was the reason that I saw less of Herr von Kleist [Ewald Christian von Kleist, Prussian soldier and poet], who was lodged with the doctor, than would otherwise have been the case. . . . I must almost fear that Gleim [Johann Wilhelm Ludwig Gleim, Prussian author of anacreontic poems and war songs] has cast me off. Herr von Haller [Albrecht von Haller, Bernese physician and author of the satirical and didactic poem *The Alps*] is here, and we expect Voltaire.

Bodmer and his friends were, of course, a tiny minority in a population that had very little understanding of, or interest in, the things that they took so seriously. This was clear enough to Ewald von Kleist, whose visit to Zürich was cut short when he was expelled for breaking the law that forbade foreign recruiting, and who wrote to Dr. Hirzel, ". . . your fatherland is no country for me. It is a place of coarseness and rage. I become angry every time I think of it and amazed that the fifty good people, who may be somewhere there, can stand it." This was a sentiment to which Bodmer himself was not immune, for especially in his last years, when his reputation was failing, he kept the windows that opened toward the city, in his home in the hills, curtained and was known to refer to the Athens on the Limmat as a *"Dreckstadt."*

At the same time Bodmer and other Zürich *Aufklärer* were perhaps not all that different from their fellow citizens. While they admired genius in the abstract, they were uncomfortable and unhappy when it arrived on their doorsteps. Bodmer was swept off his feet by Klopstock's *Messias*, but when the poet visited him he soon discovered that he was entirely too energetic and worldly for his taste and was not sorry to see him go, and he had the same experience, although it took somewhat longer to become evident, with Wieland. Foreigners, to be sure, could not always be certain of a cordial reception in Zürich regardless of their quality and talent (there had been strong opposition when Zwingli allowed the German humanist Ulrich von Hutten to take refuge on the Ufenau), but, in this case, the treatment of Klopstock and Wieland was no worse than that accorded by their native city to Johann Caspar Lavater and his friends Pestalozzi and Füßli.

Before he died Lavater's European fame far exceeded anything that Bodmer had ever enjoyed, which probably explains the scorn and rancor with which the aging sage followed his exploits. But the difference between them had deeper roots. Bodmer liked to elaborate ideas and put them into patterns and spread them before the fascinated eyes of his disciples, but he was always careful not to jeopardize his position in society by taking them too seriously; Lavater from an early age believed that ideas were nothing if not the basis for action.

A member of Bodmer's Society at Gerwy, Lavater was not content with the abstract disquisitions on civic virtue that he heard there or the debates on subjects like "Will trade harm a state more than it benefits it?" He wanted to change the things around him that prevented his country from becoming what he thought it should be. And so, in 1762, he and his friend, the theological student and later painter Heinrich Füßli, took up the case of the *Landvögt* Grebel, who had shamefully mistreated and exploited the farmers of his district of Grüningen. Grebel's misdeeds were no secret, but he was a member of the Great

Council in Zürich, the son-in-law of *Bürgermeister* Leu, connected with the city's most powerful families, and a conspiracy of silence protected him until the young men spoke up.

Their memorandum to the council listed the outrages committed in Grüningen and passionately demanded redress. "Are you asleep, Escher and Leu?" they wrote. "Are you asleep, Nüscheler and Schwarzenbach? . . . Be men! Be *Bürger!* Be fathers of the state! We lay our complaints at your feet. Shall it be said that there was no Julius Brutus among you? That Zürich no longer had a Tell, a Baumgarten? That these excellent Helvetians suffered among them such a tyrant, who was crueller than a Gessler or a Landenberg? A shame for our age if their sons had so far departed from their heroic courage that there was no one who could raise his voice against such a shameless scoundrel!" Disagreeably surprised, the council ordered Grebel and the authors of this philippic to appear before them. Lavater and Füßli cheerfully complied, but Grebel fled the canton.

The affair caused a sensation that was not confined to Zürich and appeared to some to be a portent of change in a regime that had been in power so long that its heavy weight was beginning to feel oppressive. The authors of Grebel's fall now brought charges against a notoriously corrupt guild master and an immoral cleric, and Lavater and another friend, the future educator Heinrich Pestalozzi, writing in a weekly called *Die Erinnerer,* pressed attacks upon all aspects of Zürich's life that seemed to them to be narrow, regressive, and philistine, criticizing the Great Council for not equaling the model set by the British House of Commons and declaring that its censorship of publications was demeaning.

Self-styled "Patriots," the young men dreamed not of revolution but of regeneration, of self-mastery and improvement. They felt that Zürich was being stifled by its own economic success and the materialism that it had induced, that—as Pestalozzi was to say later in his essay "On the Freedom of My Native City"—

> The wealth of the individual has always undermined free constitutions, has always destroyed the domestic happiness of the several estates, has always debauched the morals of freedom and destroyed the inner capacity of the people to govern itself, has always subordinated all public interest to

financial interest, has always debased the power of the people, which under our fathers aspired to national virtue, to the service of their sons' idol, gold.

Lavater's *Schweizerlieder*, published in 1767, was an attempt, by evoking the great men and achievements of the past, to inspire contemporaries to base their lives on republican virtue.

> *Gesundheit Dir! Du Vaterstadt!*
> *Und jedem brafen Zürcher!*
> *Wer lieb die liebe Freyheit hat,*
> *Den segnen alle Bürger!*
> *Wer nur des Staates Nutzen sucht,*
> *Stolz, Pracht und Üppigkeit verflucht,*
> *Den Ehrer des Gesetzes!*

> *Good Health to you, O Native City!*
>   *And to every stout Zürcher!*
> *Let all citizens bless him*
>   *Who loves sweet liberty!*
> *And the man who honors the law,*
>   *Seeks only the welfare of the state,*
> *And condemns pride, display, and luxury!*

But it was difficult to sustain this level of political activism in Zürich. Füßli and Pestalozzi, finding no future for their talents there, went away, the former to England, where he made his reputation as a painter, the latter to Brugg, where he began the series of unsuccessful experiments with the education of children that brought him posthumous fame. Lavater himself, always mercurial and prone to impulse and enthusiasm, gave himself over to the propagation of a highly emotional Christianity, to the conviction that there were links between the face and the soul that led him to publish a four-volume work on physiognomy in the years 1775–78 that made the subject a kind of European fad, to his obsession with modern wonders and miraculous cures, in which he sought to find divine messages, and to his enormous correspondence with friends and acquaintances, intellectuals and crowned heads, a good many of whom came to Zürich to see him, some of them—like the Grand Duke Paul of Russia, Karl August of Weimar, and the Grand Duchess of

Baden—with entourages that filled the Hotel zum Schwert to overflowing.

To these activities Zürich reacted with growing irritation. There was no doubt that Lavater, who became pastor of St. Paul's Church in 1778, was a dedicated Christian and an eloquent and persuasive interpreter of the Gospels. Eliza von der Recke wrote that in her youth his *Views into Eternity* (*Aussichten in die Ewigkeit*) and his *Secret Diary* (*Geheimes Tagebuch*) made her feel that he was one of the Lord's disciples who had come back to life again and that he had inspired her to daily self-examination. But his eccentricities were hard for Zürchers to bear, and the attention that they aroused even harder. The most malicious attacks upon his naive willingness to believe in the possibility of magnetic forces and miraculous cures came not from hard-bitten *Aufklärer* like Nicolai and Lichtenberg but from local critics, and it was the latter who seemed most resentful of the fact that their fellow citizen should arouse the admiration of foreigners, going so far as to accuse Lavater's visitors of somehow affronting the rest of the community. After Goethe's visit to Zürich in 1775, J. J. Hottinger, editor of the journal *Das Send-schreiben*, wrote a satire called "Human Beings, Animals and Goethe," in which he not only mocked the poet's attendance upon Lavater—with the jeering line "How marvelous these geniuses are!"—but went on to say that

> *Among us no one was good enough,*
> *And arrogance was written on his brow.*

During the course of the visit some members of Goethe's party explored the upper reaches of the Sihl and, taking their clothes off, went bathing. Although no one witnessed the scene, it aroused outraged discussion, and Lavater was much criticized for having befriended people—as Goethe wrote in his memoirs —"whose wild, unrestrained, yes heathen nature caused such a scandal in a moral well-regulated community." That Goethe during his visit composed perhaps the loveliest poetic tribute to the Zürich Lake that has ever been written, the final stanza of the lyric beginning "*Und frische Nahrung,/ Neues Blut*," would, even if it had been known, in no way have palliated his offense.

The dominant note in this criticism was philistinism, and indeed the Athens on the Limmat suffered from a strong disinclination to be shaken out of its complacency by new ideas. Hottinger was almost querulous when he wrote in 1775:

> I don't know what kind of an evil star plagues us, but that is the way with our destiny these days. It seems as if every five years a destructive wind blows over our land and dries out the brains of our people. When Klopstock came to Zürich many years ago, the Messiah was promptly preached from all pulpits just as he had written of him. About ten years ago every one from pensioners to chimneysweeps were Patriots. And then came Lavater with his nonsense about miracles, and our old men dreamed dreams and our young men saw visions, and it became the fashion to cure all sickness by prayer and faith. That was, as anyone can see, a desperate blow for the physicians. But ordinary people knew how to fix that and excreted the belief in miracles with their stools.

For people who thought like this, Lavater continued to be an uncomfortable oddity, yet in some ways he had a firmer grasp on reality than they did. He knew that the world was moved by ideas; he sensed that great changes were pending; he wanted his country to prepare itself lest it be overwhelmed by them. During the first years after the fall of the Bastille in Paris, he was suffering from illness and mental fatigue, but he rallied when the revolution began to extend outward and became a powerful voice for neutrality and internal reform. His sermons against the execution of Louis XVI and the excesses of the Terror alarmed the timid and infuriated the pro-French elements, who had begun to grow in influence in Switzerland. He attacked those aspects of Zürich's governance that invited revolution, coming in 1796 to the defense of the inhabitants of the lake community of Stäfa, who had sent a memorial of grievances to the Great Council and had subsequently justified their right to do so on the basis of assurances issued by that body, and countersigned by other cantons, after the Waldmann affair of 1489. Nevertheless, their leaders had been arrested, placed in that same Wellenberg in which Waldmann had languished, and charged with crimes punishable by death, from which, indeed, they were probably saved only by Lavater's sermons.

The incident in itself shows that the impact of the Enlightenment in Zürich had been a limited one and had not laid the basis for peaceful political change. With its aristocracy of wealth in firm control, Zürich remained deaf to Lavater's warnings and incapable of self-reform because it was unconvinced that it was necessary. It would take a more intimate experience of the forces released by the revolution in France to shake the provincial self-satisfaction of the city on the Limmat and set it on the course of change.

Chapter 2

THE RISE AND TRIUMPH OF LIBERALISM, 1798–1846

◆

*O Abderites, Abderites . . . struggle not so against
innovation! Everything that is old around you is
worthless; everything must become new in Abdera if
things are to go well.*
　　　　　　—CHRISTOPH MARTIN WIELAND, *Stilpon,
　　　　　　　　oder Über die Wahl eines
　　　　　　　　Oberzunftmeisters von Megara* (1774)

*Believe't or not, but the cathedral bell
Is there to speak for who has ears to hear.
Each time it tolls, a liberal is born,
Or a bandito lies upon his bier.*
　　　—GIUSEPPE GIUSTI, *Il Delenda Cartago*
　　　(1846)

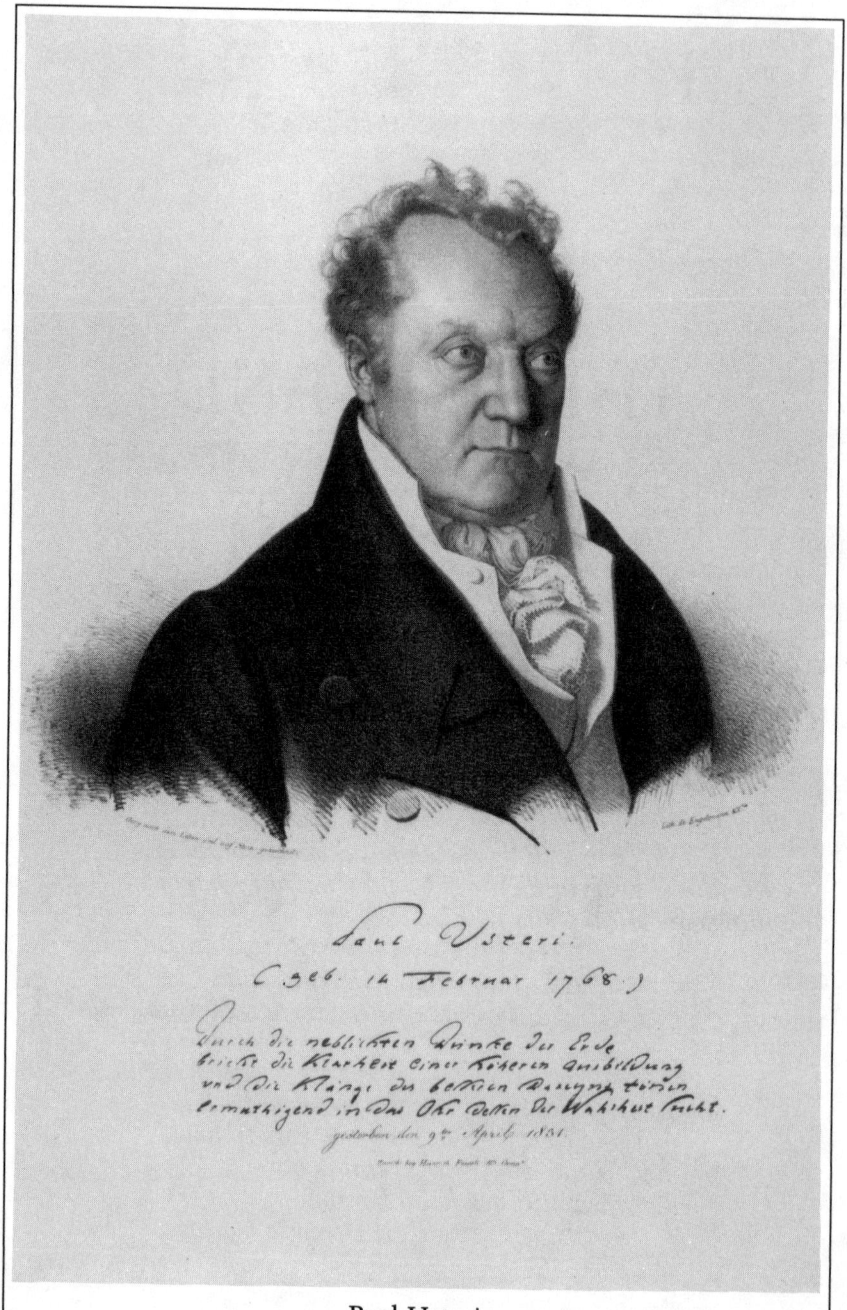

Paul Usteri

Swiss liberalism had its origins in the French Revolution, and the first liberals were men who had responded with enthusiasm to the news of the fall of the Bastille and been captivated, as Condorcet had been, by the "picture of the human race, freed from its chains, removed from the empire of chance as from that of the enemies of its progress, and advancing with a firm and sure step on the pathway of truth, of virtue, and of happiness."

Drawn for the most part from university-trained elites and the administrative and judicial bureaucracy and from the professoriate, the medical profession, and industry and trade, they shared the conviction that freedom in all of its forms—freedom from absolutism and feudalism, from economic regimentation and religious obscurantism, from occupational restriction and limitations of speech and assembly—could only improve the quality of society and the well-being of its members, and they were resolved that the old ruling class had forfeited its right to power because it was blind to this. On the other hand, they did not believe in the radical egalitarianism that was the stock in trade of the French Jacobins, they stood closer to the principles of enlightened absolutism than they did to the teachings of Rousseau, and they distrusted democracy because it placed power in the hands of the least responsible members of society. That the education of the masses would in time correct this, they professed to believe, and the ardor with which they advocated educational reform indicated that their professions were genuine. Meanwhile, however, they were inclined to the view that government should be in the hands of people like themselves, men of intelligence and *Bildung* who were capable of submerging their private motives in the desire for the common good, and who, above all, believed in progress, who regarded it, indeed, as rooted in the very law of nature and were convinced that institutions that remained static were for that very reason bad, and who held, with Condorcet again, that "there [was] no limit set to the perfecting of the powers of man, that human perfectibility [was] in reality indefinite, that the progress of this perfectibility

31

... [had] no other limit than the duration of the globe upon which nature has placed us."

This philosophy of liberty and progress was shared by Frédéric César de la Harpe and Maurice Glayre of the Waadtland, Lucas Legrand of Basel, and Philipp Albrecht Stapfer and Johann Albrecht Rengger of Aarau, who emerged as the most influential new voices in Swiss politics after the collapse of the old regime in 1798. And this was equally true of Dr. Paul Usteri, the father of liberalism in Zürich, who, through a long and varied career as physician and botanist, as Helvetic Senator and member of Zürich's Governing Council (*Kleiner Rat*) in the revolutionary and Napoleonic period and the post-Vienna reaction, as political journalist and longtime editor of the *Neue Zürcher Zeitung*, as president of the Society for the Common Good, and, finally, as Zürich's first head of government in the Regeneration of the years after 1830, remained true both to the ideas of freedom and human rights that he had derived from the writings of the French *philosophes* and to the conviction, which he shared with his friends in the government of the Helvetic Republic, that the particularism and lack of common purpose that was the persistent legacy of the *ancien régime* must be overcome.

I

At the beginning of 1798, responding to agitations in the Waadtland and to an appeal from Supreme Guild Master Peter Ochs of Basel to liberate the area from the canton of Bern, the French Directory sent an army of 400,000 men into Switzerland, which rapidly overran Freiburg and Solothurn, captured Bern, and by the second week of April had radically changed the very basis of Swiss political life by imposing a unitary constitution upon the whole country. What resistance there was—in the Forest Cantons and the Niedwald—was belated and futile. In general the old ruling class reacted to the rush of events with consternation and helplessness, and the Helvetic Republic, as the new order was called, established itself with an ease that surprised its most ardent and optimistic supporters.

Zürich was no exception to the general rule. The aristocratic government that ruled the canton was in a state of disarray as a result of a series of events that had begun with the Stäfa affair of 1795–96. Outraged by a statement of grievances from that community, and doubtless sensing the influence of Jacobinism behind it, the Great Council had sent troops to Stäfa, seized those responsible for drafting the memorial, and dragged them off to the Wellenberg in the Limmat. Here their leaders were charged with treason, and had it not been, as we have seen, for Johann Caspar Lavater's passionate sermons in their defense, they would certainly have suffered death. As it was, two of them received life sentences and three others imprisonment for terms ranging up to twenty years, while 260 other persons, who were charged with complicity, received lesser terms or were fined or banished from the canton.

This was cruel and unusual punishment and, in the context of the times, stupid. It outraged the communities along the lake-shore from which the great majority of the prisoners and exiles came. These *Seegemeinden*, in contrast to the conservative and backward rural districts of the Zürich highlands, were cultivated, progressive, and often radical in their political views; they had long chafed under their subordination to the city government, and they had a long history, dating back to the days of Hans Waldmann, of showing their resentment in violent ways. Almost immediately an agitation began for the reduction of the sentences, and when the government in Zürich was unresponsive, this became more intense, with demands for the release of the prisoners and the return of the exiles. Trees of liberty began to appear in Horgen and Meilen and Wädenswil, and the moderate members of the Great Council became alarmed and urged their conservative colleagues to recognize the necessity of conciliation.

In January 1798 three members brought the matter formally before the council: Guild Master Wegmann, J. J. Lavater, the theologian's brother, and Dr. Paul Usteri, who in 1792 had given up an established career as lecturer at Zürich's medical institute, superintendent of its Botanical Garden, and practicing physician to turn to political journalism, and who had been elected to the Great Council in 1797, despite the fact that his views were at variance with those of most of its members. They demanded a revision of the Stäfa verdicts but received no satisfaction until the end of the month, when *Bürgermeister* David von Wyss returned from a meeting of the federal diet (*Tagsatzung*) in Aarau with the sobering news that the other members of the Eidgenossenschaft, fearing the imminence of a French invasion, were of the unanimous opinion that Zürich must put its house in order. On 29 January, therefore, the council declared a general amnesty for the Stäfa defendants and began a consideration of ways in which the grievances of the lake communities might be met.

They still, however, showed no sense of urgency and dawdled so over the matter of tangible concessions that they fed rather than smothered the discontent in the *Seegemeinden*. Because of this, at the beginning of February, when the French invaded the Waadtland and Bern called urgently for military support, the Great Council could raise only a fourth of the troops needed. The return of the Stäfa exiles had touched off a series of mass meetings that called for a fundamental reordering of relations berween city and countryside and the introduction of representative democracy, and it was soon apparent that things were so far out of the council's control that concessions made by it merely became platforms for new demands. Its epochal declaration of 5 February, in which it abolished the centuries-old domination of the city over its dependencies, went almost unheard in the din caused by new manifestos and proclamations by local committees and assemblies that claimed to supersede its authority, and by mid-March, completely demoralized, it had surrendered its functions to a National Committee with a majority of country representatives. This, however, never had a chance to establish itself. The French had now completed their work, and on 12 April 1798 they forced Zürich to accept the Helvetic constitution, which abolished its cantonal independence and submitted it to the rule of a centralized national government that was a satellite of the French Republic.

Sigmund Widmer has written of the Helvetic experiment that this first attempt in Swiss history to make a modern state was later anathematized by the conservatives and regarded by the liberals as an embarrassment. This, as we shall see in the Zürich context, is entirely understandable. Yet few periods in Swiss history were as rich as this one in new ideas and aspirations for an equitable social order, and many of the reforms upon which the liberals were later to pride themselves had their roots in the Helvetic years. Moreover, even the most unpopular aspect of the Helvetic system—the sense of living under the constant shadow of France—had its positive side. By teaching the hitherto

self-absorbed Zürcher and Bernese and Appenzeller and Waadtländer to think of themselves, at least intermittently, as Swiss,
it did its bit to create the sentiment that eventuated in the
achievement of 1847–48.

Under the Helvetic constitution Switzerland was governed
by a five-man directory located first in Aarau, later in Luzern,
and finally in Bern. There were appropriate ministries, a bicameral legislature (Great Council and Senate), in which the cantons
were equally represented, and a judicial tribunal. At the head of
each canton was a governor (*Regierungsstatthalter*), who represented the directory, executed the laws, maintained public
security and disposed of the military forces, appointed the directors of cantonal agencies and supervised the civil service. In
the affairs of local communities there was some measure of
diversity and autonomy, although most important matters were
in the hands of agents who were responsible to higher authority.
Theoretically, this structure made for coherence and administrative efficiency and facilitated the reform of outworn institutions, and indeed its first effect was to establish the prerequisites
of modernity in Switzerland by abolishing such things as servitude, the remnants of feudal privilege, and the use of torture
in judicial procedure and establishing basic human rights and
freedom of trade, occupation, and religion. In the Helvetic directory Johann Albrecht Rengger and Philipp Albrecht Stapfer
in particular were prolific in plans for such things as the elaboration of a primary and secondary school system, the building
of a national university, and the cultivation of the arts and the
sciences by the establishment of libraries, museums, and research institutes, although it soon became apparent that they
lacked the financial means to implement them.

In the city of Zürich, and in large parts of the canton, the
Helvetic regime was unpopular from the start. The break with
old ways was abrupt and confusing, and the new cult of the
nation, which was propagated by the invocation of the memory
of Wilhelm Tell by means of symbolic representation and ceremony, had little positive effect. There were, moreover, two
special reasons for local disaffection. The Helvetic *Statthalter*
for Zürich was J. C. Pfenninger, who had been a leading spirit
in the Stäfa troubles and who retained deep resentments against
the city as a result. A passionate searcher after oppositional tendencies, he was suspected of wishing to set up his own com-

mittee of public safety, and his agents made a nuisance of themselves by hounding "priests and aristocrats."

More onerous were the French. In entering the Helvetic Republic, Zürchers had hoped to avoid occupation and the exactions that would go with it. This was an illusory expectation, for the French General Schauenburg made Zürich his headquarters for operations against the continuing resistance in the Forest Cantons and garrisoned it with 12,000 men. In general these troops were well-behaved, although there was some plundering in outlying villages, but the French commissioners were shameless in their demands upon the community and made off with, among other things, the greater part of the state treasury. Nor did the situation improve after the end of the fighting in Schwyz and Glarus, for in the spring of 1799 the War of the Second Coalition began, and the Austrian Archduke Charles advanced on Zürich, where he defeated the French under Masséna on 4 June. This led to local rejoicing and the flight of the Helvetic commissioners, but Masséna regrouped his forces and, on 25–26 September, decisively defeated the Austrians and Russians in the second battle of Zürich. The cost of all this to the city and the canton was great—the effects on the countryside are described with force and imagination in Albin Zollinger's story "The Russian Horses"—and included not only the life of Johann Caspar Lavater, who in the confusion of the September fighting was fatally wounded by a French soldier, but economic damages and losses that have been estimated at 14 million francs, more than a third of which fell on the city. On 3 October 1799, for example, Masséna imposed a levy of 800,000 francs on the city and demanded that it be paid within forty-eight hours.

Zürich was well served during this period by its representatives in the Helvetic government, Dr. Paul Usteri, who was president of the Senate after September 1798, and Hans Konrad Escher, who was president of the Great Council. Both were strong supporters of the revolution of 1798, which they regarded as the fulfillment of long-held desires, Escher confessing to a friend: "My belief in human rights, and in equality of such rights, was part of me ever since my youth, although I was never able to communicate them completely and systematically, since I was either howled down miserably, as is usually the case here in Zürich, or relegated with my ideas to the realm of pious wishes and fantasies." But they were at the same time outraged by the conduct and impositions of the French and stoutly opposed them, not only in speeches in the legislature, but in the pages of the *Schweizerische Republikaner,* which Usteri had founded in 1798. Indeed, it was during the Helvetic years that Usteri delineated the basic principles of a national liberal party and, with his friends Escher, Rengger, and Stapfer, formed its nucleus. He did this by taking a firm stand against the so-called Patriots, who regarded the French as liberators and were entirely uncritical of their actions, by opposing all legislative proposals that had no other justification except that provided by the rhetoric of revolution (like the abolition of tithes and ground rents, which he considered to be inequitable and self-defeating), and by resisting all authoritarian tendencies on the government's part. Usteri bitterly criticized La Harpe and Peter Ochs for their attempts to strengthen their position in the directory by silencing the press, and when they took hostages among the conservatives at the beginning of the War of the Second Coalition, he made a speech that was widely circulated in which he said, "Whether the man whose arbitrary action curbs my freedom is called Paul or Peter or Frédéric César, and whether he acts in the name of tyranny or freedom is all one to me; where there is no individual liberty, freedom is a nullity and an empty echo!"

Usteri's ambition was to build a broad middle party between the Patriots and the radical democrats on the one hand and the Aristocrats on the other, which would be dedicated to the maintenance of national unity, the preservation of the fundamental rights of the individual, and the vigorous elaboration of the Helvetic Republic's initial reforms, and his successful fight against La Harpe, which culminated in a legislative *coup d'état* that unseated the Waadtländer in January 1800, seemed to indicate that he was making rapid progress toward that goal. But this was premature, first, because some of Usteri's closest associates had a strong aversion to parties and party politics, which they regarded as potentially divisive and self-serving, and, second, because the aristocratic-conservative party, which had no such compunctions, now recovered from the paralysis of nerve that had overcome it in 1798 and launched a full-scale attack upon the whole Helvetic experiment. The next two years saw a complex struggle between self-styled federalists and unitarians in all parts of Switzerland and a bewildering series of *coups de main* and changes of government on the national level. Usteri, who was the staunchest of unitarians and who attacked the rightists as *chouans*, was an early victim of these intrigues. Driven into private life in October 1801, he had no direct role in the Helvetic Republic's last frenzy, when the new First Consul of France, Napoleon Bonaparte, cynically withdrew all French troops from the country in July 1802, apparently abandoning the Swiss to their own devices, when the Forest Cantons and Appenzell and Glarus declared their return to the old order, when Zürich was reduced to near anarchy by strife between the strongly unitarian lake communities and the federalist city and highlands, and when a tiny Helvetic force under General Andermatt ineffectually bombarded the town from the Zürichberg.

The French had, of course, no intention of abandoning their position in the country, and once the Swiss had demonstrated their political *Zerrissenheit* and ineffectuality for all to see, the First Consul summoned representatives from all of the cantons to Paris for a consultation that more closely resembled a dictated peace. Napoleon disposed of the problem that had divided Switzerland for the last three years by declaring flatly that a centralized constitution would not work in a country with such pronounced regional differences and diversity of speech, religion, and custom. He then simply handed to his auditors the constitutions that he expected them to observe, adding in each case some admonitory observations of his own.

In the case of Zürich these were not uninteresting and indicated a shrewd prescience on Napoleon's part about the country's politics. The Zürich delegation to the consultation included Hans von Reinhard, who had emerged as the ablest of the city's conservatives during the recent struggles, Usteri and Pestalozzi, who had been elected by the cantonal assembly, and J. C. Pfenninger. Napoleon addressed himself principally to Reinhard but clearly and explicitly assumed that Usteri was his opposite number. "Herr von Reinhard," he said, "you belong to a canton that is divided principally by the division between city and countryside. I regard you and Usteri as the heads of the two parties. It's up to you two to work in a moderating and conciliatory way, on the city in the one case, on the countryside in the other. . . . It's high time that the countryside . . . put aside its hatred of the city and give evidence of a conciliatory disposition. Otherwise it would deserve to fall back under the city's control or to go under in the general destruction and ruin of Switzerland." To Pfenninger, who must have found these words highly unpalatable, the First Consul said blandly, "*Bien, citoyen* Pfenninger. You are jealous of the privileges of your capital city. But take it easy! There are no longer any walls between city and countryside!"

Napoleon's Mediation Act of 1803 restored cantonal sovereignty to Switzerland, while at the same time increasing the number of cantons from thirteen to nineteen. It reestablished the federal diet and provided for a *Landammann der Schweiz* to preside over it and to coordinate Swiss policy with that of Napoleon, who guaranteed internal order. Zürich, which was assigned its present borders, regained its system of government by Great and Governing Councils, with a franchise that was limited to residents with property and an indirect system of voting that assured that the wealthiest families would exercise a monopoly of power and that the city would preponderate over the countryside. What this would mean became clear in April 1803, when the Great Council met for the first time in five years and elected the Governing Council, which would henceforth possess the initiative in all matters of policy. Four-fifths of the new members of the latter body were aristocrats, and fifteen of the twenty-five members represented the city.

This arrangement of things was hardly likely either to give an influential role to Usteri's liberal party, as Napoleon had intimated would happen, or to assure the fulfillment of his desire for peace between city and countryside. This was clear as soon as the French government withdrew its troops from the canton in May 1803, forfeiting direct restraint over the new government. Almost immediately the conservatives began to flex their muscles, and their policies, particularly their regulation of the sensitive issue of tithes and ground rents, soon led to public protests in the lake communities. When this happened the government, with a feckless display of historical amnesia, first abolished the right of petition and then sent troops to prevent public assembly and arrest agitators. This invited acts of violence on the other side, and a bad situation became steadily worse until, in March 1804, the shoemaker Jakob Willi of Horgen, who had served in the Spanish, French, and British armies, raised the flag of revolt and, with a force that never exceeded 500 men, held out in the hills until 3,800 troops from Zürich and neighboring cantons were brought to bear against him.

The government's revenge for what was called the *Böck-enkrieg* was terrible in its vindictiveness, all the more so because of the panic it had caused in the city. Military columns and civil commissioners swept through all of the communities that had had any connection with Willi's adventure, making arbitrary arrests, holding unlawful hearings, and imposing summary pun-ishments that included whippings and beatings that in some cases led to permanent injury or death. Forty communities re-ceived heavy financial penalties. As for the leaders of the rising, despite Paul Usteri's urgent protests against the procedures fol-lowed in the trial and his vain attempt to have the Governing Council intervene, and despite a message from Napoleon saying that he desired no bloodshed in Switzerland, Willi and his two closest associates received the death penalty, and two others imprisonment for life.

The memory of these brutal reprisals hung over the country for the next two decades and deprived the government of any credit it might have received for its subsequent attempts to in-stitute a more equitable system of taxation and to alleviate the burden of French levies of various kinds. Not that there was much chance in any case of the Mediation regime's developing strong public support. The most that could be said for it was that it maintained peace in the canton for ten years and allowed private enterprise to lay the basis for its later spirited growth, but even people who liked quiet times were not inclined to overlook the government's return to an almost medieval form of justice, its abolition of religious toleration, its acceptance of arbitrary guild restrictions, its censorship of books and news-papers, and its indifference to educational reform.

Even this benighted state of affairs was not enough to satisfy the reactionary wing of the conservative party—men like Junker Georg Escher von Berg, who believed that no deviation from the pre-1798 system was legitimate—and when Napoleon's retreat from Russia and his defeat at Leipzig in October 1813 indicated that his days were numbered, these people hoped that, by in-gratiating themselves with his enemies, they might gain their support for the restoration of the old regime. In this they were no more successful than the German princelings who made the mistake of thinking that the victorious coalition would be guided in its postwar planning by a rigid interpretation of the principle of legitimacy. In fact the powers that met at Vienna after Napoleon's defeat proved to be less interested in ideological questions than in seeing that Switzerland became a viable international entity and a useful contributor to the European balance of power. They turned a deaf ear to cantons like Bern, which wished to return to the Eidgenossenschaft of thirteen members (and Schwyz, which proposed returning to the basis of 1315), and they forced the contentious parties to accept a federation of twenty-two members (enlarged by the inclusion of the newly constituted cantons of Wallis, Geneva, and Neuenburg), with a diet empowered to negotiate with foreign powers and conclude political and commercial treaties, with the assent of three-quarters of the cantons, and with its neutrality and territorial integrity guaranteed by the Great Powers. Aside from this they authorized a degree of cantonal sovereignty greater by far than that permitted by Napoleon during the Mediation, but at the same time refused to encourage reactionary tendencies in internal politics, an attitude that even the Eastern Powers maintained until after the liberals took power in 1830.

Zürich was spared a retreat into complete reaction in part because of this attitude of the Great Powers and in part because of the temperament of the leader of the conservative party, Hans von Reinhard. At the Congress of Vienna the Russian Councillor Capo d'Istria, who had dealings with him, described Reinhard as "narrow-minded, timid, and guided only by the petty Zürich point of view." Certainly he lacked the daring and the imagination to be a reactionary in the grand style: he was too fearful to have ideological zeal, viewed all new ideas with skepticism and distrust, and preferred to sit tight and take no risks. He presided over a regime filled with people like himself—a new city-centered aristocracy of propertied families whose domination of the government, the courts, the cantonal bureaucracy, and clerical appointments was assured by a franchise even more restrictive and voting methods that were subject to even more manipulation than during the Mediation. For those with the right connections, politics was a profitable business, and the competition for offices and privileges was so intense that no energy was left over for the perpetration of more dramatic abuses.

Indeed, the salient weakness of the regime was that in areas where new ideas and initiatives were needed, particularly in public finance and industry and agriculture, it showed no imagination and, in general, followed the course—as Karl Dändliker has written—"of humdrumness that bordered on stagnation."

It was this, as much as anything, that contributed to the growth of liberalism by eroding the strength and authority of the government even where it was strongest. The countryside had long been in a state of sullen resentment, but fear of reprisals kept it quiet. It was in the city that the first stirrings of opposition were felt, among young people, lawyers, and intellectuals who were repelled by the government's fustiness and lack of ideas and who looked to Paul Usteri and State Councillor Ludwig Meyer von Knonau for new leadership. They found a center for their discussions in the Political Institute, Zürich's first school of law, which had been founded by Meyer and Usteri in 1808. Long an object of suspicion to conservatives, the institute became a center for jurists who had been trained in Germany by Savigny and Eichhorn and inspired by their reforming impulse, people like Friedrich Ludwig Keller, whose *Die neuen Theorien in der zürcherischen Rechtspflege*, published in 1828, called for a thoroughgoing reform of the judicial system, Ferdinand Meyer, city clerk after 1826, J. C. Bluntschli, Keller's student, and David Ulrich.

Their ideas were supported by an increasingly critical newspaper press. In 1765, Lavater had written in *Die Erinnerer* that "the freedom to speak and to write is an indispensable ingredient of true political freedom; without it the words fatherland and freedom are nothing but the sounding brass and the tinkling cymbal," but no government in the history of Zürich until the Helvetic time, and none since, had allowed itself to be influenced in the slightest by the theologian's opinion. In general the authorities had been reluctant to grant licenses for journals and, when they had done so, had insisted that they restrict themselves to the reporting of foreign news and innocuous essays on literature and the arts. These rules forced editors who had strong opinions about local or federal affairs to be ingenious in the arts of suggestion and innuendo and skillful in reporting foreign news in such a way as to hint at its relevance to the domestic scene. This was a wearying business, and the history of the press in

Zürich is filled with examples of revolt against it. In the late 1820s two newspapers took up the fight for freedom, the ← *Schweizerische Beobachter*, edited by Heinrich Nüscheler, and the *Neue Zürcher Zeitung*, edited by Heinrich Füßli and Paul Usteri. The latter, founded in 1779 by Salomon Gessner as the *Zürcher Zeitung* and rechristened when Usteri became chief editor in 1821, appeared three times a week and in its columns, which reached readers far beyond the confines of the city, constantly emphasized the aspirations to freedom and the march of liberal ideas in other lands, praising the embattled Greeks, criticizing the stifling effects of the Carlsbad Decrees in Germany, and attacking ultramontanism.

These tactics provoked the government into an attempt to tighten the censorship, and, on Zürich's initiative, the federal diet prepared and laid before the cantonal governments a regulation imposing new restrictions on the reporting of foreign news. This was clearly meant to be the beginning of a campaign to silence the opposition, but it came to the Zürich Great Council at a time when the conservative regime was shaken by two potential scandals—the collapse of a leading commercial firm amid rumors of government complicity and misuse of public funds and the suicide of a prominent state councillor in equally suspicious circumstances. The members of the council were divided among themselves and in a mood of profound self-doubt when the debate began, and they were ill prepared to defend the government's proposals when Paul Usteri rose and ripped them to shreds.

Usteri had none of the eloquence of a Richard Cobden or a John Bright, and it would have surprised, and possibly offended, his auditors if he had, for, as Lavater had once complained, the level of debate in the Great Council never rose to that in the House of Commons. A large man, with a melancholy cast of face and protruding, heavily pouched eyes, Usteri had a style that matched his appearance, wooden and repetitive and bereft of humor or illustration, but one that was, at the same time, informed by moral earnestness and deep conviction. And it was these last qualities that impressed and silenced the enemies of a free press, as he flayed the Governing Council for its reactionary philosophy and for its "failure to understand the age and its requirements . . . to understand Switzerland and what has been

happening in it in these last decades [during which] an enlightened public opinion has arisen that extends itself farther and
farther every year." Usteri declared:

> Publicity belongs to the very essence of the free state, and
> in representative constitutions the citizen has a right to
> know what his representatives are doing and what agree-
> ments they are concluding. What these representatives of
> the nation, what the administrative agencies of the repub-
> lican state do . . . is not their own property but the property
> of the whole community, to which they owe an accounting.
> The essence of the free state requires the participation of the
> citizen in public affairs; through this participation alone can
> the strength and welfare, the honor and reputation of the
> republic be achieved and maintained. Without the partici-
> pation of the citizens, or in circumstances in which the
> fatherland's affairs and relations are matters of indifference
> to them, all of this will be reduced to nothing.

It was perhaps the greatest speech in Usteri's career, both
an unanswerable argument for the free press that he had championed since the days of the Helvetic Republic and a description
in essence of the liberalism that he believed was Switzerland's
future, and its repercussions were widespread and profound. Not
only did it serve its immediate purpose, by blocking the proposed
legislation, but it heartened all of the forces of progress and
increased the pressure for change. Within a year the censorship
was dismantled, and the Great Council, tired of its subservience
to the Governing Council, had reclaimed the initiative in all
legislative matters. These were first straws, stirring in a wind
that was beginning to rise across the border and would soon
blow sharply across the land.

II

"In the steppes of the Bashkirs," Heinrich Heine wrote in the
summer of 1830, "spirits will be as deeply stirred as in the mountain heights of Andalusia. I already see the Neapolitan's maca-
roni and the Irishman's potatoes frozen in their mouths when
the news reaches them." The poet referred, of course, to the
news of the revolution in Paris, and although it is improbable

that its effect in the peat bogs and the Russian plains was as great as he fancied, there is no doubt that it electrified the Swiss cantons. There were tumultuous assemblies from one end of the country to the other, and such was the power of example that within a year eleven cantons—Zürich, Bern, Luzern, Freiburg, Solothurn, Schaffhausen, St. Gallen, Aargau, Thurgau, Tessin, and Waadt—had found their way to liberal constitutions.

In Zürich the initiative was taken, as was not surprising, by the communities on the lakeshores. For some time a group had been meeting at The Swan in Rapperswyl to discuss plans for overthrowing the aristocratic regime, and its members now entered into relations with similar bodies in all of the old centers of disaffection—Horgen, Wädenswil, Stäfa, Richterswyl, Meilen, and Küsnacht—and began to circulate pamphlets calling for a constitutional reform that would give the countryside a large majority, perhaps as much as three-fifths, of the seats in the Great Council. This alarmed the city liberals, like Usteri and Nüscheler, who were not immune to the common urban fear of *Bauernregiment*, and it seems to have aroused caution among some of the lake dwellers as well. The leaders of the reform group in Küsnacht, in any case, decided to try to frame a reasonable program of change and invited Ludwig Snell to draft one for them. A citizen of Nassau, who had been driven from his post as director of a gymnasium in Wetzlar by the campaign of thought control set in train by the Carlsbad Decrees, Snell had come to Switzerland in 1827, become a writer on educational and political affairs, and in 1829 had written an influential treatise on the freedom of the press. He possessed a shrewd political instinct and a sense for the possibilities inherent in complex situations, and he proved this now by avoiding extreme positions and drafting a document that, *mutatis mutandis*, became the foundation of the new cantonal constitution of 1831. His Küsnacht Memorial called for the recognition of popular sovereignty, representative government with a less restrictive franchise than in the past, separation of powers, an open administration with control over its decisions by elected representatives, the right of petition, and the gradual phasing out of indirect elections. On the crucial question of representation in the Great Council, it proposed a ratio of two-thirds to one-third between countryside and city, with provision for review at a later date.

The Great Council, reluctant to accept this diminution of

urban representation, resorted to delaying tactics, but the memorial was circulated widely, and on 22 November 1830 a gathering of 7,000 to 8,000 people, meeting in the open air at Uster under the presidency of Heinrich Gujer, a miller from Bauma, listened to an exposition of the Küsnacht proposals and, with enthusiasm and solemnity, accepted them by acclamation. This was such an impressive demonstration of popular sovereignty at work that the city liberals abandoned their reserve and publicly subscribed to the Uster resolution, and in January 1831 a constitutional committee that included Usteri, Ludwig Meyer von Knonau, Melchior Hirzel, Ludwig Keller, and Eduard Sulzer began work on a draft constitution. The result of their deliberations, which was laid before the Great Council in February and accepted by that body and by popular referendum a month later, remained true to the essence of the Küsnacht Memorial—that is, it celebrated popular sovereignty while making clear that it must be exercised indirectly. The constitution of 1831—which declared in its first article that the canton of Zürich was "a free state with a representative constitution" and that sovereignty rested on "the totality of the people" and was exercised "in accordance with the provisions of the constitution by the Great Council as representative of the people"—rested on principles that were to be common to all liberal middle-class parties in the West in the next decades and were to find their classic formulation in John Stuart Mill's *Representative Government* in 1861.

The acceptance of the constitution was a significant date in Zürich's history, the beginning of the regeneration of the canton along liberal lines, and it was fitting that Paul Usteri should have been chosen to serve as the first *Bürgermeister* of the new era. His tenure of office was of tragically brief duration, for he was seized of a sudden fever on 30 March and was dead ten days later, and he is remembered in history, therefore, not as the constructive statesman that he might have become but rather as the courageous fighter for liberal principles and the builder of the party that was now to give them tangible form. The most unfortunate result of his death was that the leadership of the party now devolved upon people who lacked his sense of restraint and his shrewd understanding of his countrymen and what they would tolerate. This deficiency was notable in the case of F. L. Keller, a descendant of one of Zürich's oldest families, who received his legal training in Germany and became an excellent teacher and scholar, combining a high intelligence with great analytical talent. Keller had been a leading spirit in the reform group in the Political Institute, and in 1831 he became president of the Supreme Court, while serving at the same time as the Great Council's majority leader and its most effective speaker. His work in establishing the court and expanding its functions made some people fear that he intended to make it the dominant branch of the government and led one of his critics to say that, if the courts were to become sovereign, Keller would see to it that he was "the sovereign of the sovereign." If this was unjust, it was certainly true that Keller was the dynamo of the liberal regeneration, always in favor of new experiments and skillful in finding legal justification for government initiatives in new areas, generally impatient with criticism and delay, and all too often scornful of public opinion when it did not seem to support his ideas.

In his initiatives Keller could generally count on the support of Ludwig Snell, now editor of the *Schweizerische Republikaner*, Wilhelm Füßli, a lawyer and personal friend with marked ideological propensities, and Melchior Hirzel, who represented the strong strain of idealism that animated radical liberalism, a giant of a man with a fine tenor voice and mobile features that reflected sympathy and goodwill, and a mind teeming with schemes for human happiness that were uninformed by a critical intelligence. Others among Keller's colleagues—David Ulrich, a gifted jurist who became the author of the new criminal code, and Ludwig Meyer von Knonau, a shrewd and deliberate man who was at his best in time of crisis—had doubts about the advisability of trying to accomplish too much by legislative means, but they generally overcame these and gave loyal support to their accepted leader.

The ascendancy won by Keller and his associates had two results. It contributed, in the first place, to a new polarization of politics in Zürich. At the time of Usteri's death, party lines were not clearly drawn, and party organization was nonexistent. Political groupings were amorphous and based roughly on principle and friendship, including people who, in the Great Council, would vote together on some questions and apart on others, not always very logically. Thus, Usteri's liberal movement included a good number of persons whose views on most issues could more properly be described as conservative but who had been drawn to Usteri's side because they believed that representative government might put an end to the perennial tension between city and countryside and the politics of violence that resulted from it. In 1831–32 these people were frightened away by what appeared to them to be the strong ideological tendency that animated Keller and his followers, as evidenced in a speech by W. Füßli in which he advocated the systematic indoctrination of the country by means of political unions, which would create "a compact liberal mass that would be in a position to strangle the wounded aristocracy, if they should raise their heads again, at their first breath of air." The result of this was that the right wing of the Usteri movement moved further right, merging with the moderate conservatives and the less intransigent of the old aristocrats and forming a new conservative party under the leadership of people like David von Wyss and Konrad von Muralt, both former *Bürgermeister*, Ferdinand Meyer, the father of the novelist, J. J. Hottinger, historian and publicist, and the brilliant young jurist J. K. Bluntschli, a student of Keller's who now became his most persistent critic.

In the second place, this secession of the moderates weakened opposition to Keller and his associates within the liberal party itself and heightened both their self-confidence and their radical reforming zeal. At the risk of running ahead of our story, it can be said that the long-term consequence of this was that the history of the liberal era in Zürich falls into two sharply defined phases. The first, in which Ludwig Keller was the dominant figure, may be described as liberalism's *Sturm und Drang*, years in which, amid much controversy and passionate debate, remarkable changes were set in motion, but with a speed and heedlessness that made it inevitable that, sooner or later, there would be a strong negative public reaction. This came in September 1839 with a dramatic abruptness that drove the liberals into the political wilderness and forced them to regroup their shattered and dispirited forces and to reconsider their program and their tactics. When they returned to power in 1846 it was under new leaders, whose sense of vision was no less highly developed than that of their predecessors but was less romantic, focused more upon material development, and guided by a stronger sense of political reality. The change, which can be called a growth of maturity, was reflected in the solid record of liberal achievement in the second phase of the party's ascendancy from 1846 to 1867.

III

Whatever else might be said of them, the radical liberals did not lack energy, and they set about the job of modernizing the state and giving it an effective infrastructure with dispatch and thoroughness. They completely overhauled the administrative structure of the canton, supplying the reorganized districts with effective agencies and courts and establishing rules for popular participation in community government that proved in time to be a superlatively successful means of civic education. In the field of justice they redefined the competence of the various courts, deciding who was entitled to plead before lower and superior courts, reforming trial procedures, beginning work on a new code of criminal justice, and, in general, bringing the judicial system into accordance with scientific principles. They carried through a comprehensive inventory of state property (*Staatsvermögensinventar*) that made it possible henceforth to administer such properties efficiently and to decide which estates and official residences might be profitably sold off to the public, with the proceeds turned to social purposes, and which could be converted to new uses as hospitals and schools. They set up a Finance Council and, under the skillful direction of Government Councillor Eduard Sulzer of Winterthur, drafted and secured passage of the canton's first comprehensive tax law, which taxed the property of all citizens at a uniform rate and their earnings and income at a progressive one. And, as later chapters will endeavor to show, they contributed to the promotion of economic growth in various effective ways and made remarkable progress in reforming an educational system that had, particularly on the elementary level, not improved since Philipp Albrecht Stapfer's report of 1799 had revealed its deplorable inadequacies.

Notable among the changes made by the liberals were those that modernized the cantonal capital. When they came to power Zürich was still a walled city. To be sure, the original fortifications, which ran along the Fröschengraben (roughly where the

Bahnhofstraße is today) and, on the other side of the Limmat, along the Hirschengraben and what is now Rämistraße, had been dismantled during the Mediation period, and in the 1820s some of the medieval gates, which were in bad repair, were leveled. But the outer fortifications, built under the direction of Hans Georg Werdmüller and Johann Arduser in the seventeenth century, according to the latest scientific principles of that great age of fortification, were still intact. The *Schanzen* afforded pleasant walks for citizens, and their casemates and bastions had other attractions for youth of all ages, but they were offensive to liberals for three reasons. They were a relic of militarism, which the liberals were seeking to diminish, if not to abolish (a principle that led them also to do away with garrison duty for local troops); they formed a symbolic barrier to the equality of city and countryside that was the hallmark of the liberal regime; they were an impediment to traffic and, as Ludwig Meyer von Knonau argued in the pages of the *Republikaner*, an obstacle to the natural expansion of the city, which, if allowed to take its own course, would both lower rents and improve public health. In December 1832 the Governing Council (*Regierungsrat*, formerly *Kleiner Rat*) brought a proposal for their removal to the Great Council, emphasizing the economic advantages of such action and stating further, "When these dark bulwarks against the countryside fall and friendly houses and gardens rise in their place, then gradually with this material barrier the mental one will also disappear, and the city and the countryside will extend the hand of brotherhood across the gulf that has vanished."

The council approved the proposal after a stormy debate, and the dismantling began later in the year and continued until the end of the decade, the Wellenberg and the Grendel (or Water Gate), which had barred free access to the Limmat from the lake, also being demolished in 1836 and 1837. What J. K. Bluntschli called the liberals' "destructive rage" (*Zerstörungswut*) was by no means unrestrained; parts of the *Schanzen*, like the bastion "Die Katze," were saved for the pictorial effect, and a walk along what is left of the fortifications along the Sihl River is still a pleasant diversion for a visitor to the city.

The liberals also turned their attention to the improvement of traffic through the city. For one thing, they planned new thoroughfares, like Poststraße, which was built in 1838 to connect the Münsterhof with the New Market (now the Paradeplatz) and, on the other side of the Limmat, the extension of Rämistraße, which was effected by cutting through that part of the old fortifications called the High Promenade. This made possible both an easier connection with the road to Winterthur and an extension of the town toward the north. In an entertaining account E. Zurlinden has described how, in April 1837, the main theme of Zürich's biggest annual festival, the Sechseläuten parade, was the *Durchbruch* of the High Promenade, with wagons filled with people costumed as *lazzaroni*, carrying picks and shovels, under banners reading *"E ganz neus Züri gids, e besunders Späcktackel!"* and *"Fahr hin, du altes Nest, das uns geboren, die neue Zürich reisst mächtig mich dahin!"*

In the interest of freer movement, the liberal government also built new quays and bridges on the Limmat, notably the handsome stone Münster Bridge, which was dedicated in August 1838. These works, and the erection of new public buildings like the Kornhaus and the Post Office, were made possible by the Merchants Directorial Fund, which was made up of profits from the private postal service which had accumulated since the seventeenth century and which the government now took over in large part, leaving a portion in the hands of the business community on condition that it be used for public works.

All of this activity encouraged private construction that sensibly altered and modernized the appearance of the town. The government sold a good deal of the land on which the fortifications had stood, and on it many private residences were built, particularly in areas close to the lake, on Seefeldstraße, for example, and along the Zeltweg, where the Escher houses were later to be built and where Richard Wagner lived for a time in the fifties. The late 1830s saw a building boom in Zürich, with 500 buildings under construction in 1836. The new quays were also a stimulus to building of another sort, and in the neighborhood of the Großmünster a row of new shops came into existence. On the other side of the river, at the point where the Poststraße entered the New Market, rose the city's first modern hotel, Hotel Baur, which was larger and infinitely more luxurious than the old Hotel zum Schwert at the Rathaus Bridge, which had over the years given shelter to Mozart and Carl Maria von Weber, Goethe, Mme. de Staël, Fichte and the Schlegels, General Doumouriez and Marshal Ney, and Joseph II and Alexander I.

To the cultural development of Zürich the liberal era also brought notable advances, the most important of which, because of its longtime consequences for the city's intellectual life, was undoubtedly the foundation of the university in 1833. A good deal more will be said about this in a later chapter, but it may be remarked here that this event shows an interesting coupling of two strongly held liberal prejudices: one in favor of education, the other against religion. The resources necessary for the building of a university and the elaboration of a system of secondary schools in the canton were procured only by the abolition of the Chorherrenstift and the seizure of its resources, and the liberals were driven to this highly controversial step (which Ludwig Meyer von Knonau later said had occasioned more personal attacks upon him than any other public issue that he could remember), not only by their zeal for higher education but by their view that the Stift—originally composed of those priests who read the masses for the nuns in the Fraumünster, established in the ninth century as a separate corporation in what was later to become the Großmünster, and existing since then as a privileged, highly conservative religious foundation of immense wealth— was exercising an unhealthy influence in political, religious, and educational matters.

The liberal interest in raising the cultural level of the city and promoting *Bildung* found expression also in the establishment in 1834, by public subscription, of Zürich's first permanent theater, which was housed in the former Barfüsserkirche, which, given the church's long opposition to dramatic performances, had a certain irony. The *Neue Zürcher Zeitung*, which took the lead in promoting this enterprise, declared with satisfaction on 27 November 1833:

> It is well known how little attention has been paid up till now to the question of proper diversion and entertainment for female members of the family, with the exception of a few balls and concerts, which are, however, almost exclusively dedicated to the pleasure and pride of the higher order and at which one can hardly appear except in gala attire. And so our wives and daughters have to be content to go in their dozens to women's societies or to stay at home, while the men spend their evenings in smoking clubs or in learned gatherings.

Isn't it now pleasing to think that in the theater natives and foreigners, city dwellers and citizens of the countryside, the gentry and the middle class, men and women can all, without ceremonial or embarrassment, enjoy a form of entertainment that satisfies the feeling for beauty in many ways and in full compass.

The theater opened with a performance of *Die Zauberflöte*, followed by *Egmont, Emilia Galotti, Käthchen von Heilbronn*, and Calderon's *Life a Dream*. The high point of its first season, however, was the patriotic drama *Hans Waldmann*, by a one-time resident of Zürich, Karl Spindler.

IV

That was perhaps an inauspicious omen, for within four years Zürich was to witness a repetition of the fateful events of 1488, with the liberals this time being brought down from their position of power as Waldmann had been from his. The immediate cause of this unexpected turn of events was a more than usually maladroit case of flying in the face of conventional religious feelings, but it had deeper roots. Seen in historical retrospect, the record of liberal accomplishment in the years from 1831 to 1838 was impressive. Contemporaries, on the other hand, were apt to react to the relentless process of change with fear and outrage. Too many old and familiar things were disappearing, and the liberals seemed to have too little respect for tradition and history. Watching the zeal with which they destroyed ancient institutions and beloved features of the landscape, like the *Schanzen*, in their campaign of modernization, some city dwellers were inclined to agree with Bluntschli's sour judgment that "cold reason is revolutionary. It divides, severs, plays with the world and God, builds up in order to tear down again." To people in the countryside the educational reforms were as threatening as the remorseless advance of mechanization and the factory. Because it was too hasty and doctrinaire in execution, the liberals' desire to improve the lot of the lower classes was not understood or appreciated by them, while many of the people who did understand it—who realized that the reformers wished to substitute for the indirect taxes that burdened the countryside a proportional property tax and a progressive income tax—were bitterly hostile because their own interests were hurt. Much of the gathering resentment was understandable: it was not, after all, surprising that the church disliked its diminished role in education, that parents and manufacturers alike objected to restrictions on child labor, that military officers were indignant over the abolition of garrison duty for Zürich's army and the liberals' apparent intention to reduce it to a small civilian militia, that handicrafts and formerly privileged trades regarded the law on freedom of occupation (*Gewerbefreiheit*) of September 1837 as the cause of unfair competition, that users of forests were furious over laws restricting cutting in the interest of future generations, and that simple country folk were irritated by the new decree introducing the metric system of weights and measures. The liberals, by the very energy and variety of their reforms, had inevitably created enemies for themselves. But they were also ill served by the arrogance of some of their leaders and the self-indulgence of others, which gave rise to rumors of loose living in high places that poisoned the social atmosphere. And they were hurt by events beyond their control—the machinations of Nicholas Biddle's Bank of the United States, which caused a crisis in the cotton trade and, in Zürich, led to economic failure, crises of liquidity, a fall in property values, and deep unemployment, all exacerbated by the bad harvest of 1839.

One would have thought that, in the face of all this, the liberals would have walked cannily. They did not do so. Instead, the leaders of the doctrinaire wing of the party—Ludwig Keller, Melchior Hirzel, Füßli, and Ulrich—chose this singularly inappropriate time to try to effect an internal reform of the church, a new Reformation that would modernize its spirit and awaken it to the needs of the liberal age—and in order to effect this they appointed to the chair of New Testament Theology in the university the Württemberg theologian David Friedrich Strauß.

More of a philosopher than anything else, although his critics denied him even that qualification, Strauß had studied under Hegel in Berlin and had then given lectures on modern philosophy and seminars on Plato at Tübingen before writing the book that catapulted him to fame. A two-volume work called *Das Leben Jesu*, this treated the Gospel narrative like any other historical record and rejected all of its supernatural elements as being the stuff of myths. It was a book that marked a turning point in biblical criticism, but hardly one that qualified its author for the chair once held by Zwingli. The Council of Education (*Erziehungsrat*) had approved the appointment by the narrowest of margins, by the tie-breaking vote of *Bürgermeister* Melchior Hirzel, but the theological faculty of the university were almost unanimously against it, and almost all of the canton's clergy were outraged, bombarding the Great Council with petitions to have the decision set aside. That body, however, after a long debate, confirmed the appointment, the majority taking the line that Strauß's opponents were seeking to deny reflective reinterpretation of religious writings.

In doing so they greatly miscalculated the public temper, which had been angry but now became rabid. This finally penetrated the self-assurance of even the most doctrinaire of the liberal leaders, and *Bürgermeister* Hirzel, on 10 February 1839, issued an open letter "To my fellow human beings (*Mitmenschen*) in Zürich Canton," in which, with a mawkish eloquence that anticipated the style of the Reverend Mr. Chadband, he sought to bring love and forbearance into the hearts of his critics. "Do not be angry with us any longer," he pleaded, "because we have made it possible for Dr. Strauß to cause the light that God has vouchsafed unto him to shine amongst us. Don't be angry any more! Be good!" This was greeted with derision and scores of letters beginning "*Teurer Mitmensch*" and continuing in less complimentary ways.

The more serious response to Hirzel's letter was the dangerous heating up of the public temper (to be called a "Strauß" in some parts of the countryside was now equivalent to being called a robber or a murderer) and the rapid politicization of the religious protest. In dozens of communities, committees of protest were formed, and soon a Central Committee, popularly known as the Faith Committee, was keeping them informed and soliciting their support for petitions to the government that, originally confined to the Strauß appointment, soon began to make more extensive demands. The government feebly contested the right of the Central Committee to speak in the people's name, and Ludwig Keller warned his colleagues that to make any concessions at all would be to sacrifice representative government to mob rule. But the majority of the Great Council were too alarmed to adopt his defiant stand, and on 18 March they caved in and voted to pension Strauß off before he had given his first lecture.

This act of self-repudiation did not appease the government's opponents for long. The conservatives, seeing an opportunity to exploit the ineptness of the liberal leadership, encouraged the Central Committee to demand a larger role for religion in educational appointments, and some of the committee's supporters urged it to work for broader political aims, including the dismissal of the radical leaders from the government. In late August, when the government felt compelled to order its officials throughout the canton to refuse to collaborate with, or assist, the committee in any of its activities, the opposition interpreted this as a provocation and answered by calling a monster meeting of all district committees at Kloten on 2 September. Here the Central Committee's president, J. J. Hürlimann-Landis of Richterswyl, inflamed the emotions of his audience ("*du christliches Volk des Kantons Zürich*") by telling them that they had "sensed the earnestness of the moment and had hastened here from all of the districts of your fatherland for the protection of your holy religion."

Behind this rhetoric there was no clear sense of purpose or plan of action; the plain truth was that Hürlimann and his vice president, Dr. Rahn-Escher, had lost all control of the situation. By this time the air was filled with rumors that the government had requested aid from the other cantons, that 30,000 troops were on their way from Bern, and that guillotines had been set up in the public squares of Zürich for mass executions of the committee's supporters. That was all that was needed to precipitate events. While Hürlimann and Rahn equivocated, Parson Bernhard Hirzel of Pfäffikon, a man of uncertain balance of mind with a fancied personal grievance against the government, ordered the storm signal to be rung on his church bells, and the countryside (or part of it, for many communities refused to participate in this adventure) moved against the city.

It was market day in Zürich on 6 September 1839, and shops were opening on the quays and stalls being set up when, at about 7 A.M., Hirzel and Rahn, at the head of 1,500 *Landsturm* men, armed with guns, pikes, and clubs, came over the hills north of the town. In Unterstraß they were met by *Bürgermeister* Melchior Hirzel and State Councillors Sulzer and Hegetschweiler, and there was a brief parley that came to nothing because the invaders had no clearly defined demands. As the governmment representatives withdrew, the *Landsturm* poured down through Neumarkt and the Rindermarkt to the Rathausquai on the west bank of the Limmat, singing *"Dies ist der Tag, den Gott gemacht."* At the river they paused and waited for awhile for reinforcements from the lake, and then, when these didn't materialize, decided to cross the Limmat and seize the armory in the New Market. They divided into two columns, singing *"Gott ist mein Lied, Er ist der Gott der Stärke"* as they did so, and then Pastor Hirzel led the armed contingent over the Rathaus Bridge and along the Storchengasse to the Münsterhof, with the intention of reaching the armory by passing through the narrow, crooked Im Waag at its upper end. Rahn, meanwhile, led about 800 men, armed only with staves and clubs, across the Münster Bridge and up Poststraße to the New Market, where they expected to join Hirzel's forces.

The result was a complete fiasco. Hirzel's column, after overcoming light resistance from a cavalry patrol in the Münsterhof, came under heavy fire as it entered Im Waag, wavered, lost heart, and fled back over the Münster Bridge. Almost immediately thereafter the unarmed peasants led by Rahn, who had reached the New Market without resistance, ran into the fire of 300 military cadets advancing from the garrison in the Thalacker and, as they fell into disorder, were charged by cavalry that drove them, in panic and fright, back to the Hotel Baur and down the Poststraße to the bridge, where they overran and stampeded the rest of Hirzel's column.

It was difficult at this point to say whether this was an end or a beginning, although the fact that new *Landsturm* units were on their way to the city and would be likely to want to avenge the deaths of the fifteen people who had died Im Waag and in the New Market made the latter a distinct possibility. But one man in Zürich was resolved that things must stop here, and he had the will to see that they did so. This was City President Paul Karl Eduard Ziegler. A soldier's son who had himself served in the Dutch army before taking a commission on Zürich's armed force, in which he advanced to the rank of lieutenant colonel, Ziegler had resigned in disgust in 1832 when the liberals abolished garrison duty. A man with a lively interest in civic affairs, although with a pronounced conservative cast of mind, he became a member of the City Council in 1831 and of the canton's Great Council in 1832 and, in November 1837, was elected *Stadtpräsident* (mayor) by the communal assembly. Bitterly critical of the Great Council's handling of the Strauß affair and the agitations that grew out of it, and especially of its decision to reinforce the local garrison at the beginning of December with cadets and ill-trained and ill-disciplined troops, Ziegler was appalled by the bloodshed on the morning of 6 September and promptly intervened by ordering the bells of the Großmünster to ring general alarm.

This was the signal for the citizen militia (*Bürgerwehr*) to assemble arms in hand, and it was obeyed. But the ominous clanging of the cathedral bells seemed on this occasion to affect the whole city with panic. Of a sudden the lake was covered with boats as the market people, who had come in from outlying areas, fled for their homes. The roads too were filled with fugitives, among them the radical leaders Keller, Füßli, and Ulrich, who thought it prudent to remove themselves to Winterthur. In the city that they had abandoned Ziegler was the master and, with the commander of the *Bürgerwehr*, Lieutenant Colonel Schulthess, at his side, he toured the town, seeing that order was restored and removing new sources of provocation by relieving the army commanders of their functions and ordering them to dismiss their troops and leave the city in civilian clothes. In the course of all this he came upon Melchior Hirzel, standing in a state of bewilderment in front of the Post Office. Ziegler regarded Hirzel as the main author of the day's woes—so did Gottfried Keller, who wrote after Hirzel's funeral in 1843 that he had many good qualities but had "prepared a place for the devil to lay his tail"—but, according to Zurlinden's account, he stopped and said, "Sir, you know that I do not share your opinions, but, if your life is dear to you, see to it that you get out of here." "Will you come with me?" Hirzel asked uncertainly. Ziegler answered, "With you I don't go."

Indeed, his presence in the city was indispensable, for by now the government had dissolved itself completely by flight (Meyer von Knonau, that sensible and unflappable man, was characteristically the last to leave), and the city was filling up with wild-looking figures armed with fowling pieces, pikes, halberds, and morgensterns. It was Ziegler's disciplined good sense that convinced them that the garrison that they wished to attack and loot was unoccupied, and it was under his protection that conservative and moderate members of the Great Council, along with representatives of the Faith Committee, pieced together a provisional government and promised new elections. There was no more bloodshed, and things gradually calmed down, although, as the university student (and later editor of the *Neue Zürcher Zeitung*) Johann Ludwig Meyer wrote in his diary,

> Until late in the night and all this morning, new columns from the countryside kept coming into the city. The dead were laid out in the Predigerkirche, and large crowds of peasants kept streaming past our home to see them. They are a dreadful thing to see.

V

If these events raised great expectations in conservative hearts, these were soon to be confounded. The sixth of September 1839 was no revolution in any real sense. It was merely, as has already been indicated, an end to liberalism's *Flegeljahre*, a brief exile from which it would return, sadder and wiser, to power. To be sure there was in the interim a conservative government backed by a Great Council in which there were a mere baker's dozen of liberal representatives, but in the former the men of experience and perspective—Konrad von Muralt, Ferdinand Meyer, and the intellectual leader of the moderate conservatives, J. K. Bluntschli—had too many difficulties with their allies, the *ex-altados* of the Central Committee and the extreme right, who assumed too easily that the events of 6 September had given them a mandate to set the clock back with a vengeance, to be able to govern effectively, and in the latter the conservative majority, almost from the beginning, melted like snow in the spring.

As early as the end of 1840 there were signs of a shift in the public mood. The religious zeal that had accompanied the Strauß affair died away with surprising swiftness and, when the government reformed the teachers seminar in ways that had been demanded at Kloten and gave signs of increasing the influence of the church over school administration, there was unrest in the land, attacks in Ludwig Snell's *Republikaner* upon "pharisaical pietism," and in November, on the anniversary of the Day of Uster, a large public meeting at Bassersdorf that sent an address to the Great Council expressing outrage over attacks on the schools.

The government ran into even more serious criticism when it ended up on what appeared to many people to be the wrong side of the dispute over the Roman Catholic cloisters in Aargau, which the liberal government of that canton had seized in the spring of 1841 on the basis of evidence that indicated that they were being used for subversive purposes. In April the federal diet declared this action to be a violation of the federal treaty of 1815, acting on the initiative of the Zürich Great Council, which had, however, failed to take account of the strong local support for the Aargau confiscation. This was the beginning of the conservatives' maladroitness in national affairs, and it backfired upon them almost immediately. A *Volksversammlung* at Schwamendingen in August demanded that the Great Council cease its meddling in Aargau's affairs, and the issue was still very much alive in May 1842, when elections for the Great Council brought the liberals back with a rush, giving them the same number of seats as their opponents. Even Melchior Hirzel and Ludwig Keller were elected again, although neither accepted the honor, the former no longer having any stomach for politics, the latter preferring to leave Switzerland for what became a distinguished legal career in Berlin.

The new leader of the liberal party was Jonas Furrer, a brilliant young lawyer from Winterthur who had served in the Great Council from 1834 to 1839 and had been a member of the educational council (*Erziehungsrat*) until that body was radically reformed after 6 September. Universally respected for his knowledge, conscientiousness, and eloquence, Furrer was one of the most sought-after advocates in Switzerland, and to devote himself almost exclusively to politics, as he was now called upon to do, involved considerable personal sacrifice. His public conscience and his devotion to the ideals of the Regeneration left him no choice, and he cheerfully set about the task of regaining the confidence of Zürich in his party and winning back a majority in the Great Council.

Both external events and conservative mistakes conspired in his favor. As we shall see in the next chapter, the Aargau case was merely the first of a chain of events that eventuated in the war of the Sonderbund, for it goaded the canton of Luzern into handing the direction of its institutions of higher education over to the Society of Jesus, and that provocative action embroiled the two confessions and reopened the national question with a vengeance. In this atmosphere the liberals made the national question their own. Ever since the days of the Helvetic Republic they had been enemies of Swiss particularism, and Furrer did not deviate from a tradition that had been set by Paul Usteri, making it clear, as events moved toward the final crisis, that his party stood for revision of the federal treaty of 1815 and the creation of a more perfect union.

The conservatives, on the other hand, equivocated on the issue, and their most brilliant leader, J. K. Bluntschli, took the line that a compromise must be found that would prevent civil war and the possible intervention of the powers. This was a position that did not commend itself to the majority of his fellow citizens, and this was reflected in the declining fortunes of his party, as well as in the frustration of his personal ambitions. Thus, in 1844, when Konrad von Muralt, the leader of the conservative party, retired from politics, Bluntschli's hope of succeeding him as *Bürgermeister* came to nothing when the Great Council elected the liberal physician Hans Ulrich Zehnder, who had belonged to the government in the years from 1834 to 1839, and in the spring of 1845, when the Great Council, reflecting the strong nationalism of public opinion, replaced the outgoing members of the *Regierungsrat* with liberals, Bluntschli resigned from that body, recognizing that the conservative experiment that had begun in 1839 had failed and that his own political career was at an end. It was clear that the rising man was Furrer, who was elected to the Governing Council by 107 out of 171 votes, and—urged by Bluntschli to assume the responsibility that the public clearly demanded of him—he became head of the government and, in his capacity as *Bürgermeister*, Zürich's voice in federal affairs.

The elections of May 1846, held under the shadow cast by the polarization of national politics, confirmed Bluntschli's perception of the new temper in Zürich. Only 34 conservatives were returned to the Great Council, as opposed to 158 liberals. In a letter to his friend Johann Salomon Hegi, the young Gottfried

Keller wrote that his fellow citizens had elected a council that was "never as radical even in the Thirties. Thus has the Sixth of September been avenged; it is dispersed and overcome like a vapor." About the radicalism of the new council Keller was mistaken, but he was certainly correct in discerning that the recess was over and that the liberal era had resumed.

Chapter 3

TOWARD A MORE PERFECT UNION: SONDERBUND WAR, NEW CONSTITUTION, PROBLEMS OF FOREIGN POLICY

◆

The despots and the peoples have understood the significance of the struggle in Switzerland, the struggle of modernity with the feudal past, of democracy with aristocratic and jesuitical baseness, very well. . . . The victory is to the advantage of the popular party in every country in Europe; it was a European victory.
—KARL MARX AND FRIEDRICH ENGELS, *Deutsche Brüsseler Zeitung,* 30 December 1847

Jonas Furrer

In contrast to the liberals in France and Germany, who were defeated by their failure to satisfy the national aspirations of their peoples, the Swiss liberals in the middle of the nineteenth century founded a new nation by defeating an attempted secession of the Catholic cantons in a short but crucial conflict in 1847 and then by providing the restored Eidgenossenschaft with an effective constitution and the institutions that would make it viable.

Given the cultural and confessional differences that were Switzerland's historical legacy and the passions that exacerbated cantonal politics in the 1840s, this was a remarkable achievement, and this was recognized more than a century later by Meinrad Inglin, in his novel about the cultural and ideological tensions in Switzerland during the First World War, when he put in the mouth of one of his characters words that both invoked and took comfort in it.

> Our state, as preserver of order, source of law, preserver of right, is not forced upon us by any power; on the contrary, the people will it. This desire for a common state arises in our case clearly from a rational insight, whereas, in the case of a people with one stem and the same language, it is more the result of natural national impulses. Our federal state is therefore predominantly a work of reason, of insight, of tolerance, a work of the spirit.

This was certainly true, yet it was also true that the intellectual and spiritual forces cited by Inglin did not operate automatically. They exerted themselves through human agencies; they were brought to bear upon the problems of state-making by the liberal leaders to whom the victory over the Sonderbund had given the power of decision.

No less remarkable was their ability to defend their creation from external threats during its first vulnerable decade. For the new federal state these were perilous years. The revolutions in central Europe and Italy in 1848 and 1849 posed, not for the first time but certainly in more acute form than ever before, the problem of reconciling Switzerland's policy of neutrality in time of foreign embroilments with its long tradition of providing asylum for political refugees, a problem not made easier by the fact that some of those whom it protected took advantage of this to plot new attacks against the countries that had expelled them. The conservative powers of Europe, already unhappy about the abolition of the *Bundesvertrag* of 1815, with the proud independence of the new Federal State's foreign policy, and with its absorption of Neuenburg after that duchy had in 1848 cast off its former allegiance to the King of Prussia, did not take this lightly, and intermittently from 1848 until the end of the fifties there were threats of foreign intervention in Swiss affairs in one form or another. The reactions to these by the various cantons, moreover, were not invariably uniform, and their differences imposed an additional strain upon the federal fabric.

Zürich's liberal party had the distinction not only of being the staunchest defender of the unitarian principle in the critical years 1846–1848 but also of providing the most talented of the leaders who plotted the course of Swiss policy in the stormy years that followed. This was not the least reason for its prolonged ascendancy in its canton's politics.

I

The liberal identification with the national question was not, of course, new. In the first months after the outbreak of the July revolution in France, when liberalism triumphed in some of the Swiss cantons but was rejected in others, it was the conviction of people like Paul Usteri that the resultant situation was too volatile to be safe, particularly in view of the victory of reaction in the German states, and that the cause of liberty and progress in Switzerland could only be secured against internal and external foes if an end was made to the virtually complete independence of the cantons and the country was united under an effective central government. This objective was high on the list of liberal desiderata in the first days of the Regeneration period. Ludwig Snell, the editor of the *Schweizerische Republicaner*, collected 10,000 signatures in favor of a revision of the Bund in a unitarian sense, and Heinrich Escher, a friend of Usteri's who had been a professor at the Political Institute and the president of the criminal court before becoming editor of the *Neue Zürcher Zeitung* in March 1832, wrote shortly after taking over:

> Will you be like the degenerate Greeks who, out of conten-
> tiousness and pettifoggery, wrangled among themselves
> while the Turks stormed the walls of Constantinople? If you
> don't want that, then at long last establish the union that
> can save us, the union of all! . . . The men who complete
> that work will . . . become immortal, like the men in Grütli!

The governments of the liberal cantons were not unresponsive to that appeal. In 1832, Zürich, Bern, Luzern, Solothurn,
Aargau, and Thurgau formed a Concordat of Seven for the protection of their new institutions, and in March 1833, when the
Tagsatzung met in Zürich, they attempted to force a revision of
the Federal Treaty of 1815 through the diet. Not only did this
fail, but it precipitated a major crisis in federal affairs. The conservative cantons had responded to the formation of the Concordat of Seven by establishing a league of their own (the Sarner
Bund), which now withdrew from the diet and began not only
to talk about forming a counter-*Tagsatzung* but also to consult
the governments of Austria, Russia, and Prussia about the possibility of their recognizing it. On top of this, when the liberal
proposal for revision was defeated by an unexpected negative
vote of the canton of Luzern, the conservative government of
Schwyz, apparently heartened by this, abruptly dispatched
troops to put down liberal and radical elements in the neighborhood of Küßnacht in Outer Schwyz, and rumors swept the
country that this was part of a wider plan to effect a conservative
Putsch in Luzern and then to suppress liberal groups in the Basel
countryside, which were embroiled with their conservative city
government.

In this critical situation, the diet, under Zürich's leadership,
acted with great determination, calling up 16,000 men from cantonal contingents and ordering them to advance on Küßnacht to
protect Luzern from the threatened coup and, if necessary, to
prevent violence in Basel. This firmness had a decisive effect.
The military adventurism in Schwyz came to an abrupt halt,
and when the government in Basel attempted to suppress liberalism in the countryside, the result was a fiasco. The diet then

ordered the dissolution of the Sarner Bund and the return of its members to the *Tagsatzung* and, when they complied, the crisis was over. The Austrian ambassador wrote to his chief, Prince Clemens von Metternich, "*La dernière heure du parti de la résistance a sonné en Suisse. Une manque d'entente, une précipitation impardonnable, des illusions de toute genre auxquelles une triste réalité a fait succéder la plus lâche découragement, telles sont les causes [de la catastrophe].*"

If there was a nationwide conspiracy of the right in 1833, linking events in Outer Schwyz, Luzern, and Basel (the evidence is not conclusive, although Bluntschli, for one, believed that the whole affair had been orchestrated by young patricians in Bern), then the ambassador's words were a just assessment of its amateurishness. But the liberals could take no great comfort from that, for the course of events had confirmed their apprehension concerning the connections between local and foreign reaction. They had no illusions about the depth of the ill will that Metternich and his German allies entertained toward them, and if they had had any tendency to forget this, it would have been corrected by the ominous rumblings that were heard from Vienna and Berlin and Karlsruhe in the years that followed—in 1834, for example, when Polish and Italian revolutionaries took refuge in Switzerland and radical German workers held meetings at Steinhölzli, near Bern, and in 1836 when foreign protests became so menacing that the Eidgenossenschaft found it expedient to expel Giuseppe Mazzini from Swiss soil. Metternich was entirely candid about his aversion for liberal Switzerland. He once said, "*Tout ce que l'Europe renferme d'esprits perdus dans le vague, de l'aventuriers, d'entrepreneurs de bouleversements sociaux, a trouvé un refuge dans ce malheureux pays,*" and it is wholly possible that he would have mobilized the support of the Prussians and the Russians for an attempt to correct what he considered a threat to the European order if he had not been aware that Lord Palmerston, the British Foreign Secretary, and Louis Philippe of France might have something to say about that. Even so, the thought that the fortunes of the party depended on the volatile state of the European balance of power was not comforting to Swiss liberals and strengthened their conviction that a strong union was the only real solution to the problem. But the failure of their reform plan in 1833 postponed the reopening of the national question for more than a decade.

In the mid-forties, however, the decision of the government of Luzern to place the administration of its higher educational facilities in the hands of the Society of Jesus created a national public mood favorable for constitutional reform. Why this should have been true is perhaps not easily understandable to readers in a more secular age, who may note that the Swiss Catholics had some reason for outrage over the seizure of the Catholic cloisters by the government of Aargau in 1841, a clear violation of the federal treaty of 1815 that was never completely voided, and may feel that Luzern's action was possibly an injudicious form of retaliation but at least one that lay within its legal rights. But this does not take into account the superstitious terror that the word "Jesuit" aroused in Protestant minds in the middle of the nineteenth century. In the popular consciousness the Society of Jesus, like communism in the twentieth century, was an international conspiracy with agents at work in every nook and cranny of society to win power for the papacy; ruthless, implacable, and incredibly cunning, it was the secret mover behind the scenes, the cause of much otherwise inexplicable evil in the world. This was the image purveyed by the *romans feuilleton*, like Eugène Sue's *The Wandering Jew* of 1844–45, which made its myriad readers shiver over "the dark machinations of the Jesuits," and it was this image that inflamed the imagination of many in Switzerland after the action in Luzern. This accounts for the perfervid rhetoric of the young Gottfried Keller's "Jesuit Song."

> *Preceded by the cross and banner,*
> *The poison sack tied up behind,*
> *Fanaticism as their provost,*
> *Stupidity following like a tail of beggars,*
>   *They're coming, the Jesuits!*
>
> *O Switzerland, you beautiful bride,*
> *You are affianced to the devil!*
> *Yes, weep, you poor child!*
> *An ill wind is blowing from the Gotthard.*
>   *They're coming, the Jesuits!*

The Jesuits came to Luzern on 24 October 1844. A scant six weeks later a disorderly band of irregulars from various Protestant cantons set off to overthrow the government responsible for this. This adventure had no success (the Zürich contingent got no farther than Albisrieden, only an hour's march from the city, before becoming discouraged and returning home), but it was a shocking reversion to the bad old days when such *Freischaren* made a chaos of intercantonal relations, and it startled a lot of people into realizing that, unless the federal diet were persuaded to take the Jesuit issue in hand, reversing a position that it had taken earlier in the year, a state of anarchy might soon prevail and give foreign powers an excuse for intervention. In all liberal cantons, therefore, committees and unions sprang up with the aim of petitioning the diet to consider the expulsion of the Jesuits from all of Switzerland, a movement in which Jonas Furrer played an important part, along with another rising star of Zürich liberalism. This was Alfred Escher, a descendant of a family that had had a distinguished part in the politics of the the city for generations and son of the merchant entrepreneur Heinrich Escher, who had made millions in land, cotton, tobacco, dye woods, and colonial wares and who was considerably surprised by the direction taken by his son's politics.

The Luzern government was unmoved by the negative reaction to its educational policy and responded to the *Freischarenzug* of December 1844 by arresting and imprisoning the leader of the canton's liberals, Dr. Robert Steiger, and issuing a decree that threatened the organizers of new forces of irregulars with death and authorized its citizens to take the same extreme measures against freebooters from other cantons as they would against robbers and murderers. This almost invited another attack, which, indeed, came in March 1845, when a force of about 2,000 men, including about 400 Luzern liberals and contingents from Aargau, Bern, Solothurn, Baselland, and Schaffhausen (but with only a handful from eastern Switzerland and Zürich) crossed the Luzern frontier under the command of Bernese Captain Ulrich Ochsenbein, a radical who had been a member of the Mazzinian Young Europe movement, and the Aargau militia inspector, Rothplatz. This time the fighting was bloodier and more protracted, with the Luzern forces, reinforced by troops from the Forest Cantons and led by experienced commanders, prevailing. The second *Freischarenzug* was repulsed with heavy losses, more than a hundred of the force being killed and very large numbers—perhaps in the neighborhood of 500—being taken into imprisonment, where, it was soon being rumored, they were subject to brutal treatment.

In these dramatic events Zürich's role was not a prominent one. The small column of radicals that set off to join Ochsenbein's forces, finding themselves abused by their fellow citizens in the countryside for carrying arms on the Sabbath, stopped far short of their goal and vanished into village pubs, and, as for the government, which was still led by the conservatives, its course was ambivalent and uncertain. But the effect of the bloodletting in Luzern was to increase the public pressure for a resolution of the problem hanging over the country, and this redounded to the benefit of the liberals. Jonas Furrer became the head of the government in April 1845, and a month later his party triumphed in the elections for the Great Council. Once that happened Zürich left the isolated position that it had occupied in federal affairs since 1839, rejoined the regenerated cantons of the Concordat of Seven, which the conservatives had repudiated when they took power in that year, and began, under Furrer's skillful diplomacy, to use the primacy in the *Tagsatzung* that had devolved upon it in January 1845 to push the cause of thoroughgoing reform of the federal structure.

The new energy that this change brought to the cause of reform did not bring immediate success. A clear majority for reform did not exist in the diet, some cantons that supported it in principle being intimidated by the menacing attitude of the Austrian and Prussian governments, which had informed the diet at the time of the *Freischaren* incidents that in their view the integrity and neutrality of Switzerland were valid only as long as the federal treaty of 1815 was observed. This might have continued to be a grave impediment to reform had it not been for the fact that at the end of 1845 the legal question became hopelessly contorted—and in the minds of many people irrelevant—when the treaty violation that Metternich kept warning against came not from Zürich and its associates but from the Catholic cantons. On 11 December Luzern, Uri, Schwyz, Unterwalden, Zug, Freiburg, and Wallis formed a separate federation, the so-called Sonderbund, which claimed to be purely defensive but began to arm itself in ways that made it clear that it intended to create for itself a position of independence from the rest of the Eidgenossenschaft. The *spiritus rector* of this new association was Konstantin Siegwart-Müller, who invoked as his models the confessional union of 1529, the alliance of the Catholic cantons with Wallis in 1533, and the Borromaic Union of 1586, which had been formed to combat the spread of what its members called the Zwinglian heresy. This was hardly reassuring, Alfred Escher pointed out in a speech before the Zürich Great Council in June 1846, and it was "difficult to guard against the impression that the cantons that have joined the Sonderbund would like to divide Switzerland into two parts and to represent themselves abroad as the true Eidgenossenschaft." That this was not far from the mark was shown by the fact that Siegwart-Müller had already appealed to Metternich for military and financial assistance. Escher could not have known this, but his suspicions and those of the majority of the council were strong enough to persuade them to instruct Zürich's representative to the *Tagsatzung* to support a resolution for the Sonderbund's dissolution.

The final crisis now came remorselessly on. In January 1847 the leadership of the federal diet passed, by the usual procedure of rotation, from Zürich to Bern, which increased the exasperation of the conservative powers, for Bern's government was now dominated by radical liberals of the most unbuttoned variety, and its head was the former *Freischärler* Ulrich Ochsenbein, who became the *Tagsatzung's* president. A man of unbridled temperament and uncertain judgment, Ochsenbein wasted no time in making it clear that he would force the issue with the Sonderbund, at one point announcing defiantly, "If the Allied Powers wish to play *vabanque*, we shall play with them."

It was not as courageous to strike such attitudes as it may have appeared. It is true that Prince Metternich had been encouraged by a sudden collapse of the Anglo-French entente that had since 1830 formed a liberal counterpart to the conservatism of the three Eastern Powers to think of forming a continental bloc for action against the liberals in Switzerland. But the Guizot government in France was not yet prepared for this, and Metternich, with other problems on his mind, was not disposed to take any action that would be bound to meet British opposition unless he knew exactly where the French stood. All of this was clear enough to the liberal leaders in Switzerland. They were less concerned about the possibility of foreign intervention than they were about securing a majority vote in the federal diet for action against the Sonderbund. But this problem too was resolved by liberal victories in Solothurn and Geneva, the latter by a liberal *Putsch* accompanied by street fighting, and by a conservative defeat in the elections of May 1847 in St. Gallen. As a result, when the diet assembled in July 1847, it voted for the dissolution of the Sonderbund by 12 1/2 of the 22 votes cast, after a speech by Ochsenbein in which he cried passionately that union was now at hand and that the foreign powers would be powerless to prevent it because Switzerland was "great . . . through the sympathies of all free peoples and all those struggling for freedom."

It is possible that, if the members of the Sonderbund had not been so obdurate, they might have altered the course of events even after the vote in the *Tagsatzung*. As the prospect of civil war became actual, several of the cantonal governments developed doubts and began to talk about finding a middle course. Even in Zürich the question of using military force if the Sonderbund refused to dissolve caused a long and bitter debate in the Great Council in September, and it took all of Furrer's eloquence, and his insistence that hesitation at this point would make federal reform impossible, before the council approved military execution. In the armed forces, in particular, there was considerable repugnance for the task that lay ahead, and Georg von Wyß wrote after the September vote, "Even though the Great Council has blown the trumpet of war, the mood of the people in its great majority is far from being as determined as those of the Swiss on the other side. . . . We officers will do our duty loyally and with our best powers, no matter how hard this appears to us. God knows how many will be sacrificed for this heavy task! In no sense is it an elevating one, in no sense an enjoyable one."

The members of the Sonderbund showed no disposition to exploit these doubts and hesitations. Trusting perhaps in the inspiration afforded by their religious conviction and the strength of their strategic position, and encouraged by weapons shipments from Austria, they mobilized their forces and soon had 30,000 regulars and 50,000 *Landsturm* under arms. Their commander was Ulrich von Salis-Soglio, who had served with distinction in the Bavarian and Dutch armies. That his relations with his chief of staff, Colonel von Elgger, were not good was a debilitating factor but went unremarked as the Sonderbund opted for war.

On the other side the question of command was initially a matter of some controversy. Ochsenbein had ambitions of his own in this regard and was backed by his government, but this was deftly sidetracked by Furrer, who pointed out that such an appointment might hearten rather than discourage the other side by evoking memories of the second *Freischarenzug* and that a not inconsiderable number of officers might, as professionals, simply refuse to serve under him. The second point was a telling one—earlier in the year one of Switzerland's best military talents, Colonel Ziegler, had resigned from the *Tagsatzung's* war council when Ochsenbein became its president—so the diet passed Ochsenbein over and gave the command of its troops to *Oberstquartiermeister* Henri Dufour, an officer whose known experience and reputation for integrity and energy outweighed liberal concern about his conservative politics. Dufour had an advantage over the Sonderbund in numbers—37,000 regular troops and 48,000 *Landsturm*—but hardly a decisive one. His principal strength lay in his clear-sighted recognition that he could not fight a protracted war without risking foreign intervention and his skill in adapting his strategy to that requirement.

The war of the Sonderbund was, indeed, a *Blitzkrieg*, but one that was unaccompanied by the dreadful losses of twentieth-century examples of that style of warfare. On the basis of an operations plan drafted by the Zürich Lieutenant Colonel of Engineers Nüscheler, Dufour at the outset of hostilities turned his whole force against Fribourg, which, isolated and cut off from the possibility of reinforcement, capitulated on 14 November. Without pause the federal commander then concentrated his army against Luzern, the *Schwerpunkt* of his enemy's resistance. The decisive battle was fought at Gislikon, where Ziegler took what Zürchers regarded as revenge for their defeat at Kappel in 1531, returning to Zürich, after hostilities were over, with Zwingli's weapons, which had been held in Luzern ever since. After Gislikon further resistance by the now disorganized Sonderbund army was impossible, and it laid down its arms.

The collapse of the Sonderbund's army, after a resistance of less than a month, shocked those contemporaries who remembered the historical reputation of the Forest Cantons for bravery and élan on the offensive and for dauntless resistance when faced with overwhelming odds. In truth, Salis-Soglio's troops—in part, perhaps, because of inadequate psychological preparation that seems to have led them to underestimate the determination of their opponent—showed little stomach for the fight when it was pressed against them, sometimes abandoning positions that they had successfully defended if the enemy renewed the attack. Lack of discipline, moreover, almost invariably marred performance, disrupting offensive operations and making orderly withdrawals impossible. At Gislikon, for example, the Sonderbund's forces were unresponsive to the commands of their officers and, in the end, simply ran away. Dufour's army, thanks to the superior training of its field officers, was held under tighter control, at least while on the march or during engagements; in bivouac, troops were inclined to assume that they were off duty and to get drunk.

Fire discipline was miserable on both sides, the expenditure of ammunition being out of all proportion to the losses suffered (74 dead and 377 wounded on the Eidgenossenschaft's side, 24 dead and 116 wounded on that of the Sonderbund), which does not say much for the marksmanship of the Swiss militia and the highly regarded sharpshooting companies, although Erwin Bucher in his assessment of the war has suggested that, when they found themselves in real firefights, the Swiss may have preferred not to try to kill each other. If this were so, they were less scrupulous about pillage, rapine and other excesses reminiscent of an earlier age, and one observer said after the fighting was over, "*Les Suisses ont l'instinct décidément pillard. Cet instinct s'est fait jour partout, de tout temps, dans tous les guerres, nos voisins s'en souviennent, hélas. Malheureux vaincus lorsque les Suisses sont vainqueurs.*"

All in all, the Sonderbund war did not redound to the glory of Swiss arms, and the *Karlsruher Zeitung* wrote in December 1847, "If you Swiss are everything possible, soldiers at this time you are not!" Bucher points out that it was awareness that this impression, if it became general, would be dangerous to Swiss independence that inspired General Dufour's efforts, during the revolutions of 1848, to bring the federal state's new army to a high level of performance in the field. In an army order issued during the mobilization of 1849, he did not hesitate to appeal to history, saying, "*Vous feriez en un mot, tous vos efforts pour qu'on dise de vous: 'Les enfants de la libre Helvétie n'ont pas dégénéré de leurs ancêtres.'*"

The speed with which the victory was won confounded the

European powers. Both Metternich and Guizot would have liked a collective intervention by the concert of Europe, which would have forced a cessation of hostilities and the submission of the intercantonal dispute to an international conference at which the Sonderbund would have been represented on equal terms with the federal diet. A precedent could have been found for such a meeting in the London Conference of 1831 on Belgium, which had also dealt with an attempt to amend by violence an arrangement that was sanctioned by the Final Act of the Congress of Vienna. This time, however, the conference idea failed because the British Foreign Secretary, Lord Palmerston, a firm supporter of Swiss liberalism, while not refusing to collaborate, raised so many procedural objections that the collective note did not arrive until after the victory had been won. Palmerston was also responsible for discouraging ideas of military intervention, which occurred at various times to both the Prussians and the Russians, by pointing out that a declaration of the powers of 20 November 1815 obliged them to respect Swiss neutrality and thus barred them from violating or occupying any part of Switzerland unless Switzerland itself engaged in offensive action against its neighbors.

The frustration of the powers increased when it became apparent that the Swiss liberals had no intention of standing on their military victory but were proceeding at full speed to reform the federal structure and create a unitary state, with little regard for the treaty of 1815 and without consulting other governments. In a joint note quivering with indignation, the governments of Austria, France, and Prussia informed the federal diet that this violated the public law of Europe, that no new state could be established without the consent of the Vienna powers, and that this would not be forthcoming unless all of the cantons agreed with the changes. This seemed less an attempt to assert the authority of the European concert than an effort to rehabilitate the cause of the Sonderbund, and, rightly diagnosing its purpose, Jonas Furrer, now Zürich's *Bürgermeister* and chief representative to the diet, rejected it flatly.

He did so without resorting to the kind of slanging that characterized Ulrich Ochsenbein's allocutions to other governments but in language that was measured, reflective, and determined and with a persuasiveness of argument that made his reply, in the opinion of Edgar Bonjour, a note that hardly has its equal in the history of Swiss diplomacy. Recalling the circumstances in which the Eidgenossenschaft, by a decision made by its diet on 27 May 1815, had adhered to the Vienna treaty, he reminded the powers (as Palmerston had done recently) that, on 20 November 1815, they had signed the documents "that confirmed in the most formal and solemn manner their earlier promises with respect to Switzerland's everlasting neutrality and independence." It was in the light of these circumstances that the present legal situation must be judged. Nothing in the events of 1815 or the documents signed then gave the powers the right to limit the inner form or the further growth and development of the Eidgenossenschaft, "which did not grow out of that time but had existed independently in various forms for centuries." Furrer continued:

> But the great powers did show evidence of a great interest in the speedy reconstitution of Switzerland, in its relations with the states surrounding it, in its strength and unity and all of the things that would enable it to protect its independence and neutrality. . . . It is from these memorable events and from the clear text of the pertinent documents that the diet is completely convinced that the [old] federal constitution itself was never guaranteed and that, in addition, the neutrality that was promised to Switzerland was never tied to conditions about specific forms of federal arrangements.

The firmness of this note did not please its recipients, nor was it persuasive to all of them (the Tsar of Russia suspended his recognition of Switzerland on the grounds that it had violated the conditions recognized as the very rationale of its existence and, in addition, was harboring revolutionaries), but it removed any basis for further discussion. In any event, the state of Europe discouraged that. In February, Guizot and his king were driven from power; in March the all-powerful Metternich followed them into exile, and there were barricades in Berlin. With relief the *Neue Zürcher Zeitung* announced on 12 March 1848:

> The latest revolutionary storm in France has also swept away a host of hazardous circumstances in Switzerland. As it dispelled the diplomatic storm clouds that hung heavily over our fatherland and drove them away toward the north, it brightened the heaven above us, and every Swiss breast

breathed more freely than ever. We have never desired anything more from foreigners than that they should not hamper us in our movements and that Switzerland should be left to itself. Yet even that modest wish remained unregarded. . . . Now everything is different, and Switzerland, free and unrestrained, can turn its eyes exclusively to its own interests.

II

During this lull in the diplomatic crossfire the work of constitutional reform moved briskly forward, thanks to the political experience of the twenty-three men chosen to form the Revision Commission, to their familiarity with the issues involved, and doubtless also to the fact that the conservatives were largely unrepresented. The commission began its work on 17 February 1848, and six weeks later, after thirty-one five-hour sessions, completed it and submitted its draft constitution to the *Tagsatzung* and the individual cantons. In May the majority of the *Tagsatzung*, acting on cantonal instructions, voted to accept the draft, with some amendments, and it was sent back to the cantons for popular referenda. Finally, on 12 September, after receiving the results of the vote and and settling disputes rising out of it, the diet decreed that, in view of the fact that fifteen cantons and one half-canton had voted for it, the new constitution was the law of the land.

It is hardly necessary, in a book that deals with the liberal achievement in Zürich, to describe the constitution of the new federal state in any detail. Perhaps only two points need be made. It was, with respect to the cantons that had resisted reform with arms in hand, a remarkably conciliatory document. Indeed, the restraint that characterized those parts of it that affected the former members of the Sonderbund most nearly was admirably designed to overcome their bitterness and to persuade them to accept the new order of things. No attempt was made to diminish their territory; no effort was made to infringe upon their freedom of religious belief, apart from the provision that permanently forbade the Society of Jesus to carry on its work in Switzerland, and they were even spared the extreme centralization that radicals like Ochsenbein and Druey had so ardently desired and that they themselves had so deeply feared.

In the second place, the new constitution more closely resembled the American than the Helvetic model. The powers of the central government, now embodied in a bicameral legislation, a collegial executive, and a federal supreme court, were enhanced in order to enable it to discharge its stated purpose, which was "to strengthen the union of Eidgenossen, to maintain and promote the unity, strength, and honor of the Swiss nation," and to "assert the independence of the fatherland against the outside world [and watch over] peace and order at home, the protection of the freedom and rights of Eidgenossen, and the promotion of their common welfare." For these purposes it was given exclusive control of foreign policy, broadly defined prerogatives in the field of military affairs, including selection and administration of the general staff and the right to take measures to improve the coordination between cantonal contingents, and —as one might expect in a constitution written by liberals— very extensive functions designed to promote economic growth (maintenance of uniformity of currency, weights and measures, and postal service; responsibility for tolls and customs; oversight of freedom of trade and occupation, and the like). It also received the financial support necessary for effective discharge of its powers and duties from the proceeds of tolls, the postal service, interest on the federal war chest, and contributions from the individual cantons.

On the other hand, extensive powers were reserved to the cantons. To be sure, they could no longer conclude military capitulations with foreign powers, or maintain more than 3,000 men under arms, or violate any right guaranteed by the federal constitution (like freedom of the press), and they were enjoined to refrain from the use of force in disputes with other cantons and to supply the assistance requested when any part of the federation was under attack from without. But they had sovereignty in local affairs; they controlled their own educational establishments and judicial system and police; punishment of crime and infringement of civil and commercial statutes lay within their jurisdiction, and they kept the power of direct taxation. And, even in those areas where their former powers had been curtailed or—as in the case of foreign affairs—eliminated, they were enabled, through the institutions of representative government and a free press, to criticize, modify, and change policies that they did not like.

The canton of Zürich accepted the new constitution with

enthusiasm, the Great Council unanimously, the electorate by a vote of 25,119 to 2,517. In doing so, however, it suffered two losses. The first was a personal one. Jonas Furrer's work on the Revision Commission, his skillful steering of the draft constitution toward acceptance, and his masterful service as interim foreign minister not only impressed a broad public but convinced it that he was the person best suited to lead the new federal state in its first years. On 4 October 1848 the Zürich Great Council elected him as the canton's representative on the *Ständerat* (the national chamber of cantonal delegates). On 6 November he became its president and, on 16 November, the first member of the executive *(Bundesrat)*, or *Bundespräsident*. For the rest of his life (he was *Bundespräsident* for four terms) the focus of Furrer's life was on the federal capital and national affairs, and that meant that Zürich was largely deprived of the services of its most distinguished statesman and the Zürich liberals of a shrewd and sagacious leader. The canton and the party were fortunate in finding in Alfred Escher a talented successor.

In the second place, the price of the liberals' victory in the national question was the final defeat of Zürich's old ambition to be Switzerland's capital *(Hauptstadt)*. Peter Stadler has pointed out that, because of the nature of federal politics, polycentrism was the rule until the middle of the nineteenth century, with various cities having the right to serve as the meeting place of the federal diet and being considered *Vorort* when this happened. The Helvetic Republic, true to its principle of centralization, had a permanent capital, first in Luzern and then, in its last throes, in Bern, but after its fall the old system was restored, and after 1815 this was modified to provide for a regular rotation of the *Vorort* between Zürich, Luzern, and Bern.

The war of the Sonderbund severely weakened any claim that Luzern might have had to primacy in the new federal union, and when the constitutional debate began in 1848 it was clear that the choice lay between Zürich and Bern. Jonas Furrer had high hopes that his city would be chosen; the liberal-conservative *Eidgenössische Zeitung* pointed out on 14 November that it was entirely appropriate that it should be, for this would prevent an otherwise inevitable confrontation between Catholic Luzern and radical Bern; and Ludwig Snell, in an anonymous pamphlet, cited, as special recommendations, the natural beauty of Zürich's location, the public buildings and other accommodations and amenities that it could provide for the federal parliamentarians and officials, and the cosmopolitanism and hospitality that had characterized it since 1830. But Zürich's salient disadvantage was the fact that it lay in eastern Switzerland, uncomfortably remote—in days before the full development of the railway net—from other centers at home and abroad. This was a point that Bern's politicians, who actively campaigned for their city (in contrast to the Zürchers, who thought such tactics were demeaning) emphasized effectively. In the end the National Council (*Nationalrat*) chose Bern over Zürich by 58 votes to 35, with six votes falling to Luzern, and the Council of Cantons (*Ständerat*) confirmed this by a 21–13–3 vote.

This was a disappointment, although, in the course of their campaign to secure votes for their own city, the Bernese had proposed that there should be a national university whose seat would not be in the capital, and Zürich clearly had the strongest claim to be the home of that institution when it was built. Aside from that, with Jonas Furrer as *Bundespräsident* and Alfred Escher soon to be president of the *Nationalrat*, there was no possibility of Zürich's being excluded from the direction of national policy. Indeed, the fact that it now became a principal goal for refugees from the reactionary persecution that followed the suppression of the revolutions in Germany and Italy placed it in the very middle of the heated debates over neutrality and right of asylum that marked the dangerous period of Swiss foreign policy that opened even before the new constitution was ratified.

III

In the spring of 1848 many Swiss citizens must have had feelings similar to those put into words by the English liberal Thomas Babington Macaulay, who wrote at this time, "All around us the world is convulsed by the agonies of great nations. Governments which lately seemed likely to stand during ages have been on a sudden shaken and overthrown. . . . Meanwhile, in our island, the course of government has never been for a day interrupted. We have order in the midst of anarchy." Gottfried Keller doubtless spoke for many of his fellow Zürchers when he echoed Macaulay and wrote, "With what superiority and calm can we poor little Swiss look down—down in a literal sense, from our mountains—upon the spectacle!"

This detachment did not, however, please everyone in the new federation. Leaders like James Fazy of Geneva, Henri Druey of Waadt, and Jakob Stämpfli of Bern felt that Switzerland should play a more positive role in the European fight for freedom, which had, in their view, received its first stimulus from the Swiss example, and their more radical followers called upon the federal government to raise a military force of 120,000 men to go to the aid of the revolutions in Germany, Hungary, and Italy and described anyone who demurred as a traitor to the liberal cause and a supporter of the Holy Alliance. In some cantons the majority of public opinion opposed the policy of neutrality. This was true, for example, of Tessin, whose predominantly Italian population had no compunction about sending *Freischaren* into Lombardy to aid the rebels there, although this flatly violated federal policy. Tessin was one of the six cantons that voted for acceptance of the offensive-defensive treaty that Carlo Alberto of Piedmont-Savoy offered the Swiss Confederation in April 1848, a proposal of which Druey was a strong supporter, arguing that Switzerland could not simply stand aside in the struggle between democracy and absolutism

In the national capital the majority of the cantonal representatives took a more realistic view of the probable outcome of the European revolutions and wanted no gambles at the expense of Swiss independence. They agreed, moreover, with Jonas Furrer's strong insistence that policy in this respect must be set by the federal government and not by the individual cantons, and that violations of national policy must be prevented and punished by the interposition of federal force in cases where cantonal governments proved ineffective in enforcement. Thus, in April 1848, when the redoubtable Johann Ludwig Becker, whose record as a fighter for democracy went back to the Hambach Festival and who was later to be the friend of Marx and Engels and one of the founders of the First International, began to recruit a German Legion to fight alongside Friedrich Hecker in Baden, the federal government dispatched troops to help the government of Basel seal off its borders with Baden and Alsace and prevent the passage of men and munitions, an action that was perhaps the first manifestation of the determination and will of the new *Bundesstaat*. Later, when Becker resorted to the same methods to aid the Badenese rising of 1849, this time in Biel in the neighborhood of Bern, he was expelled and forced to join the revolutionaries in Rastatt without followers and with little more than the clothes on his back. Throughout the revolutionary period the federal government was equally vigilant in Tessin, although at the cost of not inconsiderable local dissatisfaction.

On the question of neutrality the Great Council in Zürich stood foursquare with the federal government, remaining true to a principle first laid down by Zwingli, and found general support in the local press. In the *Neue Zürcher Zeitung*, both Ludwig Herkules Daverio and his successor as editor, Peter Felber, were sympathetic to the revolutionary cause in Germany and Italy but opposed to any form of intervention. In June 1849, when the Badenese revolution was close to collapse and radicals were rashly calling for the dispatch of troops to save it, Felber pointed out that such a palpable breach of neutrality would invite retaliation and added, "With our German, French, and Italian sympathies, we have of late almost forgotten that we are Swiss and that a people has above all to think of itself." The same note was struck in Spyri's moderate-conservative daily, the *Eidgenössische Zeitung*, a paper that generally took the line that "for the anarchists, phantasts, socialists, and communists of other countries, Swiss citizens should not pull chestnuts out of the world's fires." On 26 June 1849 it warned that it was "possible that the King of Prussia, after he has conquered the anarchy [in Baden] and doubtless the freedom along with it, will develop a craving to have a little word with Switzerland, which people have said so often, although certainly with exaggeration, supplied the impetus for the whole European revolution through its Sonderbund war. . . ." Only strict observance of neutrality could discourage that prospect or give Switzerland the moral strength to withstand it if it came.

The only time in the whole liberal period that Zürich came close to wavering in its position was during the Crimean War, which in the eyes of many people was a special case, in which all of the European powers, liberal and conservative alike, were united against Russian absolutism. The *Neue Zürcher Zeitung* declared that this was a war for the highest values of civilization and called for the creation of a Swiss auxiliary force of 12,000 to 16,000 men to support the allies, a position that found wide agreement in the national press. The federal government in Bern did not see fit to act on this suggestion, but it chose to avert its eyes when its nationals joined Swiss Legions in Britain and France, Ulrich Ochsenbein actually serving as brigadier in the latter force. These formations never got to the front, but their very existence was an evasion of the *Nationalrat's* decision in May 1849 that there should be no more recruiting for foreign armies in any part of Switzerland and, by extension, of the principle of neutrality itself.

Equally difficult to interpret and apply in ways that satisfied all of the parties concerned, whether domestic or foreign, was the counterpart of neutrality, namely, the right of asylum. In its circular note to the cantons of 28 February 1848, the federal government had stated, "Should refugees, armed or unarmed, of whatever origin, cross the territory of the Eidgenossenschaft, a peaceful sojourn is to be granted them, in accordance with the application of the right of asylum and the laws of humanity. The former, however, are to be disarmed immediately and further to be watched over so that the granted asylum is not misused for intrigues against neighboring states."

At the time that that was written, no one had any idea of the potential dimensions of the problem it treated. Switzerland had a long record of giving refuge to political refugees, but the numbers had always been relatively modest: in Zürich, for example, there were in the whole canton only four political refugees in 1843 and five a year later. That changed with dramatic suddenness in the years of revolution, as the remnants of Hecker's column and Herwegh's German Legion from Paris and the participants in Struve's September Putsch straggled across the Swiss borders in 1848, and as the barricade fighters of Dresden and Lombardy and the shattered armies of Sigel and Mieroslawski sought refuge a year later.

Even before the Badenese Army had become a body of refugees in a technical sense, it posed a difficult problem for the Swiss government and caused a curious modification of the doctrine of right of asylum. In the first days of July 1849, after the Prussians broke the Badenese line of resistance along the Murg River at Rastatt, the revolutionary army flowed southward, past Donaueschingen, to an improvised line running eastward from Lörrach. Command had shifted from Mieroslawski to Sigel, an unfortunate soldier who never realized his full potential until he fought in the western theater during the American Civil War. But no one could fault Sigel's courage, and the spirit of his troops was generally good, especially in the workers battalion fighting under the former Prussian Lieutenant August Willich. It seemed not unlikely, then, that a major battle might be fought almost within sight and sound of Swiss territory.

This greatly alarmed the Swiss government, which had no desire to see the Prussians (with whom, as we shall see, the Neuenburg question had poisoned relations) on its border. It took the unusual step, therefore, of sending a commissioner to Sigel to tell him that he must either withdraw from his present position to a line farther from the Swiss frontier (which was, of course, a military impossibility) or come across the border without any further fighting. In the latter case he should lead his army in the direction of Zürich and Winterthur, where it would be divided among the cantons of Zürich, Glarus, St. Gall, Schwyz, and Zug. The terms of Sigel's own internment would depend upon the manner in which he crossed the border. If he did so fighting, he would be met by the fire of federal troops commanded by Colonel Ziegler.

This was, in effect, a threat to deny asylum unless the revolutionary army capitulated before it was utterly defeated, but, although it was bitterly resented, it left Sigel and Willich no choice. The passage of the Rhine began on 11 July, 2,000 men with cannon crossing at Rheinau, 1,400 with twenty-eight field guns at Eglisau, and other units coming over at Lotstetten. On the twelfth the *Neue Zürcher Zeitung* reported the arrival of the higher officers of the defeated army at the Hotel Baur in Zürich on the previous day, Sigel and his general staff, uniformed and wearing galloons and epaulets, in one carriage and the free corps leaders, in blouses and red sashes, in a second. More interesting to the reporter than the arrival of these notables was the presence in one of the columns from Lotstetten of a young woman in man's clothing, whom the authorities carefully detached from her companions and interned separately.

Sigel's army had been preceded by remnants of the revolutionary army of the Palatinate, and it was followed by other columns of refugees in the weeks that followed. On 23 July it was officially estimated that there were 9,000 German refugees in Switzerland, plus 150 Poles and several thousand French and Italians, and more were expected after the imminent collapse of the Roman Republic.

The costs of maintaining this number even for a considerable period did not pose a serious problem, for the revolutionary army was disarmed as it crossed the frontier, and the arms were subsequently sold back to the government of Baden or to other interested parties at a profit. The dislocation caused by the sudden infusion into the local scene of hundreds of "unattractive youngsters, in a considerably miserable state, some dressed in Bavarian uniform (light blue and red) and supplied with *casquets*, others in the dress of *Freischärler*, still others quite fantastic in appearance," as one observer described the remnants of Blenker's corps as it entered Zürich, was quickly alleviated by the distribution of the refugees among the various cantons in accordance with their population. Thus, Zürich's initially heavy share— about 4,000—was quickly diminished, and by the beginning of 1850 there were only slightly more than 600 refugees in the city, most of whom had already found employment.

Some of these were civilians of distinguished reputation in the field of scholarship, like the historian Theodor Mommsen and the classical philologist Hermann Köchly, who had been involved in revolutionary activities in Germany and Italy, and had had to flee when the tide of revolution turned, and these people, as we shall see, found positions in Zürich's university and schools and soon played a prominent role in its social and cultural life. Others had private means and could support themselves, like the former Bonn student Karl Schurz, who had fought in Baden and been caught in the fortress of Rastatt when the Prussians encircled it but had escaped through a drainage canal and made his way to Zürich. Here he lived quietly, studying the history of the Reformation in the university library and, in the evening, being tutored in military history and strategical theory by Alexander von Schimmelpfennig and other young officers in the exile community, until February 1850, when, responding to the appeal of the wife of Gottfried Kinkel, who had been imprisoned by the Prussians in Spandau, he went to Berlin and engineered a daring rescue of his former professor, fleeing with him to England and subsequently making his own way to the United States. Thirteen years later, when Schurz commanded a division of the Union Army at the battle of Chancellorsville and

Schimmelpfennig was one of his brigadiers, he reminded him of the time in Zürich and told him that what he knew of the military art he had learned from him there.

The less fortunate of the military refugees profited from the efforts of the Committee for the Support of German Refugees, which had been founded in Zürich in July 1849 under the presidency of J. J. Sulzer and with a board that included prominent lawyers, manufacturers, and merchants, as well as representatives of the church and the university. This body solicited cash donations and gifts of shoes and clothing, not only from Switzerland and Germany but also from Great Britain and the United States, distributed these among the neediest of the refugees, and, with considerable success, provided them with jobs. Those refugees who preferred to live in the military garrison at state expense soon discovered that refusal to work led to severance of support and termination of the right of asylum. This freed the community of the least desirable elements among the exiles, and an agreement with the French government to allow transit for those refugees desirous of going to England or America at their own expense also reduced the overall total.

From the very beginning of the mass incursion of refugees it was clear to the federal government in Bern that the political aspect of the problem was more difficult than the economic and administrative ones. They were aware that the Badenese, Prussian, and Austrian governments would resent the presence in Switzerland of large numbers of revolutionaries who might be tempted to use their sanctuary as a jumping-off place for new *coups de main*, and that they might use this as an excuse for intervention in Swiss affairs. To forestall anything of the sort the federal government, on 16 July 1849, instructed the cantons that all political and military leaders who had taken part in the risings in Baden and the Palatinate must leave Switzerland. This was greeted with considerable indignation, not only in Geneva and Bern, where the radical governments of James Fazy and Albert Galeer in the former and Jakob Stämpfli in the latter protested strenuously and where there were agitations among the university students, but also in Zürich, where both the government and the press felt that the *Bund* decree was in contravention of Switzerland's historical policy. The *Eidgenössische Zeitung* found it demeaning that, with the new federal state only a year old, the first government elected freely by the deputies of the people should have issued an order that flatly violated tradition, and the *Neue Zürcher Zeitung*, in articles on 20–21 July ridiculing the government's arguments in support of its decree, asked, "What is the good of *raison d'état* toward foreign governments if it provokes in our own country the creation of a refugee and an antirefugee party?" and wrote, "We have no words for our sorrow."

Jonas Furrer reacted with some irritation to these complaints from his own canton. "Of late," he wrote to Alfred Escher on 21 July, "people have been practicing a real idolatry in respect to the right of asylum. A right of asylum for foreigners, that is already formally assumed, we recognize in no way at all, but rather the right of asylum that every independent state has in relation to other states, combined with a moral obligation, as far as humanity demands it and the highest interest of the state permits it." The government elaborated this position in new notes to the cantons in the weeks that followed and gave assurances that there was no intention of handing the revolutionary leaders over to the governments they had fought against and that every effort would be made by negotiation to secure them transit to democratic countries.

It was easier to appease the cantons than it was to convince the foreign governments that Switzerland was not—as one newspaper put it—"the great lodging place of the honorable guild of demagogues." In February 1850 the government in Karlsruhe accused Zürich of tolerating the presence of groups that had clandestine ties with subversive groups in Baden and Württemberg, and it became known that representatives of the French, Prussian, and Austrian governments had met to discuss the possibility of an ultimatum that would insist upon the expulsion of all refugees from Switzerland. With the atmosphere becoming as tense as it had been in 1847, the federal government took urgent steps to appease foreign opinion, arresting and expelling Mazzini, who had come to Switzerland after the fall of the Roman Republic, breaking up a number of radical workers unions and deporting their foreign members, warning the cantons to tighten their regulations against political activity by refugees, and to see that they were kept away from international borders. This was enough to prevent the powers from agreeing on an interventionist policy, and it met with the general approval of the cantons, particularly Zürich, which had by now become convinced that Furrer's view was correct and whose press was highly critical of actions that jeopardized his policy, like those of Fazy in Geneva, who, after Louis Napoleon's *coup d'état* in December 1851, made his city, as one critic said, a kind of "democratic Koblenz" and gave the refugees a dangerous political latitude. In general, however, federal policy prevailed and, because of its success, the refugee question was resolved and, despite some local incidents and an occasional flurry in the foreign press, the debate over neutrality died down. This did not, however, put an end to the country's foreign worries, for the long-simmering dispute over Neuenburg now came to a head.

Like many other complicated matters, this had resulted from the deliberations of the Great Powers in Vienna in 1815, who had, here as elsewhere, chosen the ambiguous over the simple solution. They had decided that the princedom of Neuenburg, a possession of the King of Prussia, should become a canton of the Swiss federation, with rights and duties equal to those of other cantons but without relinquishing its Prussian connection. This was anomalous enough in the conservative post-Vienna years; it became more so with the opening of the liberal era in 1830, for all of Neuenburg's officials owed their allegiance to the King of Prussia and its government was inflexibly conservative. Thus, in 1833, Neuenburg was a member of the Sarner Bund, and in 1847, while not belonging to the Sonderbund, its government so far sympathized with it that it declared its neutrality in the war that it precipitated. This was far from being to the liking of Neuenburg's liberals, who tried twice during the thirties to overthrow their government, and in 1848 tried again, more successfully, declared the republic, and entered the new Swiss federal state as such.

This result the King of Prussia refused to accept. Frederick William IV assured his party in Neuenburg that he would not abandon them and appealed to the other Great Powers, who, to oblige him, further compounded the confusion in 1852 by recognizing both his rights in Neuenburg and Neuenburg's union with Switzerland, the British government adding a codicil to this protocol to the effect that the King had no right to intervene by force to secure his rights. With this Frederick William professed to be content, but the royal party in Neuenburg was of another mind and, in September 1856, they attempted a singularly ill-planned *Putsch*, which was put down with ease, all of the participants being arrested. The King of Prussia demanded their immediate release; the Swiss government replied that this would be contingent upon the King's relinquishment of all his rights in Neuenburg.

These events precipitated the most dangerous crisis in Swiss foreign relations before the First World War. The Prussian government seemed to be spoiling for a fight, perhaps to make up for its inglorious role during the Crimean War and the snubs that it had received at the Paris Conference of 1856, and its general staff elaborated a war plan that would have involved a three-pronged attack upon Switzerland by a force of 120,000 to 130,000 men. Undaunted by this, the Swiss government prepared to defend its neutrality with all of its resources, ordering full mobilization at the end of 1856, placing General Dufour, the victor in the Sonderbund War, in supreme command and deciding that, instead of waiting for the Prussians, it would adopt an offensive strategy that would hit their columns separately before they were fully deployed.

In the end everyone had second thoughts, the South German governments not least of all, who had no desire to see Prussian troops in their territory again, and in this situation British diplomacy, ever fertile in expedients, was once more able to find a compromise. In May 1857 the Prussian crown renounced all real power in Neuenburg while retaining a shadow title. In return the Bern government quashed the indictments against the Neuenburg insurgents, a small price to pay for what was clearly a successful demonstration of its will to defend its independence and neutrality.

In the canton of Zürich patriotism ran high during the Neuenburg crisis, and if there was some apprehension among the most distinguished members of the refugee community about what might happen to them if the Prussians arrived (Friedrich Theodor Vischer and Gottfried Semper were said to have their bags packed for imminent departure), there was also a considerable degree of belligerence in the local population, which, according to the *Neue Zürcher Zeitung*, expressed suspicion of the diplomatic process and held the view that war was necessary to avoid a compromise at Switzerland's expense. This ebullient overestimation of the country's military capacity, which a clearer recollection of the lessons of the Sonderbund War might have tempered, was again characteristic of the public mood three years later, during the crisis caused by Emperor Napoleon III's annexation of the Duchy of Savoy.

There is no doubt that the Swiss government had sound reason for complaint in this matter. The signatories of the Final Act of the Congress of Vienna had recognized that possession by a Great Power of that part of Savoy that bordered upon the Lake of Geneva would represent a threat to Switzerland's independence, and they had therefore extended the principle of neutrality to cover northern Savoy and had granted to the Eidgenossenschaft the right to occupy it militarily in time of crisis. Napoleon III was not unmindful of this and, after he had demanded the cession of Nice and Savoy as the price for his support of the Kingdom of Piedmont in its war against Austria, he declared that it was his intention to leave the northern provinces of Chablais and Faucigny to the Swiss, a declaration that sensibly modified the indignation that had been expressed over the annexation in Great Britain as well as in Switzerland. In April 1860, however, a referendum in Savoy strongly supported union with France and rejected the idea of separating the northern provinces from the rest of the duchy, and the French Emperor immediately announced that he could not ignore this clear expression of the people's will.

This about-face caused an explosion of fury in Switzerland, and there were demands for an immediate military occupation of the contested area before the French annexation was completed. To the hotheads who took this line—who found a national leader in the Bernese statesman Jakob Stämpfli and, in Zürich, included Gottfried Keller, admittedly not a very knowledgeable person in military and diplomatic matters—it never seems to have occurred that the kind of military action that they proposed would almost certainly elicit a massive response from France and Savoy and that Switzerland could not expect military support from any of the other powers, least of all from Great Britain, which, in the wake of its unhappy experience in the Crimean War, had no stomach for new adventures and would for the next decade and a half follow a policy of nonintervention in European affairs. The federal government in Bern was more sensible than the activists who followed Stämpfli, largely because of the strong lead given by Zürich, where Alfred Escher's colleague Jakob Dubs wrote a series of five articles in the *Neue Zürcher Zeitung*, pointing out that it would be foolhardy to jeopardize Switzerland's profitable economic relationship with France for a cause that was not incontrovertibly sound from a legal point of view and made little political or military sense.

After his election as president of the Zürich Great Council in December 1860, Escher himself delivered a programmatic address on foreign policy in which he argued that, if Switzerland had a world mission, it was one that could be accomplished not by the use of the bayonet but rather by the example it provided of the ways in which freedom could be put to positive use, adding that the best defense of independence lay not in a strong army but in fiscal integrity and economic stability and growth. In their reprobation of adventurism in foreign policy, Escher's remarks had a strong Manchesterian flavor. He did not go so far as to say, as *Punch* did a few years later, after a British retreat in the Schleswig-Holstein question that was more humiliating than Switzerland's acquiescence to the cession of Savoy, "What is prestige, after all? A piece of diplomatic and political slang!" but some of his critics claimed that that was what he meant.

Even so, after the first mortification of spirit had passed, most Zürchers (the Genèvois were naturally of a different persuasion) were inclined to agree with Dubs and Escher. Zürich was, after all, in the middle of a vigorous and exciting economic boom, and it was not difficult for its citizens to redirect their attention from the prospect of a dubious military gamble to the profitable works of peace.

Chapter 4

THE ECONOMIC TAKEOFF

♦

A people is idle when it does not fulfill the task that its age demands of it, or leaves it half-done or half-addressed. From 1830 to 1848, our people's work was the creation of constitutional circumstances and a common legislative system based upon universal suffrage as well as on the interests of the separate cantons. The work is done; the house is built, and the enterprise goes its way. Now, time, ever creative, makes another demand on us, a demand for which we have already in some part prepared ourselves by the concentration of our political forces but which must now be pushed forward by other means. Steam is creating a new world, and all peoples are making haste to see that they are ready and equipped for the new division of the world.
—*Neue Zürcher Zeitung*, April 1852

Zurich's first railway station

If the center of political gravity in Switzerland was from 1848 onward to be found in Bern, Zürich in the same years became the economic capital of the new nation. This was partly due to the fact that, as early as the eighteenth century, it had outpaced all potential rivals except Basel and Geneva as a manufacturing and trading center and had a geographical position more suitable than theirs for the extension of influence over the whole nation and a stronger preindustrial base to build on. But it was surely not accidental that its rapid progress toward national dominance took place during the years of liberal ascendancy in Zürich's politics and particularly in the second phase of that ascendancy, the period after 1848. In the first years after 1830 the triumphant liberals worked effectively to remove incumbrances upon freedom of trade and occupation, and their programs of public works were certainly beneficial to the economy. But the radical ideologues who led the liberal movement in its first years had too long an agenda to permit systematic concentration upon economic goals, and it was only after the shock of 1839 had unseated them that greater influence in party councils fell to the kind of people whom Charles Morazé has called *"les bourgeois conquérants,"* apostles of growth who believed, with an almost religious intensity, in the development of productive forces.

Chief among them was Alfred Escher, to whose vision and energy Zürich owed both its leading role in the development of a Swiss railroad system but the establishment of the kind of credit facilities that made this possible. It was not for nothing that people spoke of the years after 1848 as the Age of Escher, and that Theodor Mommsen, who lived and worked in Zürich in the early fifties, could say, "He stands as the compleat sovereign, all the more so because he doesn't have the title." It should be remembered, however, that Escher's dominance was due not only to his economic accomplishments but in equal measure to his leadership of the liberal party, and that this was distinguished by important services to the common welfare. In Zürich liberal humanitarianism was the concomitant of economic growth, and that was the reason why it was spared much

95

of the social dislocation and suffering that accompanied the rapid advance of industrialism in other parts of Europe.

I

It was characteristic of the general economic history of Switzerland that the limited supplies of rich agricultural land, the lack of natural resources, and limitations upon possible territorial expansion forced its subjects to find alternative methods of making and enlarging their livelihoods. In the Middle Ages the favored method was the selling abroad of military skills; at a later time this was supplemented and then supplanted by the export of products that Switzerland's neighbors could not themselves produce economically, clocks and watches, for example, and silks and linens of such fine quality that "Swiss cloth" enjoyed an international reputation.

From an early time Zürich's economic development was bound up with the production of textiles: since the sixteenth century, silks and woolens; since the beginning of the eighteenth, and in ever greater volume, cotton yarn and fabrics. Except in the case of silk, the process of production was concentrated not in the city but in the countryside, where farmers with modest holdings who wished to increase their income and escape the drudgery of an exclusively agricultural life set themselves up as producer-merchants on a small scale. Ulrich Bräker, who was not a Zürcher but lived not far away in Zwingli's birthplace, Toggenburg, was describing a common experience when he told, in his widely read memoirs, *Lebensgeschichte und natürliche Ebentheuer des Armen Mannes im Tockenburg,* of how, in April 1759, because his fiancée didn't want to marry a mere peasant and boiler of saltpeter, he bought forty-six pounds of raw cotton, at two gulden the pound, and went into the yarn business, later teaching himself to weave it into cloth. Bräker sold his product to a merchant in Glarus; the peasants of the Zürich Oberland who followed his example sent their cloth, either individually or through local brokers or *Landfabrikanten,* to merchant houses in the city on the Limmat, which controlled the export trade.

Heinrich Pestalozzi once praised this combination of industry and agriculture—which was concentrated for the most part in the Tösstal, the right shore of the Zürich Lake between Küsnacht and the cantonal border near Rapperswyl, the left shore between Richterswil and Horgen, and the vicinity of Winterthur—as an ideal arrangement, one that represented "the non plus ultra of the economic welfare of a people." Yet it is clear that the 34,100 spinners and 6,400 weavers who were engaged in this kind of home industry in 1787 had become dependent upon an occupation that was highly vulnerable to disruptions caused by competition and the introduction of new techniques. How true this was became clear when the Helvetic Republic, by doing away with the power of the guilds to restrain industrial expansion and by establishing the freedom to create new establishments, encouraged the first experiments in mechanization. In 1801, Marc-Antoine Pellis, a citizen of Vaud who had served as the Helvetic Republic's commercial attaché in Bordeaux, established the first mechanized spinning establishment in Switzerland when he installed in a cloister building in St. Gall twenty-six spinning mules with 206 spindles that he acquired through his contacts in France. This pioneer venture was badly managed and continually in deficit, finally collapsing in 1819, but it inspired imitation. In 1802, at Wülflingen, members of the Winterthur families Sulzer, Ziegler, and Haggenmacher, which had long been active in the cotton trade, established the first mechanical spinning concern in the canton of Zürich by importing and installing forty-four Arkwright machines with 8,000 spindles from France, and a year later Christian Naef of Toggenburg founded a mechanical spinning establishment at Rapperswyl, an event that caused outrage and rioting in the Oberland. Once it had gotten this far, however, the tendency was irreversible. The spinning concern Neumühle, founded by the Zürcher Kaspar Escher in 1805, developed rapidly into the Escher, Wyss and Company machine works, which manufactured, among other things, spinning machines, and in 1826 the Winterthur firm of J. J. Rieter and Company began to do the same. As early as 1813 there were sixty mechanical spinning establishments in the canton; in 1827 there were 106, with 180,000 to 200,000 spindles.

The introduction and spread of mechanical spinning caused widespread distress and disruption of life in the mountain districts. Cottage spinning had been a not unpleasant occupation in which all members of the family, young and old, could participate, around the hearth or in the open, to the accompaniment of music or the telling of tales. Now, unable to support themselves by agriculture alone, many families left the land to seek employment in the new factories, in environments uncongenial to them and under conditions that were destructive of family ties and injurious to the health of the children, who were often, in view of the lowness of wages, forced to supplement the family income by going into the workshops themselves. The social problem came into existence at the same time as the machine. As early as 1815 the government felt compelled to address the problem of child labor and passed legislation forbidding the employment of children under ten, and in the 1820s the Swiss Society for the Common Good, whose purpose was to relieve indigence and social distress, was encouraged by Paul Usteri to begin an investigation of their possible causes, among which he listed the impact of factories and mechanization.

Even so, after the first shock had passed, the home cotton industry survived. By driving down the price of yarn, the spinning machine increased the profits to be made from the production of cloth and served as an inducement for former hand spinners to turn to weaving or to go into business as *Verleger*, or small village entrepreneurs, who hired their neighbors to weave for them. This development was encouraged when the breakdown of Napoleon's Continental System caused an economic boom in the years 1813–16. Between then and 1827 the number of looms in use in the Zürich Oberland doubled and profits were high. These were years in which the weavers themselves—uneducated people who were often barely literate, who were ignorant of politics, wholly provincial in outlook, and without any inkling of understanding of how their own condition was affected by external forces—lived, ate, and dressed not only well but luxuriously, leading Johann Hirzel, the pastor of Wildberg, to complain about their falling off from the piety and industry that marked the life of the average peasant, their proneness to the pleasures of the flesh, and their unresponsiveness to the warnings of the church.

The retribution that he hinted would come to them was, in fact, on the way. At the end of the decade British cotton firms increased their production sharply and, thanks to the lower prices that cheaper labor costs made possible, began to invade Swiss markets. In 1831–32, Zürich exports of cotton cloth sank by 60 percent, and all of a sudden there was much talk of the necessity of mechanizing cotton weaving. A few mechanical looms had already been installed in other parts of Switzerland, with ambiguous results, and in 1829 the Zürich commercial house Trümpler and Gysi had begun to experiment with mechanized weaving in its spinning establishment, Corrodi and Pfister, at Uster. But it was only in 1832, when machine-made cloth of foreign origin began to reach Zürich in considerable volume, that Corrodi and Pfister, with new mechanical looms imported from Alsace, went into production, and it became known that other Oberland entrepreneurs were making plans to follow suit.

To the thousands of handweavers in the canton (in 1827, 12,000 hand looms were in use, two-thirds of them in the Oberland), and to the *Verleger*, who served as middlemen between them and the commercial houses of Zürich and Winterthur, this news seemed to promise poverty and ruin. Among some of them the coincidence in time between the announcement of Corrodi and Pfister's intentions and the second anniversary of the day of Uster on 22 November 1832 aroused muddled expectations —surely the government that had profited from the common people's revolt against the aristocrats two years earlier would protect the people now from threat of the new machines?— which turned to blind rage when it became apparent that they would not be fulfilled. The result was that during the anniversary fête at Uster the crowd got out of hand, stormed the Corrodi and Pfister *Spinnerei*, smashed the new looms with iron staves, and put the building to the torch.

For this collective breach of peace and destruction of property, both unusual in Switzerland, public authorities arrested and tried twenty-nine persons, of whom it turned out only seven were full- or part-time weavers and only one a *Verleger*, the others being involved because of private resentments or surrender to the pleasure of destruction. Their leader, Hans Felix Egli, commonly called Rellstenfelix, was known to be subject to religious mania and fits of melancholy, and his wife testified that the excessiveness of his generosity to the poor during the winter of 1831–32 was a certain sign of madness. His defense attorney, the twenty-four-year-old Jonas Furrer, who was at the beginning of his brilliant career as a trial lawyer, made the most of this information and argued that his client had been obsessed with the idea that the mechanical looms would inevitably mean death and starvation for his family and that he had been in such a rage during the events of 22 November that he was not responsible for his actions. This defense did not prevail, for the liberal government, still uncertain of its hold on power and aware that the conservatives were looking for ways to use the incident against them, felt that they could not afford to be lenient, and Rellstenfelix was, therefore, sentenced to twenty-four years in prison, his accomplices also receiving long terms of punishment.

What had happened in Uster did not, however, rest lightly on the liberal conscience, and on 12 January, Heinrich Escher, the new editor of the *Neue Zürcher Zeitung*, published a long leading article which began:

> Anyone who has intimate knowledge of the situation and the misery of that class among the residents of our canton who until now have supported themselves and their families by weaving, and knows how they are scarcely able, by sixteen hours of daily work, to still their own hunger and that of their wailing children with boiled potatoes and thin milk or to cover their nakedness, will, if he has anything like a human heart in his breast, wish that their condition will not only not get worse but, if possible, improve. In this connection, the introduction of the weaving machine demands earnest and conscientious discussion, which cannot be satisfied in the interest of only one class or by coldly invoking the word freedom of trade.

Human sympathy alone, Escher continued, might seem to require the government to forbid the use of mechanical looms. But the burden of available information indicated that, without them, Zürich's textile industry would not be able to compete with other nations, whose machine-made fabrics would be both cheaper and perhaps even of finer quality than the local product. In the long run prohibition of mechanical looms, even if legally possible, would spell the decline and eventual disappearance of cotton weaving in Zürich, in which case the weavers would have gained nothing from it. It was obvious, of course, that, if the introduction of mechanized weaving inflicted serious hardship upon the handweavers, the state would have to come to their aid. Studies would have to be undertaken to discover how many people were affected, and in this connection—and here Escher's article reflected its author's study of Adam Smith and Thomas

Malthus in his youth—some attention would have to be paid to the fact that "in no district of our canton and in no other class is early marriage and the production of a great number of children more common than in the weaving districts and among the weavers." If large-scale relief were necessary, consideration would have to be given to means for restraining the current birth rate, either by moral means or by the establishment of poor houses in which the sexes were separated. On the other hand, one must hope that, if the condition of the industry counseled the unrestrained introduction of weaving machines, they would gradually absorb the handweaving population, "just as the spinning machines, which were so deeply hated at the beginning, later provided bread and even more or less adequate employment for many thousands."

Escher, a close associate of Paul Usteri's and a professor of law at the Political Institute, was a moderate liberal who did not find the radicals of Ludwig Keller's stripe congenial and was, indeed, considered by them to be a hopeless conservative. Yet, although he was more troubled than they by the conflict between faith in freedom and progress on the one hand and humanitarian concern over their results on the other, in the last analysis he was at one with them in regarding economic growth as the means for alleviating social problems, and his position in this respect was characteristic of liberalism in general at this time, particularly in France, where Escher had studied in his youth, and England, whose political economists had influenced him.

In the case of the cotton weaving industry, his view was justified, although other crises had to be surmounted before this was clear. Handweaving did not disappear in the thirties. On the contrary, the explosion of popular rage at Uster in 1832 had the effect of slowing down mechanization for a generation: Corrodi and Pfister were not back in operation until 1837, and other entrepreneurs seemed unwilling to risk the damages that it had suffered. Meanwhile, handweaving continued and, thanks to an abatement of foreign competition, held its own for at least a decade, the number of hand looms, which had stood at 12,000 in 1827, increasing to 17,000 in 1842.

The real crisis came in the forties, when the prices for calico, that is, plain white cotton cloth, began to fall catastrophically. About two-thirds of the Zürich handweavers worked in calico and, unless they could shift to the weaving of colored wares or to silk, which was still in a robust condition, they were fully exposed to the incursion of cheaper foreign cloth. Thousands were forced to the wall in the decade that earned the name "the hungry forties" all over Europe because of its crop failures and disastrous potato famine. These did not spare the Zürich Oberland, and the government was hard put to it to mount relief programs and to seek new occupations for the indigent at a time when it was distracted by the disorders that accompanied the onset of the Sonderbund War. Paradoxically, the same people who had railed against the onset of mechanization in 1832 now pleaded with entrepreneurs to establish new factories, and there was a general complaint that the canton had allowed its chief industry to lose its competitive advantage by neglecting industrialization.

If this was true, this condition did not last for long. The economic depression came to an end almost simultaneously with the founding of the new federal state, and amid the buoyant optimism engendered by the latter event Zürich was not long in making good its industrial deficit, the Oberländer Caspar Honegger of Rüti playing a major role in the vigorous industrialization of the weaving trade. Rudolf Braun has called the fifties a veritable *Gründerzeit* in this respect, pointing out that in 1856 there were already 2,600 mechanical looms in operation in the canton of Zürich and that, in the sixties and seventies, the expansion assumed hectic proportions. That it was accompanied by all the psychological and social problems that industrialization breeds goes without saying, and the liberal government was unable to eliminate these, not least of all because its humanitarian impulses were checked by its economic prejudices. Before 1837 there were no legal restrictions upon hours of labor, although in that year the Great Council issued orders regulating child labor, eliminating the worst abuses and forbidding the employment in factories of children who were attending school full-time. In 1858 the Governing Council convened a commission of experts, and the Great Council set up a special inquiry of its own to consult on comprehensive factory legislation, and the resultant law of 24 October 1859 introduced a series of safety regulations and measures for the protection of workers' health. On the crucial question of working hours, the law, while forbidding child labor at night under any circumstances, established a legal daily limit of thirteen hours for adults and children alike. Repeated attempts during the debates and consultations to reduce the hours of child labor further were defeated on the grounds that this would constitute an unwarranted interference with the freedom of trade, would tend to make the factories uncompetitive, and would lower the standard of living of the working class, with unforeseen social consequences. It is interesting to note that this was the position taken by the commission member J. J. Treichler, a former socialist, whereas Gottfried Keller, in the press, was a vigorous critic of this aspect of the law.

In general, it can be said that the transition from hand-weaving to industrialized production had been accomplished without major social dislocation, and the cotton industry not only played a major part in making Zürich the leading Swiss industrial center but helped to encourage and support the industrialization of other trades—silk manufacturing, machine tools, printing, papermaking, bookbinding—which, by 1860, were an important part of the Zürich scene.

II

Economies that are ambitious to acquire more than regional scope require efficient systems of transportation, and in this respect Zürich, like all of Switzerland, was badly served until the second half of the nineteenth century. The cantons were, of course, bound together by roads and canals that were superior in quality and maintenance to those in many parts of Europe, including the German states, but travel by coach and barge was slow and impeded by the multitude of toll booths that interrupted the journey at cantonal boundaries and often in between. A merchant carrying a shipment of clocks and watches from Geneva to Zürich could count on having to stop dozens of times to pay customs duties, a procedure that not only slowed delivery but sensibly raised the market price of the product. Moreover, at a time when other European nations were investing heavily in railroad construction, Switzerland seemed entirely indifferent to this revolution in the transportation of goods and persons. In the mid-forties, when there were already 3,600 kilometers of railway line in operation in Great Britain, 7,500 in the United States, 1,750 in Germany, and 882 in France, there were no Swiss railways at all.

This is not to say that there was no interest in railways in the Eidgenossenschaft. The liberal press championed construction from an early date, and in 1836, noting the brisk market in Germany for shares in projected lines between Frankfurt-am-Main and Mainz and between Dresden and Leipzig, the *Neue Zürcher Zeitung* wrote, "Will Switzerland alone remain wholly behind? Should something similar not be undertaken between Zürich and Winterthur, Basel and Zürich, Bern and Neuenburg?" If the first of these questions continued to be answered affirmatively, this had three principal causes: the fact that, before the creation of the Confederation in 1848, the kind of national economic policy or vision that might have encouraged railway construction did not exist; the conservatism of the business community, which deprived construction products of the capital needed to support them, and the absence of any public pressure for railways. Indeed, Ferdinand Gubler once compared the popular view of railways in the 1830s with that of "the free Toggenburgers at the end of the eighteenth century [who] protested against the construction of the post roads and cursed them as a work of Satan."

In the canton of Zürich at least the third of these obstacles proved less formidable than it originally appeared, and the change was effected by another application of steam. In 1834, Caspar von Rorschach and a mechanic named Lammlin from Schaffhausen founded a company in Zürich for steamer service on the lakes of Zürich and Wallen and ordered an iron steamship, complete with engines, from England. This vessel, *Vulcan*, sailed via Rotterdam and the Rhine to Basel and Kaiserangst, where it was dismantled, carried overland to Zürich, and reassembled, refurnished, and renamed *Minerva*. On 19 July 1835, amid the firing of cannon and the ringing of bells, with flags flying and music playing, she made her first voyage from Zürich to Rapperswyl and back, and regular service began the next day. The experiment was so successful that Escher, Wyss and Company started competition a year later with its steamer *Linth-Escher*, and by the mid-forties there were five steamers on the lake. There were always lots of passengers, for the service lent itself equally well to business and pleasure trips, and in the autumn, when columns of pilgrims went to Einsiedeln, they were apt to use the steamships for part of their journey, traveling from Zürich to Wadenswil or Richterswyl by water.

The success of the steamship changed popular thinking about railways all over Switzerland and opened many eyes to new possibilities. In December 1837 a liberal journal in Graubünden argued vigorously for the railway as the key to economic expansion and prosperity. "What travel by steamship is to lake and river traffic," its editors exclaimed, "travel by steam railway is to traffic on land. A Hercules in the cradle, that will free the peoples from the plague of war, from inflation and famine, from national hatred and unemployment, from ignorance and routine, that will fertilize their fields and put new life in their workshops and mines, and give the lowliest among them strength to educate themselves by visiting foreign lands, to seek work in distant places, to seek the restoration of their health in far-off springs. . . . A new invention is all the more important and beneficial in proportion to its effect upon the well-being and the intellectual improvement of the working class, that is, the great majority of the people. Measured by this criterion, railways are really popular welfare and education machines."

Most of the cantonal governments were still, however, reluctant to embark on programs of construction or even to make concessions of rights-of-way to private entrepreneurs, and investors remained for a long time timorous about the soundness of participation in railway companies. In 1838, when a group of Zürich businessmen under the presidency of former *Bürgermeister* Conrad von Muralt formed a company to construct a line from Zürich to Basel, they encountered endless difficulties in their negotiations with the Basel cantonal government, which seemed bent on preserving its toll rights on the post roads running eastward and to prefer to have the railway come to it from the west, as it did in 1844 in the form of a line from Straßburg, which crossed only 1,800 meters of Swiss territory. The Zürich company persisted in its efforts, but it suffered a heavy blow when only 9,178 of the 30,000 shares it offered for public subscription were taken up and, after fruitless efforts to obtain government support, it went into liquidation in December 1841.

There was, however, a happy ending to this story. When the company auctioned off its documents and plans, which included scientific studies and geometrical sketches of levels, contours, and gradients along possible routes, these were acquired for a trifling sum by Martin Escher-Hess aus dem Wollenhof. The man who was to be remembered in local history as "Steam Escher" (Dampf-Escher) had already demonstrated his imagination and energy as the head of the Kaufmännische Direktorium in the thirties, when he had been responsible for much of the new construction along the Limmat, including the Münster Bridge and the Kornhaus. He had since become inspired by the vision of integrating the economy of his native city into the rapidly growing European railway net, and in 1845 he formed a planning committee of friends and local businessmen, opened negotiations with the governments of Zürich and Aargau for the necessary concessions of rights-of-way for a line that would run from Zürich along the left bank of the Limmat to Baden and then, following the Limmat and the Aare, to Koblenz and eventually to Basel, and went to Vienna to recruit the services of engineer Negrelli of the Austrian State Railway, who had designed and built the Münster Bridge.

Martin Escher's self-confidence was contagious. When the difficulties with Basel once more proved to be insurmountable, he decided nevertheless to go ahead with the construction of the Zürich-Baden-Koblenz stretch and, once the concessions were in hand, offered the public 40,000 shares of stock, at 500 French francs a share, in a company to be called the Schweizerische Nordbahn. This time there was little evidence of distrust and timidity among investors. By October 1845, 10 percent of the capital was already in hand, and by March of the following year 32, 939 shares were paid up, the company holding the remainder. By this time—with the newspapers reporting daily on Negrelli's plans for bridging the Sihl River and the designs of the local architects Wegmann and Stadler for the new Zürich railway station, which was to be built in the Schützenplatz—railway fever had Zürich in its grip, and in March 1846, during the Sechseläuten festival, there was an explosion of almost frenzied enthusiasm, which began with a ceremonial laying of the cornerstone for the new station and culminated with a gigantic torchlight procession to Martin Escher's home on the Seilgraben, in which 800 torchbearers, 13 guild masters, 26 marshals with staff and banner carriers, and hundreds of local dignitaries participated, songs composed especially for the occasion were sung, and a silver beaker engraved with the arms of the city and images of the Münster Bridge and the Kornhaus was presented to the man of the hour.

All of this was nothing to the excitement on 7 August 1847, when—despite a year of unexpected problems (difficulties with the bridging of the Reppisch at Diätikon, the correction of the terrain between Spreitenbach and Baden, and the shoring up of the tunnel walls at Baden against massive rock slides)—the Northern Railway had its formal dedication, and the steam locomotive *"Aare"* (one of four built by Emil Kessler's works in Karlsruhe) made its first run from Zürich to Baden. The *"Aare"* was bedecked with flowers, and two of its three engineers wore ancient costumes and carried banners, the third directing the engine. It was followed by an open carriage filled with musicians, who played throughout the voyage, and the passenger coaches, filled with 140 leading citizens and stockholders, followed. Crowds cheered their progress at Altstetten, Schlieren, and Diätikon, and at Baden they passed through a large garlanded arch of triumph to a tumultuous reception in the station and a banquet of rich foods and oratory at the Gasthof zum Schiff. This exuberance did not seem out of place. Zürich had won the distinction of having built Switzerland's first railway, and the *"Spanische Brötlibahn,"* as it was immediately nicknamed after a much-loved baked confection that was made only in Baden (and which, thanks to the railroad's shortening of the trip there from four hours to thirty-five minutes, one could now have for breakfast in Zürich on the same day of baking), was immensely popular. Regular service, of four trains a day in each direction, began on 9 August, and in the first three weeks of operation the Northern Railway carried 24,836 passengers, traffic that was not discouraged by Switzerland's first train accident, when on the third day of operation the engineer leaned out as the train crossed the Reppisch and was torn from the cab and killed.

After this exhilarating beginning, however, nothing much happened for a considerable period. The atmosphere of intercantonal strife and foreign menaces was not conducive to economic innovation, and, although many projects were conceived, none came to fruition, and even the Northern Railway had to abandon its intention of extending its line toward Koblenz. Thus, when the federal state was established in 1848, the *Spanische Brötlibahn* was still the only Swiss railway in existence. At the same time the new constitution created conditions that were much more favorable to planning in the grand manner. In November 1849, in his opening speech to the second session of the National Assembly, Dr. Alfred Escher, its president and the new leader of Zürich's liberal party, reminded his fellow deputies of the services that the new federal state had already performed for the economic growth of the country: the creation of a national postal service, the abolition of internal customs and the establishment of free trade, and the acceptance of a common currency that had put an end to the "Babylonian confusion" that had reigned previously. It was now essential, for the sake of its own survival, for the government to take the railroad question in hand. The iron rails were approaching Switzerland from every direction, the question of how they were to be coordinated was ever more actively debated, and there were actually plans to bypass Switzerland completely. If that should happen, the country would be reduced to the condition of a melancholy hermitage, and this would be accomplished, ironically enough, by means of an invention that had been called one of the greatest agencies of peace at the expense of a nation that had just proved itself to be an island of calm in a European ocean racked by tempest. Escher urged the assembly to rise to the challenge and "weigh the full significance of the present situation with respect to the question that, without exaggeration, can be called a matter of life or death for Switzerland."

The involved rhetoric of this statement made it difficult to discern what it was exactly that Escher wanted the national government to do, and it may well have been that at this point he did not know himself, for the issues were complicated ones. Article 21 of the federal constitution of 1848 authorized the federal state, in the interest of the whole country or a large part of it, to engage in or to support public works and for this purpose granted it the right of expropriation with full compensation, a right defined in greater detail by an expropriation law passed in 1850. It was clear that these provisions opened the door for intervention by the national government in railway planning and building, and the *Bund* availed itself of the invitation to engage the engineers Henry Swinburne and Robert Stephenson to draft a plan for a Swiss national railway system; simultaneously it entrusted Councillor Geigy of Basel and the Winterthur engineer Ziegler with the task of estimating costs and proposing a scheme for financing the construction. Swinburne and Stephenson's plan, which was completed at the end of 1851, called for the construction of a main trunk line that would run east and west, connecting Geneva, Lausanne, Yverdon, Bern, Olten, Brugg, Zürich-Winterthur, Rorschach, and Lindau with branch lines from Bern to Thun, from Olten southeast to Luzern and northwest to Basel and the railroads of Baden and Alsace, and from Rorschach south to Chur and beyond, a plan that was simple and reasonably comprehensive and would allow for easy expansion into unserved local areas. This might have generated a lot of support had it not been for the difficulty of reaching agreement about financing, and more particularly about the issue of state or private ownership of railways.

The experts Geigy and Ziegler clearly came down on the side of state ownership, although they envisaged collaborative financing arrangements between the *Bund* and the interested cantons, and the majority of the National Assembly's railroad commission were of the same persuasion and drafted a railway law which said in so many words that "the establishment of the Swiss railway network, as well as the organization of the construction and the company itself, is the subject of federal legislation." But this was a very narrow majority, and the minority had the support of that part of the country that did not stand to profit directly from the railways and objected to the national plan on economic and moral grounds, as a scheme for building "pleasure trains" for politicians who wished to flee from the piety of Bern to the fleshpots of Europe, as well as the great body of liberal opinion that viewed state ownership as objectionable on various grounds.

The debate over the ownership question marked the beginning of a duel that was to dominate national politics for more than a generation between the leader of Bernese radicalism, Jakob Stämpfli, and Alfred Escher. They had in the past been allies and collaborators, both in their opposition to conservatism and the separatist ambitions of the Sonderbund and in the creation of the new federal constitution, but on the railroad issue they divided, and, because of their personalities, their differences hardened into an implacable hostility. Both men—the relatively uncultivated Bernese politician, who had made his way, despite the gaps in his formal education, by sheer energy and will, and the Zürcher aristocrat to whom eminence and power had come easily and at an early age—possessed extraordinary energy, absolute dedication to their immediate task, whatever it might be, and a ruthless determination to succeed. They were alike in their impatience with opposition, their unconditionality, and their desire to dominate, and this temperamental kinship alone made their mutual animosity all but inevitable.

Escher's wealth made it easy for his critics to demean his own motives and those of his supporters. But his position on the ownership issue in 1852 was influenced neither by this nor by any desire to increase his belongings. His opposition to state ownership of railways was rooted in the individualism that lay at the very heart of the liberal philosophy, in his aversion to any unnecessary increase of government power, and his conviction that, in the economic sphere, private enterprise and the laws of free competition should be allowed to prevail and would in the long run bring greater benefit to the community than government *Dirigismus*. In addition, there is no doubt that Escher represented a shift of emphasis within liberalism from the strong unitarian impulse of Paul Usteri's time to a jealous regard for cantonal sovereignty now that a stronger union had been achieved. He saw no reason why Zürich's economic development should be at the mercy of federal bureaucrats and Bern politicians. In this sense his dispute with Stämpfli was from the beginning more than a debate about abstract principles—state ownership/private ownership, centralization/states rights. It was—and this was recognized by both great antagonists—another phase in the struggle between Zürich and Bern for leadership in the Eidgenossenschaft, and one in which the city on the Limmat sensed its industrial potential and was determined to achieve it, while Bern, proud of its political primacy, looked on with jealousy and suspicion.

In 1852, when the Railway Bill came up for a vote, its fate was probably determined less by Escher's personal intervention, although he was certainly regarded as the leader of the opponents to state ownership, than by the strength of liberal sentiment in the country. With Zürich's representatives, and those of St. Gall, Appenzell, Thurgau, and Graubünden, expressing the most unimpeachable Manchesterian sentiments, and the deputies from western and central Switzerland divided, the National Assembly left the future development of the country's railways to private enterprise, provided the exercise of this privilege did no harm to the national interest.

The law of 1852 opened the way for Zürich to build a rail network that would complement its already healthy industrial development, and Alfred Escher charted the course with skill and restraint. Unlike his Bernese adversary, who continued to draft grandiose state rail systems for the next two decades while continually attacking "Escherism" and accusing the Zürich leader of seeking to establish a nationwide "private railroad monarchy" for the profit of "an interested caste," Escher moved with caution and deliberation and restricted his activities for the most part to eastern Switzerland. In the early spring of 1853 he became head of the board of directors of the newly established Zürich-Bodensee Railway and almost immediately entered negotiations with the Northern Railway, which had lost its original momentum and was suffering from financial problems. In July the two companies amalgamated under the presidency of Martin Escher, with Alfred Escher as chairman of the board of directors, and a vigorous program of construction got under way. By May 1855 the new Northeastern Railway (*Nordostbahn*) had built a line from Winterthur to Romanshorn, in the vicinity of the Bodensee, and by June 1856 the route from Winterthur to Zürich via the Oerlikon tunnel was in operation. Meanwhile, the extension of the *Spanische Brötlibahn* toward its original objectives made progress. The line from Baden to Brugg was complete by September 1856 and by May 1858 had reached Aarau, where passengers bound for Basel could transfer to the Swiss Central Railway and travel toward their objective via Olten and Liesthal. Escher's company also opened a line from Winterthur to Schaffhausen in 1857, after acquiring the Rheinfall Railway, which owned the original concession, and in 1859 a line from Turgi, on the main line between Baden and Aarau, to Koblenz and Waldshut.

Nor did these activities exhaust railway building in eastern Switzerland. In 1852 and 1853 three other companies were founded: a St. Gall-Appenzell Railway, which planned a line from Winterthur over St. Gall to the Bodensee; a Swiss Southeastern Railway Society, which projected connections between Rorschach and Chur, with connections to Rapperswyl and Glarus, and the Glattal Railway, which planned to connect Zürich with Wattwil via Uster. All three of these companies experienced financial difficulties, which they reduced by fusing, in April 1857, as the United Swiss Railways. The completion of their projected lines, and their connection with the Northeastern Railway system at Winterthur and Wallisellen and with the steamship service on the Zürich Lake at Rapperswyl, created a comprehensive and well-articulated transportation system with Zürich as its hub.

These developments were followed with enthusiasm by the Zürich press. The *Neue Zürcher Zeitung* had been a strong advocate of railway construction since the 1830s; Ludwig Herkules Daverio, its editor from 1845 to 1849, had written shortly before assuming that office, "Zürich must make haste, lest our canton be circumscribed from the direction of Basel or the Bodensee. Let us get to work quickly! Whoever builds the first Swiss railway will have an advantage over all followers and the most secure prospect for a fortunate continuation of its undertakings," and, under his successor, Peter Felber, who was editor until 1868, the paper strongly supported the fight for private ownership and saw in the success of Escher's construction plans a manifestation of the soundness of liberal economic policy. The liberal conservative *Eidgenössische Zeitung* was even more zealous and constantly urged expansion and fusion. After the Northeastern Railway had completed its line to Schaffhausen, it began to urge haste in making connections with the Badenese and Württemberg lines between Tuttlingen and Tübingen, and in 1858 it carried an article that spoke of Zürich's interest in becoming "the central point in the trade basin that extends toward Italy and upon which the rich industrial districts of Toggenburg, Glarnerland, and the eastern part of Aargau impinge."

By the end of the liberal era the railway promoters had completed their work in eastern Switzerland, and the greatest among them, Alfred Escher, was turning his attention to what would be his greatest challenge: the building of the Gotthard Railway through the Alps, an enterprise that would, before it was finished in 1880, require the construction of a main tunnel fifteen kilometers long and fifty-five smaller ones with a combined length of forty kilometers, as well as thirty-two bridges and ten viaducts. Yet what he had already accomplished at home was remarkable enough, for the Northeastern Railway, by galvanizing Zürich's existing industries and encouraging the growth of new ones, had transformed the city on the Limmat into Switzerland's leading industrial center.

This transformation had brought many other changes in its wake, not least of all to the traffic passing through the city. One victim of this was the railway station that had been designed and built by Gustav Albert Wegmann and inaugurated with such ceremony in 1847. In the graphics department of Zürich's Central Library, one can find lithographs of that original station, an unpretentious building set in the wooded area close to the confluence of the Limmat and the Sihl. Its main hall had four tracks, separated by a fifth with a turntable at its end for switching, and it was flanked by a modest administrative building on the side facing the city and shops and service buildings on the side facing the Promenade Platz. Trains approached from the northwest, crossing the Sihl Bridge before they entered the station, and when one approached barriers were set up for the protection of pedestrians until the train was safely in the station. There must have been many people in those first days who walked out from town to see the trains come in, and in one of the romanticized artists' representations we see some of them—elderly gentlemen with walking sticks strolling along the bank of the Limmat, a governess with her charges, a fraternity student with sash and long pipe lounging against a tree, a servant girl sitting on a bench in the shade, two boys fishing and a barge slipping downstream, its six occupants watching with interest as two horse-drawn coaches cross the bridge to the station, laden with passengers and their luggage for the train, which can be seen in the distance, trailing a long plume of smoke as it approaches. The scene is rural and almost idyllic, dominated not by the locomotive and its carriages but by the trees that gird the station, the river in the foreground, and, rising above the Sihl valley, the green hills, their slopes terraced for cultivation, their tops crowned by forests.

By 1860 it was clear that Zürich's economy had outgrown this simple facility, and the railway board of directors asked the city's leading architects—Gottfried Semper, whose work will engage our attention in a later chapter, Leonhard Zeugheer, Ferdinand Stadler, and Johann Jakob Breitinger—to submit designs for a new station. All did, but the jury chosen to decide among them voted in the end for one laid before it by the new city architect, the thirty-one-year-old Jakob Friedrich Wanner, whom Semper had strongly supported, even to the extent of permitting him to borrow features of his own design. Wanner's new station, construction of which began in 1865 and was completed in 1871, was situated where its predecessor had stood. It was a Neo-Renaissance hall-like structure without pillars, covering 7,000 square meters of space (which made it one of the biggest stations in Europe), with six tracks, without perrons, that led to the east facade. This Wanner crowned with a figure of Helvetia, surrounded by allegorical figures signifying public transportation by land and water. The station's location was criticized by some in the sixties for still being a bit remote, but time and the economic growth of Zürich were to correct that. By 1889, when a statue of Alfred Escher was erected opposite the east facade, it was already in the very heart of the city, and the railway king's eyes looked down the street that was to become the fashionable shopping center of the Zürich of the future.

III

At the beginning of his economic history of Switzerland, Jean-François Bergier has cited the words of a character in Racine's *Les plaideurs* of 1668: "*Point d'argent, point de Suisse.*" However true this may be as a general proposition, it is incontestable that the impressive development of industry that raised Zürich to a position of economic primacy among Swiss cities in the latter half of the nineteenth century would have been impossible without money, in its abstract rather than its concrete form, as credit. And for credit one needs banks.

Zürich had never been a great banking center. In the late Middle Ages credit for the expansion of local business, or for the liquidation of the debts of the aristocracy, or for major communal enterprises generally came from Jewish and Italian money lenders. In the purchase of Winterthur from Duke Sigmund of Austria in the fifteenth century, for example, the Jews provided a fifth of the 10,000 florins needed to complete the transaction. After they and the Italians faded from the local scene in the fifteenth century (they never seem to have been very welcome and were subject to intermittent violence and expulsions), local *Bürger* who had acquired wealth from trading in mercenaries set themselves up as money lenders, but never on a very grand scale and apparently without sufficient success to establish a family tradition in banking. When private banking began to be recognized as a Swiss specialty, at about the time when Racine was writing *Les plaideurs*, it found its main center in Geneva, where in the course of the eighteenth century the names Thélusson, Saladin, Necker, Mallet, Candolle, Pictet, Lombard acquired a European resonance.

Nothing comparable was to be found in the city on the Limmat, and there were no intimations of that distant time in which a British Foreign Secretary would coin the term "the gnomes of Zürich." This was tolerable as long as the economy was purely regional in scope, but when the textile industry began to expand its export activity and when interest in railways began to grow, it soon became clear that an improvement of the city's financial facilities was urgent. In the 1840s, Zürich had two private banks, the Bank in Zürich and Leu and Co., and it was due to their support that the *Brötlibahn* was able to complete the construction of its line to Baden, but the resources of these houses were completely inadequate for the extension of the kind of credit that would have enabled the *Nordbahn*, to say nothing of the more ambitious Northeastern Railway, to expand. That meant that the railway lines would have to seek financing from foreign banks, which were eager to enter the Swiss railway scene, with resultant loss of local control and the diversion abroad of a large part of the return on investment. In 1853, when the Northeast Railway was seeking credit for its Winterthur-Romanshorn line, it had to go to the Rothschilds in Frankfurt for the necessary support, and it looked for a time as if this would be the normal procedure.

In the spring of 1856 the Universal German Credit Institution in Leipzig (Allgemeine Deutsche Kreditanstalt in Leipzig), acting on the advice of its deputy chairman of its board, who was also the Swiss Consul General in Leipzig, decided that investment in Swiss railway development would be profitable and proposed to set up a branch office in Zürich. This galvanized Alfred Escher into action, and in June he formed a local committee, procured a concession from the government, and announced his intention of founding a Swiss credit institution, inviting the bankers from Leipzig to participate on the condition that they abandon their plans for a branch of their own in Zürich. Agreement was quickly reached; shares were offered to the pub-

lic and taken up with celerity, and the result was the foundation
of the Schweizerische Kreditanstalt, which has been called Escher's most important achievement and which he himself said
later, in his autobiographical notes, gave Zürich a financial importance that it had not possessed before.

While the negotiations were proceeding, the *Eidgenössische
Zeitung* published a series of articles under the general title
"Credit Institutions," which were apparently designed to educate its readership in the choices that Zürich had if it hoped to
pursue a policy of vigorous economic growth and to explain the
importance of Escher's initiative. One could, the editors wrote,
reject the whole course of industrialism out of hand, on ethical
and other grounds, if one was willing to deny the advantages it
brought in the way of daily conveniences and comforts of many
kinds. But it was not to be stopped and, in view of the growth
of urban population and the necessity of providing it with co-
mestibles and supplying its other needs, such things as the expansion of food services on the one hand and transportation on
the other were indispensable. Credit institutions existed to make
such things possible. The question was what kind of institutions
were the most effective and desirable. Experience had demonstrated clearly that old-style private banks were incapable of
funding large projects. Government banks were, and the Great
Council in Bern had just perpetuated the life of its State Bank
because the people of Bern apparently believed that the state
should supply all of its needs at whatever cost. But, the editors
wrote, in a burst of liberal orthodoxy,

> We must emancipate ourselves from that spirit. . . . It is a
> sad thing to want to be regimented in all things, and espe-
> cially in money matters. For every attempt on the state's
> part to mix in such things goes wrong. . . .
>
> The government can always direct commerce, but it does
> so badly, as it does all other business. Let the private sector
> do what is appropriate to it, and the government the same.
> Let them manage the police for us, instead of playing the
> banker!

What was needed then was a new kind of credit institution,
like the *Crédit Mobilier* in France or the old Brussels bank of

1822, *La société générale des Pays Bas pour favoriser l'industrie nationale*—banks with large accumulations of capital that were provided by selling public shares on a large scale and which existed not to pay out big dividends but to serve a public interest by investing in its economy. The Schweizerische Kreditanstalt was such an institution, and not the least of its advantages was that it was a Swiss bank—despite the fact that it had accepted investments from Leipzig, Augsburg, and Berlin—for only an independent Swiss bank could make a proper assessment of Swiss needs and provide for them.

Escher's new bank—for he not only inspired its foundation but directed its fortunes from 1856 until 1877 and again, after a short break, until his death in 1882—lived up to this encomium. It helped free Switzerland from its dependence on foreign banks, and it gave Swiss citizens an opportunity to invest in their own future, to which they responded with alacrity. From the beginning its activities were extensive, although the focus was generally on eastern Switzerland. Its first great loans were made to the Western Railway and the Northeastern Railway, but it was by no means a predominantly railway enterprise. Indeed, the industries that were its beneficiaries were diverse in kind even if all were central to the development of the country—in the first instance, texiles and the machine industries, later food and the luxury trade, later still the chemical and electrical industries. It extended loans to cantonal governments and, in 1870–71, came to the aid of the federal state in supporting the costs of mobilizing and maintaining the army along the country's borders. It was also active in laying the foundations of Switzerland's insurance industry and in financing the Gotthard railway. Indeed, in the crisis of 1877–78, it played a prominent part in preventing the collapse of both that enterprise and the Northeastern Railway. All in all, its services to the country's economic development and its importance in making Zürich the center and motor of that development can hardly be overstated.

IV

In his memoirs the Luzern politician Philipp von Segesser described the two greatest political figures of his time, Jakob Stämpfli and Alfred Escher, and in a passage in which the implied contrast was clearly designed as a defense of the former, wrote:

> Escher was the heir of millions, on whose education nothing was spared. Around him gathered the men of high finance and industry, who held their noses high and luxuriated in the fine pleasures of life—those modern feudal lords who, with no less appetite than that of their forefathers in their castles, pose as the benefactors of humanity—and also those who in this society of interest saw a chance of getting ahead themselves, hungry professors and scribblers from all over, and journalists for hire—and, naturally, many respectable people also, who believed that their well-being and convenience were better served by Herr Escher than by his opponent. Because for his obedient partisans—it cannot be denied—his yoke was light and pleasant; with his fine tact he knew how to appeal to everyone's weak side and to bind him to him in proportion to his usefulness. But woe to the disobedient! A wave, and the name of the unhappy wretch was crossed out of the golden book.

This portrait is doubtless malicious, but it does prompt one to ask whether, in the so-called Escher Era, the principles that had guided the liberal party when they first came to power in 1830 had been subverted by the profit motive. There can be no doubt that some liberals worried about the power of the "modern feudal lords," and their fears were formulated sharply by a writer to the *Eidgenössische Zeitung* in 1856 who complained that "until the end of the year 1852 we in German Switzerland, and especially in Zürich, knew nothing about stock market gambling and swindles with paper. At that time there was a *Züriputsch* with Northern Railway stock!"

It seems highly likely that these fears were, at least in the first stage of the economic takeoff, exaggerated. Gottfried Keller had a very good nose for such things, and it is worth noting that his growing pessimism about encroaching materialism came at a much later time. It is true, of course, that the number of industrialists and great merchants who supported the liberal party and had a voice in its councils was greater in the fifties and sixties than it had been at the beginning of the liberal era, and there is no doubt that they were drawn to liberalism by the fact that it protected and advanced their economic interests. But the time was still far distant when such people were forming trade associations to lobby for special privilege, and it would be a mistake to think that they were untouched by a sense of social responsibility or uncommitted to those parts of the liberal program that expressed such responsibility in action.

It has often been said that early industrialism retained elements of an older patriarchal concern for the rights and interests of the working class. This was true in Zürich, where, in addition, the corporate spirit that was so deeply rooted in the city's history discouraged unrestrained Manchesterism. If some liberal men of affairs had been startled in November 1833, when the *Neue Zürcher Zeitung* printed an article on "Associations of Workers," in which it defended such unions as justified by liberal principles and respect for human rights and said that, basically, they were a necessary protection against "capitalists, agriculturists, and entrepreneurs" who sought maximum profit at the expense of the consumer, they had come to accept the proposition that the vulnerable classes in society had special problems that required attention. In general they believed that economic growth was the best panacea, in which they were not entirely wrong, since for the period 1836–60, with the exception of the depression years 1847 and 1855, the percentage of Zürich's population on relief was only 3 to 4.8 percent, less than half of the percentage for the largely agricultural cantons. But they knew that this was not the only answer, and this was demonstrated by the careful investigation of working and living conditions that they undertook before the passage of the Factory Act of 1859, as well as by their support of hospitals, of public charitable organizations, with which Zürich was richly endowed, and of public education.

No one embodied the corporate spirit more completely than Alfred Escher himself. In 1847, Gottfried Keller wrote an appreciation of him that began where Segesser's did, but took a different direction.

> The son of a millionaire, he submits himself to the sternest labors from morning until night, and takes on difficult and protracted duties at an age when other young men between twenty-five and twenty-eight would, if they possessed his wealth, devote themselves above all to enjoying life. It is said, to be sure, that he is ambitious. That may be; it merely

delineates a firmer shape. For my part, I should find it difficult, even if I had his education, to sit all day at a desk—even if I had his money too!

If Escher was ambitious for himself, it was because he was ambitious for his canton; if he enjoyed authority, he used it for the enhancement of his community. All of his work in politics and all of his creative achievements—the Northeastern Railway, the Kreditanstalt, and the Polytechnic Institute, to which we shall turn in the next chapter—were directed to that end, and, since he was the leader of his party in every sense, it is probable that his example was not without influence upon his colleagues. It is perhaps true that the liberal philosophy that inspired his own career, with its emphatic insistence upon the representative principle and its opposition to direct democracy, could not have been expected to satisfy the people he served indefinitely. Peter Stadler has written that his speech to the National Assembly in November 1849, urging the elected representatives to make "courageous and determined progress along the road delineated by the constitution and followed by us until now" and describing them as "the priests to whom the people has entrusted the flame . . . for careful nurture," made a religion, if not a mystery, out of parliamentary politics. To a people with Stäfa and Uster in their history, to say nothing of 1488 and 1839, this was perhaps never completely congenial. But when they finally overthrew the "Escher System" it was because they felt it gave them insufficient opportunity for participation in the political process, not because they believed its creator had been motivated by self-interest.

Chapter 5

THE LIBERALS AND EDUCATION: SCHOOL REFORM, UNIVERSITY, POLYTECHNIKUM, 1830–69

♦

I came to see popular instruction as a measureless swamp, and I waded around in its muck energetically until I got to know the source of its waters and the causes of its blockages and got some idea of how its wet destructiveness might be drained off.
> —J. H. PESTALOZZI, *How Gertrude Teaches Her Children* (1801)

All of the reflective people in the country recognized that the sound foundations of real freedom lay only in a higher and more general education of the people; religion and morality, active understanding and useful knowledge could make the use of democratic institutions possible and permanent.
> —EDUARD SULZER (1836)

The Polytechnikum, after an etching by Gottfried Semper,
circa 1860

If it is true that one of the greatest achievements of liberalism in the nineteenth century was the progress made in overcoming illiteracy and extending education to the masses, it is also true that the relative pace at which this was done, country by country, was highly uneven and that the countries that were usually regarded as being the most progressive politically were not in the vanguard. In France—despite the interest shown in popular education by the *philosophes* of the Enlightenment, the experiments made during the revolutionary and Napoleonic periods, and the passage of Guizot's Educational Bill in 1833—there were more than a thousand communities without any schools at all when Victor Duruy became Minister of Public Instruction in 1863, and in 1870 the rate of effective literacy has been calculated as being no greater than 50 percent. In England the Reformed Parliament of 1833 made the first state grants for the establishment of popular schools, but the funds voted were small, and no provision was made for primary education that was either compulsory or free. In 1839, 41.6 percent of Englishmen were illiterate, and the percentage was not appreciably lower in 1871. Nor did this seem to worry the ruling orders of society, most of whom probably agreed with the member of Parliament who said in a debate in the Commons in 1833 that education would only teach the masses "to despise their lot in life instead of making them good servants; instead of teaching them subordination, it would render them fractious; it would enable them to read seditious pamphlets, vicious books, and publications against Christianity; it would render them insolent to their superiors." Momentum for a real measure of educational reform did not begin to gather until the third quarter of the century, and the motive was largely economic, since it was clear by then that the efficient functioning of industrial society depended upon clerks and operatives and manual workers who possessed the ability to read and write.

Things were different in the German-speaking areas of Europe, where, for example, 60 percent of Prussian children of school age regularly attended school in 1816 and 82 percent (95 percent in Saxony) in 1846, where the rate of illiteracy among Prussian army recruits was 9 percent in 1841 and 4 percent in 1868, and where the Bavarian and Saxon recruits in 1865 had an illiteracy rate of only 7 percent and 1 percent respectively. This relative superiority can be attributed in some part to the energetic initiative of enlightened rulers during the period of the *Aufklärung* and, in the Prussian case, to the high priority given by Stein and the other reformers to popular education in their struggle to free their country from the yoke of Napoleon. But one is tempted in addition to wonder whether the fact that the German-speaking countries applied themselves to the task of educating the masses sooner and with greater determination than their western neighbors was not due to the fact that the liberal-minded bureaucracies that governed them approached education not pragmatically, as was true in France and England, but philosophically. Writing of the Prussian reform movement, Thomas Nipperdey has pointed to the important influence of Kant's ethics and his concept of man not as a means or a cog in the machine but as an autonomous being, self-determining and self-acting, of Fichte's extension of this to a belief in the state's duty, out of moral obligation and self-interest, to develop the full capacities of its subjects, and of Johann Heinrich Pestalozzi's demonstration of how this could be done pedagogically.

Pestalozzi was, of course, not a Prussian but a citizen of Zürich, and the mention of his name reminds us that the modern movement for educational reform in Switzerland predated the work of Stein and his colleagues. In 1798, when the Helvetic Republic brought the Swiss cantons into a short-lived union, the revivification of the educational system at every level was one of its most eagerly sought goals, and most of the ideas that the Zürich liberals actualized in the years after 1830 were conceived during the half decade of the Republic's existence. The driving force behind the Helvetic effort was Philipp Albrecht Stapfer, a native of Bern who became Minister of Arts and Sciences when the Republic was established. Like his colleague on the Helvetic Directory Johann Albrecht Rengger, Stapfer was deeply imbued with Kant's doctrines and, as professor of theoretical theology and director of the Bernese Political Institute before 1798, had written widely on educational problems. An enthusiastic unitarian, like La Harpe, Glayre, and Rengger, he dreamed of a uniform national educational system, and once he became minister drew up elaborate plans for the transformation of all existing secondary schools into coordinated preparatory institutions for a single national university and the establishment of a Central Institute composed of leading scholars and writers that would have oversight over the whole educational hierarchy.

Stapfer recognized that such a national system could not hope to be successful without a thorough overhauling of the existing elementary schools, which, despite some halfhearted attempts at improvement in the more progressive cantons during the period of the Enlightenment, were in a state of utter neglect at the end of the eighteenth century. With great energy Stapfer carried through a national survey of existing facilities, working through an Educational Council (*Erziehungsrat*) and a system of school inspectors, and, mindful that in the rural areas existing schools were largely dependent upon church support and staffing, he addressed a memorandum to the *Geistlichkeit* in 1798 stressing the fact that the goal of popular education must be "the moral improvement and elevation of the people" and urging that the churches vie in improving their educational methods.

Stapfer was a strong supporter of Pestalozzi, who had rallied to the Helvetic regime from the beginning and lent his talents to the writing of pamphlets defending its aims and to the editing of its principal organ, the *Helvetisches Volksblatt*. Through Stapfer's influence, Pestalozzi was appointed to head the War Orphans School at Stans, an experience that was decisive in convincing this remarkable man, sometime political activist and unsuccessful farmer, who, in Friedrich Dürrenmatt's phrase, "wandered through the land, from one disaster to the next, poor, shabby, and glowing," that his future lay in schoolteaching. He had already, in the fourth part of his peasant novel, *Lienhard and Gertrude* (1787), taken up arms against the two salient prejudices that stood in the way of state aid for the extension of popular education: the idea that the masses were incapable of intellectual improvement and, its corollary, that attempts at popular education could only endanger government authority and social order. Now at Stans and—after the French had taken over the Orphans School and turned it into a military hospital —at the elementary school at Burgdorf, where he was director from 1799 to 1805, he formulated the pedagogical principles that were to win him a European reputation and to have a profound influence upon the educational systems of many countries besides his own.

Pestalozzi flatly rejected the prevailing method of teaching children by rote learning and insisted that effective education must take into account the individuality of the child and be adjusted to its natural development and concrete experience. In *How Gertrude Teaches Her Children* (1801), a treatise in the form of a series of letters that became his most influential work, he argued that education begins with birth, as the newborn child becomes susceptible to the impressions of nature and begins the process of becoming a human being.

> All instruction . . . is nothing but the art of extending aid to this natural striving for self-development, and this art is based essentially upon the proportionality and the harmony of the means used to impress the child with the precise stage of his developed powers. Therefore, in the impressions that must be made upon the child through instruction, there must be a sequence, whose beginning and progress must keep exact step with the beginning and progress of the child's capacities that are to be developed.

Strict discipline and the memorization of written materials serve no useful purpose. Effective education depends upon gifted and well-trained teachers who love children and believe that it is their duty to turn them into responsible moral and social beings and who are aware that, in the early stages of education, the use of tactile objects (plants, minerals, and the like), the learning of skills (gardening, spinning), and the singing of songs and playing of instruments are as important as the reading of books and the calculation of sums. By all appropriate means the developing mind must be led from confusion to definiteness and from there to clarity and the ability to explain.

The confusion of the times, the lack of funds at the disposal of the Helvetic regime, and the brevity of its tenure of power prevented either widespread or permanent application of the ideas of Stapfer and Pestalozzi, and the Mediation years and the period of the Restoration were not congenial to educational experimentation and reform. Still, all was not lost. In August 1812, Stapfer wrote to Paul Usteri that his school inspectorate had survived all of the other accomplishments of the revolution and was still operating successfully in some of the Swiss cantons. Could he have looked into the future, he might have taken additional satisfaction in the thought that he had helped to establish a liberal tradition of educational reform that was to find its realization in the Regeneration in Zürich after 1830.

I

Even before the liberals had taken over power in Zürich in 1830, Melchior Hirzel, later *Bürgermeister*, had sent the Great Council a memorandum, written with his characteristic verve and moral earnestness, on the urgent necessity of improving elementary education in the countryside, and this made such an impression that in the spring of 1830 the Educational Council empowered a special commission to solicit reports from all school inspectors and country parsons in the canton about the condition of the schools in their localities. The replies were analyzed and coordinated by J. J. Hottinger, and in an interesting report that he issued before the end of the year he revealed that, despite much dedicated work by school inspectors and schoolmasters since the passage of the still-existing School Law of 1803, there had been a steady deterioration of conditions and standards. This was evidenced in such things as inadequate facilities, forty-one communities being without buildings designated as schoolhouses and many others having schools that were badly in need of repair, a wide variation of standards of instruction, excessive emphasis upon religious instruction (memorization of catechisms and repetition of passages from the New Testament), an almost total lack of adequate schoolbooks to complement this and prepare students for practical life, and badly trained and badly paid teachers, some of whom had other jobs that prevented adequate attention to their pedagogical functions.

The leaders of the Regeneration set out to correct these conditions without delay. The constitution of 1831 declared unequivocally that "care for the improvement of the instruction of the young is the duty of the people and its representatives. The state will to the best of its abilities maintain and support the lower and higher schools and educational institutions." With this as its mandate, the new liberal government proceeded to elect a new Educational Council (*Erziehungsrat*), charged with the complete overhaul of the existing system, a Teachers Seminar to supply and train those who would run it, and—the inspiration of Melchior Hirzel—a Teachers Synod to articulate the principles and supply the inspiration that would maintain the reform once it was accomplished.

Viewed from the standpoint of the talents of its members and the magnitude of its achievement, the new *Erziehungsrat* was certainly the most distinguished in Switzerland's history. At its first meeting, in July 1831, it divided into two sections, the first, for the reform of higher education, comprising J. J. Hottinger, Johann Caspar von Orelli, Government Councillor Eduard Sulzer, Dr. Friedrich Ludwig Keller, the leader of the radical wing of the party, Professor Heinrich Escher of the Political Institute, who was to be the chief editor of the *Neue Zürcher Zeitung* from 1832 to 1833 and again from 1834 to 1837, and Court Councillor Horner. The second section, which was assigned the task of reforming the *Volksschulen*, had as its members Melchior Hirzel, Rector Troll of Winterthur, Parsons Füßli and Weiss, Ignaz Thomas Scherr, who had during the 1820s attracted widespread attention by his work as director of the Blind, Deaf, and Dumb Institute in Zürich and was now, as editor of the *Neue Zürcher Zeitung*, arousing controversy by the outspoken radicalism of his political leading articles (a new feature of the newspaper for which he was responsible), district teacher J. J. Dändliker of Stäfa, and the composer and choral leader H. Georg Nägeli, the last two, like Orelli, ardent followers of Pestalozzi. Working with a speed that in retrospect seems incredible, these men completed their work by the end of 1832—Scherr being primarily responsible for the draft of the law on primary education, Hirzel for the new regulations concerning secondary schools, and Orelli for the reform of higher education—so that the total reform could be put into effect at Easter time in 1833.

The system that it outlined and that took tangible shape in the decade that followed was far in advance of anything that existed in England and France. The law made school attendance obligatory from the sixth to the sixteenth year, and while parents had to pay fees set by the local school boards, those bodies were also authorized to provide reduced rates for children from needy families and free education for those from indigent ones.

Children began their education in communal *Volksschulen*,

spending three years in elementary instruction (*Elementarklassen*) and three in more advanced (*Realklassen*) and completing a program of work, set by the Educational Council, that embraced religious instruction, the German language, arithmetic and geometry, the elements of natural philosophy, history and geography, singing, handwriting, drawing, and gymnastics and, for the girls, needlework. At the age of twelve they either went on to the cantonal schools (*Gymnasium, Industrieschule*), which had much higher fees and prepared students for the university or for careers in business and technology, or they were obliged to remain in the *Volksschule* system for another three years. In the latter case families who could afford it normally sent their children to the so-called *Sekundarschulen*, which had higher yearly fees, although the law required that one student in eight be admitted as a free scholar. Requiring twenty-eight hours of weekly classes for forty-four weeks of the year, these schools provided an extension of the courses taught in the lower schools, plus instruction in the French language and some attempt to prepare students for future work in agriculture and trade. The law allowed parents whose means were insufficient to keep their children in a full-time school program after they had reached the age of twelve to send them for three years either to an *Ergänzungsschule*, or finishing school, which required eight hours of weekly instruction (which could be performed in two mornings), or to a *Singschule*, which combined musical and religious instruction and required two and a half hours practice and instruction a week.

An important part of the reform was the establishment of new cantonal schools of higher education to replace the existing preparatory schools and other institutions like the Art Institute and the Technical Institute. The new creations, which students entered at the age of thirteen and where they remained for five and a half and six and a half years respectively, were the School of Industry (*Industrieschule*) and the gymnasium. The former, which was designed to train students for careers in industry, engineering, and technology, provided in its first years a broad curriculum that included religious instruction, German and French, arithmetic and mathematics, natural history and geography, drawing, writing, singing, gymnastics, and military exercises; in the upper grades students specialized in either mechanics, chemistry, or business and had courses in English and Italian. In the gymnasium, which prepared students for entrance in the university, the emphasis was classical, and during the first four years the curriculum included Greek and Latin in addition to all of the subjects taught in the lower *Industrieschule*. In the upper grades the subjects of the lower gymnasium were carried further, and there were classes in Hebrew and logic.

Of fundamental importance to the success of the work of the primary and secondary *Volksschulen* was the improvement of the quality of teaching and the correction of the abuses noted in Hottinger's report of 1830. This task was taken in hand by the new Teachers Seminar, which was established, after long debate in the *Erziehungsrat* and the Governing Council, at Küsnacht, a town that was proud of its reputation as "the radical community" and had, in its petition to the Governing Council, stated emphatically that "the schoolteachers must propagate and strengthen progressive ideas throughout the whole canton, and this will take place if they are educated in the most progressive atmosphere that is possible, and this is the case in Küsnacht." Provision was made for the training of thirty students at a time for a period of two years, in subjects ranging from theory of numbers, form and speech (the Pestalozzian Triad, which was the basis of all elementary education) to Christian doctrine, knowledge of the Bible and historical catechesis, musical composition, national history, and an introduction to geography, husbandry, and biology.

The seminar's director was Thomas Scherr, already a controversial figure and soon to become even more so as a result of his authorship of the School Law and the rigorous standard of excellence that he required of his seminar pupils. But Scherr asked much more of himself than he asked of his charges, often teaching from six to ten hours a day and spending the evening hours on administrative tasks or the writing of schoolbooks and pedagogical tracts, and his ability to communicate his own enthusiasm to his students made the Teachers Seminar a success from the start, a fact reflected in the eagerness with which its graduates were sought after, the number of visitors who came to view its methods, and the growing confidence of the government in its work, which led it to increase the number of students admitted, the stipends at their disposal, and the size of its faculty.

In addition to making this basic and permanent contribution to the success of the new School Law, Scherr performed an important interim service by taking on the difficult task of examining, and if need be dismissing, the teachers who were in service before the law came into effect. With the aid of his chief assistant in the seminar, Eduard Dändliker, the son of the *Erziehungsrat* member, Scherr examined 400 of these—discovering, according to his later account, some remarkable cases of inadequate knowledge of the Bible and ignorance of basic facts of history and the sciences—and in the end felt compelled to retire seventy-five of them, most of whom were doubtless in the vanguard of those who called for his head in September 1839.

A sign of the ideological zeal that animated those who effected the educational reforms was Melchior Hirzel's successful insistence that the new system would be incomplete without an organization that would bind the teachers together and serve to animate and strengthen their common purpose. This was the origin of the Teachers Synod, which comprised all of the teachers and all of the educational administrators in the canton and which held yearly meetings, always in a different locality, to discuss questions of general interest. While its activities were innocuous enough, its very existence was provocative to large numbers of people, for its name seemed to indicate an intention (which in Hirzel's case was unquestionable) of supplanting the primary role of religion in the old educational system. Indeed, the distillation of Pestalozzi's ideas into the frequently iterated declaration of intention "to form the children of all classes, in accordance with commonly accepted principles, into intellectually active, socially useful, ethically religious human beings" seemed a kind of intimation that the new breed of teachers felt themselves better qualified than churchmen to undertake instruction in moral and religious values.

It was of course the ideological element of the reform movement that triggered the reactionary backlash of September 1839, which, as we have seen, reflected the resentment of the church, the short-sighted selfishness of certain business interests who regarded mass education as a threat to a docile and cheaply priced labor force, and the superstitious dread of change of parts of the rural population. Yet it is important to remember that, while the conservatives were able to unseat Thomas Scherr (that abrasive man had made so many enemies in his own camp that he was doubly vulnerable), they were unable to undo his work, and their first intimations of a desire to do so were answered by an angry mass meeting at Bassersdorf and a petition to the Great Council that said, in effect, "Hands off the schools!" The fact was that by 1840 the results of the reform, in terms of the progress made by children in basic skills, were so palpable that a reversion to older ways was unthinkable. All over the canton communities were expressing pride in their schools and vying with each other for the best teachers, and there was a growing realization that the canton of Zürich led the nation in educational progress and that its schools were attracting the enthusiastic interest of foreign educators.

This satisfaction became even stronger as a result of the reforms of the second period of liberal ascendancy. In 1859, after three years of close collaboration with the body of teachers and members of the press, Jakob Dubs completed an overhauling, codification, and emendation of all regulations and administrative decrees on education that had been issued since the law of 1832. One of the great legislative achievements of the liberal era, the Educational Law of 1859 not only confirmed the basic principles of Thomas Scherr's initial reform but significantly improved the economic position of teachers, tightened up the existing system of school inspection, provided regulations to prevent the overcrowding of school facilities, and, for the first time, established schools in the practical arts (*Arbeitsschulen*) for women.

In 1865 the English poet Matthew Arnold, who was also, for thirty-five years of his life, an inspector of schools, was commissioned by the Schools Inquiry Commissioners to investigate school systems in France, Italy, Germany, and Switzerland. The Swiss part of his report, which he submitted in 1867, was restricted almost exclusively to an examination of the educational system in Zürich, which, he wrote, was "on the whole the best provided with schools of all the Swiss cantons" and where "the continuity between the primary and the higher schools" was more complete than elsewhere. "A territory with the population of Leicestershire," Arnold wrote, "possesses a university, a veterinary school, two great classical schools, two great *real* schools, a normal school for training primary and secondary teachers, fifty-seven secondary schools, and three hundred and sixty-five primary schools, and many of these schools are the best of their kind in Europe."

Arnold was particularly impressed by what he called the

democratic nature of the system. Every primary school was administered by its own school partnership, or *Schulgenossenschaft*, a community body that appointed the teacher, set his salary, and supplied him with housing, decided how much the school fee should be and which students should receive reductions, appointed a steward to administer the school funds, and provided, furnished, and heated the school premises and kept them in good repair. Oversight of teaching and discipline in the school was the duty of the local school board (*Gemeindeschulpflege*), which was composed of four locally elected members sitting with the parson as ex officio president. This body made regular inspections of the schools in its jurisdiction and reported to the district school board, which was composed of three members chosen by the teachers of the district and six to ten members elected by the local residents by universal suffrage. The district boards had oversight of all community schools and were charged with seeing that the community school boards were exercising their functions properly, that the schools were in good condition, that children were attending school regularly, and that the regulations of the Educational Council were being obeyed. The district boards reported directly to the Educational Council, whose president, the director of education for the canton, was also a member of the canton's Governing Council. Thus, Arnold wrote, the system, while intensely democratic and intensely local, was "not insanely democratic, so that the idea of authority, nor insanely local, so that the idea of the State, shall be lost sight of."

Democratic in nature, the system also promoted democracy in society, a fact demonstrated by the way in which the *Volksschulen* tended to supersede private education. The School Law allowed parents to have their children taught at home or in private schools, provided that the standards of the *Volksschulen* were observed and the school fee paid. As the years passed and the excellence of the state schools became increasingly evident, fewer and fewer parents availed themselves of this option, and by the time that Arnold was making his report he could write, ". . . the public day schools being really good, few children go elsewhere, and one finds all classes of society mixed in them."

Arnold's enthusiasm for all of this was not unalloyed. In the conclusion of the Swiss part of his report, he wrote that it was his feeling that the aim of Swiss education was not the highest educational aim, that the idea of what the French call *la grande culture* did not have much effect in the country, and that it was "not in the line of what is specially called a liberal education" that it was most successful. The spirit that reigned in Zürich, he felt, was "a spirit of intelligent industrialism, but not quite intelligent enough to have cleared itself from vulgarity." Even so, he added hastily:

> ... the grand merit of Swiss industrialism, even though it may not rise to the conception of *la grande culture*, is that it has clearly seen that for genuine and secure industrial prosperity, more is required than capital, abundant labor, and manufactories; it is necessary to have a well-instructed population. So far as instruction and the intelligence developed by instruction are valuable commodities, the Swiss have thoroughly appreciated their market worth, and are thoroughly employing them.

We need not accept this judgment at face value, for it is clear that the motive for educational reform that Arnold attributed to the Swiss was really the only motive that he believed would galvanize his own government to do something to correct the deplorable state of popular education in England. He was honest enough to make a half admission of this in his final paragraph, in which he wrote:

> Meanwhile let us be grateful to any country, which, like Switzerland, prepares by a broad and sound system of popular education the indispensable foundations on which a civilizing culture may in the future be built; and do not let us be too nice, while we ourselves have not even laid the indispensable foundations, in canvassing the spirit in which others have laid them.

II

The educational edifice created by the Educational Council of 1831 and passed into law by resolution of the Great Council in September 1832 was not complete until the new university, the first to be established on Swiss soil since the creation of the University of Basel in 1460, opened its doors in the spring of 1833. The new *Hochschule*, as it was called until the twentieth century, was not, of course, without predecessors in the city on the Limmat. In 1525, Zwingli had founded a school of theology in the Großmünster, and that institution, which came to be called the Carolinum, not only continued to exist over the centuries but was gradually enlarged to include instruction in philology, natural sciences, and history. The late eighteenth century saw the establishment of a Medical-Surgical Institute, which rapidly gained in reputation and in the distinction of its faculty after it became a state institution in 1804. And in 1810, at the initiative of Paul Usteri and Konrad Escher, the Educational Council had authorized the establishment of a Political Institute for training in legal studies and preparation for careers in the civil service. There was, however, no organic connection between these institutions, and standards were not of the highest, particularly in the Carolinum, where the professorships were reserved for residents of Zürich and were often awarded for reasons that had nothing to do with scholarly excellence, so that many talented young Zürchers with an interest in humanistic studies preferred to go to German universities for their degrees.

The leaders of the liberal party in 1831 regarded the creation of a new university as a symbol of the modernity of their aspirations and as a means of initiating and maintaining the intellectual revival of their city, and they were unimpressed by the fears that were expressed concerning the financial burden of a new institution or by the sentimental opposition of graduates of the Carolinum. The first of these they alleviated, as we have seen, by expropriating the resources of the Chorherrenstift, which gave them the financial underpinning for all their reforms of higher education; the latter, they simply disregarded. An additional reason for their urgency was their desire not to be overlooked when the time came to actualize at long last Philipp Albrecht Stapfer's plan for a single national university. At the meeting of the federal diet in Luzern in 1822, the historian Charles Monnard, the delegate of the Waadtland, had revived this project, naming Zürich and Bern as appropriate locations. In the end nothing came of Monnard's suggestion, the issue remaining in abeyance until the 1850s, but in September 1832, when the Zürich Great Council was debating its educational reform plan, it was not known that this would be so, and members responded positively to J. J. Heß's urgent message from Luzern, saying that it was clear that a national university would not be built in a city in which an institution of higher learning did not already exist.

In the end the council voted 148 to 9 for the establishment of a university, and the work of planning the curriculum and recruiting the faculty began at once. Here the leading spirit was the philologist Johann Caspar von Orelli, a student of Lavater and Pestalozzi and, since 1819, a professor at the Carolinum, where he had made persistent but unavailing attempts to promote reform and collaboration with the other existing institutes. As member of the first section of the Educational Council of 1831, Orelli was responsible both for the creation of the new gymnasium and School of Industry and the basic draft plan for the university, to which he now, with unflagging energy, added form and scholarly substance. It was due to his influence that, at a time when the radical zeal of the liberals was at its height, the university was conceived of on the German model as an institution in which academic freedom would prevail and which would stand above politics, with scholarly considerations being decisive in all questions of policy and administration. In this respect the Strauß affair of 1839 was a kind of exception that proved the validity of his general rule.

The new foundation had four faculties, theology, medicine, philosophy, and law, thus absorbing the functions of the Carolinum and the Medical-Surgical and Political Institutes, which were dissolved when it began its operations. In the matter of appointments, it was Orelli's desire—born of his bitter experience in the Carolinum—to break through the parochialism of the past and to bring new ideas and vitality to the top faculty positions. He persuaded the Educational Council, therefore, to call scholars from southern and middle Germany to the professorial posts and, because of the atmosphere of reaction that prevailed in Germany in the early thirties, succeeded in attracting men of undeniable distinction—the natural philosopher Lorenz Oken and the surgeon Johann Lukas Schönlein, for example, both from Bavaria, where their liberal political opinions had caused them difficulties, and, from Baden, the man whom Ernst Gagliardi has called "the strongest personality in the founding phalanx" of the university, the philologist and Old Testament scholar Ferdinand Hitzig, who became the moving spirit in the new theological faculty. There was some talk of inviting Friedrich Schlosser's student, the brilliant Heidelberg *privat dozent*

Georg Gottfried Gervinus, who was about to embark on his magisterial *History of German Literature*—an appointment that would undoubtedly have made Zürich an exciting center of humanistic studies but deprived Gervinus of his fame as one of the Göttingen Seven of 1837—but nothing came of this. In the end all of the full professorships went to Germans—in addition to those named, the Württemberger Friedrich von Pommer in medicine, the theologian Michael Rettig from Giessen, the Germanist Karl Ludwig von Löw and the jurist Wilhelm Snell from Nassau (the latter via Basel), the anatomist Hermann Demme from Saxony, and the philosopher Eduard Bobrick from Bonn. The associate professorships were reserved for Zürchers, generally persons who combined their scholarship with work in politics or state service, like Orelli himself, who was *Extraordinarius* for classical philology, Friedrich Ludwig Keller, Heinrich Escher, and Johann Caspar Bluntschli, associate professors respectively for private law and legal procedure, for civil and international law, and for Roman law, Ludwig Snell, associate professor of philosophy, and J. J. Hottinger, associate professor of history.

When the university began its work in the summer semester of 1833, in a building on the Fröschengraben next to the Augustine Church, it had 139 students and a faculty of forty-six, and the collective distinction of the latter made it easy to disregard the jeering that had occurred in the press of some of the other cantons over the new creation. In particular, the conservative *Baseler Zeitung*, which seemed to be irritated that its own university would no longer occupy a unique position in Switzerland, had since the end of 1832 been taking the line that an institution that had only one full professor in its philosophical faculty could hardly claim even the title of academy, pointing out that the University of Basel had nine professorships in that faculty, three in theology, two in law, and four in medicine. This kind of sniping was offset by the knowledge that the foundation of the university had impressed more cantonal governments than it had left indifferent, and that the Great Council of Bern was already hastening to emulate the Zürich example, founding a university that opened in 1834.

Despite the ebullience of its founders, the first years of the university were difficult ones. The opening ceremonies took place only three weeks after the storming of the watch in Frank-

furt am Main on 3 April 1833, and in the eyes of the reactionary
regimes of Germany there was a natural connection between
these events. They chose, in any event, to regard the crowning
educational accomplishment of the Zürich liberals much as
West German conservatives of the 1970s regarded their universities, as a center, if not of political terrorists, then at least
of *Sympathisanten*, as a source of subversion that must be isolated and, if possible, eliminated. Noting the number of young
people crossing the Swiss frontier in order to escape persecution
for political agitations, the Prussian and Bavarian governments
declared it illegal for their subjects to enroll in the new university
in Zürich, the German *Bundestag* issued a similar prohibition,
and the government of Württemberg announced that anyone
who had matriculated in Zürich would be denied the privilege
of serving in the Württemberg civil service. These decrees made
it difficult for the new university to profit from the normal tendency of German students to study at more than one university
and made it more heavily dependent on Swiss students than it
had hoped and desired to be.

The university did very little to justify the political suspicion that it attracted, for it had no *Burschenschaft* or other political societies. But even the actions of nonstudents could bring
foreign threats down upon its head, as in the spring of 1834 when
German exiles in Zürich participated in Mazzini's freebooting
raid into Savoy, and the political turmoil at home in cantons
like Basel and Schwyz made it easy for conservatives to believe
that the new *Hochschule* must be involved in some obscure but
malevolent way. That newcomers to the faculty often held extreme political opinions did not help this situation. Lorenz Oken,
the first *Rektor* of the University of Zürich, was a radical democrat who had participated in the Wartburg assembly in 1819,
and he was interested in bringing young German scholars who
were driven from their positions for political reasons to Zürich
as *privat dozenten*. One of those who benefited from this interest
was the dramatist and medical student Georg Büchner, a fugitive
from the Hessian police because of the incitation to revolt contained in his 1834 pamphlet *Der Heßische Landbote*. Forced to
flee to Straßburg, where he completed his medical degree, Büchner went on to Zürich and, in the winter semester of 1836–37,
submitted his dissertation, "On the Nervous System of Barbels,"
to Oken, gave a trial lecture on the nerves of the cranium, was

appointed *privat dozent*, and began immediately to present a course on comparative anatomy of fish and amphibians. Büchner did not live long enough to become a *cause célèbre*—his fatal illness began only four months after his appointment—but the latter was doubtless noticed and considered provocative by conservatives at home as well as abroad.

Even before the Strauß affair of 1839, the university had many enemies in the canton, and the Educational Council's unfortunate appointment of the author of *Das Leben Jesu* brought it into the most extreme jeopardy. The resultant crisis not only mobilized all of those who hated the university as a symbol of political radicalism, a cause of foreign complications, and a financial burden but rather irrationally drove some of the radical leaders to take the position that, if the Strauß appointment were to be invalidated, then the university might as well be abandoned as well. When Government Councillor Bürgi, speaking for twenty-four members of the Great Council, proposed on 18 March 1839 that the university be dissolved, most of the Governing Council rallied to its support, but Ferdinand Ludwig Keller and his closest followers remained silent in the debate. They were doubtless acting from obscure tactical motives rather than from any real desire to see the university dismantled—the Bürgi resolution was perhaps an attempt to push the university issue into the foreground in order to deflect the full-scale assault upon the *Volksschule* reform that the radicals feared—but there is no doubt that this increased the university's vulnerability while inflicting other wounds. The news of the Bürgi motion was enough to make the reigning star of the medical faculty, Lukas Schönlein, who heard it when he was abroad, begin the negotiations with Berlin that led to his departure from Zürich before the beginning of the winter semester in 1839.

Worse was to follow. Although the Bürgi motion was defeated, and the Great Council, after an investigation of all of the charges against the university, voted in June 1839 to leave it unchanged, the coming of the conservatives to power after the September *Putsch* created a situation that threatened to destroy the morale and efficiency of the faculty. The purge of the Educational Council by the triumphant leaders of the Faith Committee deprived Johann Caspar von Orelli of his seat on that body and, in a stroke, left the university without the vital leadership that had sustained it during the first six years of its existence. The stepchild of the new dispensation, it had for the next three years to fight against constant interference, inadequate budgets, and blatant assaults upon its academic freedom, which took the form of attempts to dictate the choice and content of courses. That the university was able to repel the worst of these attacks was due to the kind of solidarity that adversity sometimes produces, in this case a firm alliance between the student body and the beleaguered faculty, but the cost was great in terms of damage done to the university's true functions, scholarship and teaching, in loss of gifted faculty (like the leaders of the medical faculty Carl Pfeufer and Jakob Hänle), and in the decline of student enrollment. By the winter semester of 1841–42 the number of students had sunk to 97, as compared with 159 in 1833, and although there was a sign of recovery as the first signs of a liberal return to power became apparent after 1842, the average enrollment for the period 1839–49 was only 129, compared with the average of 176 for the university's first six years. Since most of the deficit was in foreign students (despite the Prussian government's having lifted its ban in 1842) and in students from other cantons, and since the greatest losses were in the medical and philosophical faculties, there was some fear that the university was being reduced to a small provincial theological academy, as in the days of the Carolinum.

That fate was averted by the return of the liberals to power in May 1846. When that happened the canton once more had an Educational Council that understood and supported the principles of the reforms that had been inaugurated in 1831 and a Great Council that was sympathetic to the university's purposes and jealous of its reputation. The great crisis that led to the Sonderbund War not only united the canton behind the national effort but increased the prestige of the university by reawakening the hope that it would be the basis of the future national university. Funds became available for improvement of salaries, for new appointments, and for new institutes and scientific equipment, and a policy of vigorous recruitment got under way to repair the losses of the conservative interim. The revolutions that broke out in 1848 in neighboring countries and the persecution that followed their repression aided the process of growth and renewal by bringing many distinguished foreign scholars— the historian Theodor Mommsen, and the classical philologist Hermann Köchly among them—to the city on the Limmat. The student enrollment grew slowly but steadily and by the winter semester of 1853–54 had reached 200, the highest of any university in Switzerland.

Ernst Gagliardi has entitled that part of his history of the university that covers the years from 1847 to 1868 "A Calm Sea and a Lucky Voyage" after the Mendelssohn overture and the two Goethe poems upon which it is based. It is an appropriate enough description, for certainly the university had to suffer no more of the frustration and harassment that had been its lot in the wake of the September *Putsch* and could once more go about its proper business. Indicative of the changed attitude toward the university was an incident in 1856, when the Educational Council, having failed to attract the brilliant pathologist Rudolf Virchow to Zürich, followed his advice and invited Jakob Moleschott to accept a chair in physiology. The medical faculty was not happy about the appointment, because, in contrast to Emil du Bois-Reymond, the alternate candidate, Moleschott was less a specialist than a writer of scientific books for the cultivated lay public. More interesting than this criticism (which rapidly faded once Moleschott began his work in Zürich) was the unsuccessful attempt by the conservative *Eidgenössische Zeitung* to block the appointment by charging in a series of articles at the end of 1855 that Moleschott was unsound on Christianity and that the materialistic views that he had already adumbrated in his studies of the physiology of nutrition and his books *The Cycle of Life: Physiological Answers to Liebig's Chemical Letters* (1852) and *Georg Forster, the People's Scientist* (1854) would be destructive of the morals of his students. This campaign fell completely flat, proving perhaps that even the churchmen realized that Moleschott's kind of materialism was not out of tune with the railroad age (the Sechseläuten parade of April 1856 was a joyous celebration of the railway, with brightly painted locomotives representing the different lines and hundreds of people dressed as Laplanders or Tatars to indicate the ultimate destinations of the Nordbahn and the Ostbahn) and that they were disinclined to attempt to make another Strauß out of the physiologist. Moleschott's inaugural address on "Light and Life" was a notable success, and during his career in Zürich his scholarship, on such things as the nerves of the heart and the effect of the changing count of white blood corpuscles in illness, was as brilliant as his lectures.

The university's success in establishing itself in the popular consciousness as an institution that brought honor and intellectual stature to the city was manifest in the ceremonies in April 1858 celebrating its twenty-fifth anniversary, which were considerably more expansive than the modest inaugural celebration of 1833. Through streets crowded with enthusiastic onlookers, the academic procession made its way to the Großmünster, accompanied by the pealing of the bells and the singing of a chorus made up of two local *Gesangvereine*. In his anniversary speech Professor Ferdinand Hitzig recalled the university's modest start and rapid progress, its victory over the forces of reaction in the early forties, and its rapid recovery since. Born from the realization that a university was not only the best proof of the intellectual vitality of the community that created it but also the guardian of its traditions and, through its teaching functions, the guarantor of its future, the *Hochschule*, Hitzig declared proudly, had fulfilled the hopes of its founders, a fact richly illustrated by its literary and scholarly accomplishments, the excellence of its faculty, and the alumni who were now applying what they had learned in its lectures and seminars to their service in industry and government.

A festive banquet followed in the casino, which had been richly decorated for the occasion. Some of the university notables expressed annoyance over the absence of certain city fathers, who had elected to attend the launching of a new steamboat on the lake instead (although Professor Moleschott expressed the perhaps frivolous view that this competition between nature and art and trade and scholarship added to the zest of the occasion), and those guests who found themselves, because of the large number of diners, consigned to a second hall, remote from the high table, felt unhappy until someone reminded them that the Commons was the more important part of Parliament, that the wine was the same, and that they had in their midst the people's poet, Gottfried Keller, who had composed two Hutten songs for the occasion. So all went merrily below, while in the upper hall the official toasts were given to state and country, to teachers and students, to friends of the university, to the sister universities of Basel and Bern, and not least of all to the new Polytechnic Institute, which was just beginning its life in Zürich. *Rektor* Köchly's toast to the university's new partner was perhaps not wholly felicitous—he said that the two institutions stood not arm in arm but back to back, one sending its search columns into the zone of materialism, the other seeking conquests in that of idealism—but other speakers felt that the founding of the Polytechnikum would mark the opening of a fruitful new era for the university as well, and it was on that note that the guests dispersed, going out into the streets to enjoy the torchlight parade that ended the birthday celebration.

III

The Polytechnikum was not, of course, what the liberals had hoped for, for ever since the days of Paul Usteri it had been their ambition to build the Swiss national university that had been Philipp Albrecht Stapfer's dream in their own city. No one had been more intent on this objective than Alfred Escher, who became the *princeps* of the liberal movement after Jonas Furrer's removal to Bern. One of those graduates of the university mentioned in Ferdinand Hitzig's *Jubiläumsrede* in 1858, Escher had shown a keen interest in educational affairs from the moment he entered politics in the forties. As a member of the Educational Council, he had been the prime mover of a series of reforms in the cantonal schools—making study of the French language compulsory, and revising instruction in German, the natural sciences, history, and philosophy in ways designed to make those subjects a better preparation for life—and then turning his attention to the *Volksschulen*, which had not survived the years of conservative reaction completely unscathed. In January 1846, on the occasion of the centenary of Pestalozzi's birth, Escher gave a widely reported speech in Außersihl in praise of the primary school teachers and their services to democracy, and in the subsequent period he began the investigations that in the long run led to the comprehensive reform of the system of primary and secondary education that was carried through by his friend and successor Jakob Dubs in 1859.

But it was the issue of the Swiss university that was closest to Escher's heart, and as a member of the National Assembly in Bern he took it up in earnest as soon as the railway question had been laid to rest in 1852. By that time, however, what had seemed, at the time of the debate in 1848 over the location of the national capital, to be an assurance that Zürich would be the new university's home had become much less certain. On 14 June 1851 the *Neue Zürcher Zeitung* reported that the press in Geneva was conducting a campaign against the Zürich solution on the grounds that this would be an attempt to extend *Deutschtum* over all of Switzerland and that it was ludicrous to think that the kind of German liberal dreamers who currently occupied the professorial chairs in Basel, Bern, and Zürich, all of whom had themselves been born and raised under despots, could educate Swiss youth in the uses of freedom. While dismissing this as nonsense, the Zürich paper admitted that the religious question was bound to cause difficulties. In a national university there would have to be two theological faculties, and there was no doubt that the very idea of educating Catholic priests in Zwingli's town, where a pension was still being paid to Professor Strauß, would strike some people as being ridiculous and others as being offensive.

Escher argued that it was precisely because of the distrust between the nationalities and the confessions that Switzerland needed a national university, which would be the natural complement to the creation of the new federal state. The best way of promoting a truly national consciousness was to provide an opportunity for young people from all cultures and confessions to live and work together; what Bonn and Tübingen had done to inspire a new sense of German unity, a Swiss national university could do for the Eidgenossenschaft. As for the location, the advantages possessed by Zürich had been adequately canvassed in 1848, and these had not changed or been surpassed by other cities. In the interests of equity, however, it would perhaps be possible, if Zürich became the university's home, for a polytechnic institute to be founded in western Switzerland.

The idea of a Polytechnikum was not new, but the creation of the new federal state had given it a greater urgency, for the closer national union opened the way to a greater degree of centralized planning of public works like railway and road building, the damming and diversion of streams, and the creation of security measures against flooding and avalanches. For this Switzerland would need greater numbers of engineers, just as industry would need more of technicians of many kinds, and it seemed bootless to go on depending upon Karlsruhe, Paris, Munich, and Vienna to train them. The hero of the Sonderbund war, General Dufour, was a strong advocate of the creation of a Swiss polytechnic institute, and the idea attracted many people who were unenthusiastic about the idea of a national university, particularly in the Catholic Church and the world of business and not least of all in the existing universities, whose existence, some people felt, would be threatened by a national *Hochschule.*

Inevitably, then, the Polytechnikum tended to supersede the national university in the minds of the legislators in Bern, who could not help but be impressed by the breadth and depth of the opposition to the latter, and in the crucial debate in January 1854, despite an eloquent and incisive speech by Escher, they tabled the university plan *sine die.* A month later the National Council voted to establish a Polytechnikum in Zürich, but all that Escher and his supporters could salvage from the wider scheme was the right to include a political-humanistic faculty in the new institution, presumably to provide some courses in general culture for the engineering and science students.

In a leading article entitled *"Aut Caesar, aut nihil,"* the *Eidgenössische Zeitung* on 8 February expressed bitterness over the National Council's decision and said that it made a mockery of the ideal for which the supporters of the national university had fought and deprived the Eidgenossenschaft of what could have been its crowning glory. But this kind of disappointment did not long survive the publication of the regulations for the Polytechnikum (drawn up by a committee of experts chaired by Stefano Franscini of Tessin, one of the new institution's prime movers, and with Alfred Escher as one of its members) and the release of details about its organization and curriculum, and after Zürchers became aware of the excitement that its establishment was arousing in scholarly circles in Germany, they warmed to their new acquisition. From the very beginning the Polytechnikum was planned on a generous scale. Its director, J. W. von Deschwanden, the *Rektor* of the School of Industry, took as his model not the École Polytechnique in Paris but the technical universities of Karlsruhe and Stuttgart and, as was true in their case, set up five separate faculties, devoted to professional education in architecture, engineering, technology and mechanics, chemistry, and forestry, plus a sixth section for courses in the humanities and political science.

In advertisements published in the European press, the new school announced that it had over forty positions to fill, and within three months it had received 189 applications, over half of which came from Germany. As the appointments were made, journalists with a historical sense began to write that no institution of higher learning since the University of Berlin had begun its career with such a wealth of talent. This was hardly an exaggeration. In its humanistic section alone, the Polytechnikum could boast of such luminaries as the future historian of the culture of the Renaissance, the Ranke student Jacob Burckhardt, who had already published his *Age of Constantine the Great* and in the year of his appointment as Professor of Archaeology and History of Art was to follow it with his *Cicerone,* an erudite guide to the art of Italy; Friedrich Theodor Vischer, the writer of widely known and respected treatises on aesthetics, a dynamic and combative personality whose career at Tübingen had been plagued by continued surveillance because of the independent role he had played during the troubles of 1848, when he had been a member of the Frankfurt Assembly; and the future historian of Italian literature and Minister of Public Instruction, Francesco De Sanctis, who had been on the barricades in Naples in 1848 and came to Zürich from Turin and in a short time became a brilliant and much-loved lecturer. To the school of architecture the Swiss Educational Council called a man whose long-term effect upon Zürich was to be greater than any of these, the builder of the Dresden Opera House, Gottfried Semper, who since his flight from Saxony after the May rising of 1849 had been in exile in London, where his contributions to the Exhibition of 1851 had won him a post in the London Department of Practical Art. This he now left in order to come to the Polytechnikum, of whose future home, high on the right side of the Limmat, dominating the old town, he was to be the architect.

The other professional schools were almost as fortunate in their faculty recruitment, with known talents like Karl Culman in engineering and P. A. Bolley in chemistry. In physics in particular the appointment of the former professor of physics at the cantonal school, Albrecht Mousson, and the brilliant young director of the physics institute at Würzburg, Rudolf Clausius, made possible a combination of technical and theoretical work that became traditional in Zürich and had rich results. During his Zürich years Clausius continued the researches that he had begun at Würzburg on the mechanics of heat, and in the opinion of James Clerk Maxwell, his contributions to the molecular theory of gases, and his concept of "mean free path," opened up a new field of mathematical physics. On the practical side, Mousson and Clausius built up the Polytechnikum's scientific collections and acquired the apparatus needed for the most advanced kind of current research as well as a collection of instruments for lecture demonstrations in the general course on experimental physics. Clausius's departure from Zürich in 1867 caused no diminution in the excellence of the program, for his position was filled by highly talented young physicists like August Kundt and Friedrich Kohlrausch and later by H. F. Weber, in whose laboratory Albert Einstein was a student.

IV

From the beginning of their existence both the university and the polytechnic institute depended heavily upon the importation of foreign talent for their highest posts. There is no doubt that the newcomers made a rich contribution to Zürich's cultural activity, as we shall have occasion to see in the next chapter. But it should not be imagined that their reception in the city and in the academic community was completely without strain. In his memoirs Friedrich Theodor Vischer wrote that the Swiss had a deep-lying aversion for the Germans that perhaps went back to the Schwabian War and that, even in educated circles, a German had the sense of walking on mined ground and was never sure that he might not "be forced to hear something against the *Dütschen.*" It was only natural, in addition, that the foreign stars would be the targets of some malicious remarks from colleagues who were not as well-favored as they in salary and perquisites. Jakob Moleschott's lectures received less respect from his juniors than from his auditors, and one Swiss colleague said spitefully that he was a prophet and virtuoso with words who needed a hall filled with white-clad maidens before he could perform effectively.

On the other hand, the outsiders, even those whom their Zürich appointments saved from political persecution or positions not worthy of their talents, were sometimes less than grateful once they had taken up their duties. By no means all of them reacted with the enthusiasm of Ferdinand Hitzig, who wrote after joining the university faculty in 1833, "Everything is amazingly pleasant and beautiful! . . . It would be hard to make me ever regret that I had wandered here!"; and again: "Zürich is, from all that I see, hear, and read, the only place in German Switzerland where I would like to be. Here is the greatest amount of scientific feeling . . . and much virtue, honesty, and straight-forwardness is also at home here."

The historian Theodor Mommsen, for example, shared none of Hitzig's strong attraction to the city on the Limmat. Active in the abortive revolution in Schleswig-Holstein in 1848, Momm-sen had received an appointment at the end of that year as as-sociate professor of jurisprudence at the University of Leipzig, but his political stance during the May troubles of 1849 alienated the Saxon government, which revoked his appointment in 1851. Thanks to Alfred Escher's success in winning funds for the cre-ation of a second chair in Roman law, Mommsen almost im-mediately received the offer of a professorship at the University of Zürich and began his teaching in the summer semester of the following year. His time in Zürich was fruitful, for, in addition to important epigraphical work, he completed the first and began the second volume of his *Roman History* during his three years in the city. From the very beginning, however, as his letters to his friend the Mozart biographer Otto Jahn make painfully clear, he was far from happy. "The university has no foundation here," he wrote on 1 June 1852, "not because the number of auditors is small, but because the public does not respect it." The creation of the radicals, it was, he continued, tolerated by the towns-people as an evil that had to be borne and was completely de-pendent upon the government, which had the result of making the majority of the faculty unpleasantly servile. For the greater number of those colleagues Mommsen had scant respect, and he seemed to fear that continued contact with them would lead to the deterioration of his own powers. "That's the way it is in these little nests," he wrote, "one declines without really knowing how." Reassurance was to be found only in the thought that this was a mere way station. On 3 April 1853 he wrote to Jahn:

> I live here like a haughty intelligence in exile or a Prussian postmaster in Kerzkowska and make an angry face, not with-out intention. If one doesn't kick the Swiss, then they kick you, and thus the choice is not difficult. To be serious, every-thing goes reasonably well here as long as I hold on to the

thought that it won't last forever; if that disappeared on me, then things would be quite different.

In general scholars from southern and central Germany seemed to find it easier to fit into the Zürich atmosphere than northerners or scholars from France and Italy. Francesco De Sanctis arrived in Zürich on a bleak day in early 1856, with scant personal baggage but a number of caged canaries whom he had named after figures in Italian literature—Boccaccio, Poliziano, Aretino ("because he dirties everything, including my books and furniture")—and the like. He found it difficult to adjust to the weather—"What a life I live here, Camillo," he wrote to a friend. "One needs a will to live in such a place. I have not left my room for a week, except to go to class. Outside there is snow and rain and loneliness"—and even more so to get used to his new colleagues. "These German professors are strange," he wrote. "They have red faces from drinking so much, and every night they get drunk as Templars"; and apparently the greatest honor a student could pay his professor was to invite him to drink *usque ad inebrietatem*. De Sanctis went out once with Jacob Burckhardt to what he thought was going to be a learned society. "Whether it was or not," he wrote later, "I found that beer was the order of the day."

In the lecture hall De Sanctis found his colleagues wooden and often inaudible, hiding behind ancient lecture notes, which they read badly. His own lectures, on the other hand, were masterpieces of dramatic art. He repeated them to himself half an hour beforehand, walking up and down on the bridges of the Limmat, his face dark and lost to the world, and when he entered his classroom, according to Jakob Moleschott, "it was not as a prophet with promising mien and gesture but as an unconstrained man of the world among his friends," and within five minutes his students had forgotten Zürich, the Limmat, and De Sanctis himself and were *himmelweit weg* with Orlando or Angelica or Astolfo on the moon. His success as a teacher gratified De Sanctis but didn't make him any happier with Zürich. When he finally found a female friend, she turned out to be suffering from consumption. He was confirmed in his worst impressions. "*Povera Minna!*" he wrote. "Beautiful and passionate! In Zürich it is impossible to find passion except in the company of consumption!"

De Sanctis's friend Paul Armand Challemel-Lacour was no less forlorn in his new home. Expelled from France after the *coup d'état* of December 1851, he had taught in Brussels with great success and was shocked by what he found in Zürich. *"Ah, Paris!"* he lamented. *"Ah, Bruxelles! Pas de maitresses, pas de bals, pas de soirées! Mais c'est un pais sauvage, où la civilisation n'a pas encore pénétrée!"* The lack of applause after his lectures disconcerted him. *"Ils sont des statues, ces coquins là!"* He feared that his hair would turn gray and that he would lose his teeth in Zürich. *"Maudite ville! Je grisonne!"*

These were perhaps exaggerated views. Zürich's cultural life was livelier than it appeared at first sight. Indeed, in the 1850s there was enough going on to tempt the interest of even the most misanthropic of its visitors.

Chapter 6

CULTURAL LIFE
IN THE
LIBERAL AGE

◆

Men and women lust after Bildung *here as the mice do after the grease pot.*

—THEODOR MOMMSEN to his brother
Tycho, 18 November 1852

I have already been present at various Zürich banquets. They cook well here, and there is no lack of subtleties, so that it was high time that I came home to preach morals and moderation to my countrymen, for which purpose, however, I had to taste things one after another in order to obtain a thorough knowledge of what it was I wanted to attack.

—GOTTFRIED KELLER to Lina Duncker,
13 January 1856

Zürcher Stadt-Theater.

12. und letzte Vorstellung im ersten Abonnement.

Freitag, den 8. November 1850:

Don Juan,

oder

der steinerne Gast.

Große Oper in 2 Akten von Mozart. Mit neuer Bearbeitung des Dialogs und mit Recitativs von Richard Wagner.

Personen:

Don Pedro, Gouverneur	Hr. Windwart.
Donna Anna, seine Tochter	Fr. Rauch-Wernan.
Don Oktavio, ihr Geliebter	Hr. Wihrler.
Don Juan	Hr. Dupont.
Donna Elvira, Don Juans Geliebte	Frl. Kral.
Leporello, Don Juans Diener	Hr. Ubrich.
Masetto, ein junger Bauer	Hr. Feistmantel.
Zerline, seine Braut	Fr. Dupont.
Ein Gerichtsdiener	Hr. Richter.

Bauern und Bäuerinnen.
Die Scene ist in Spanien.

Der Feuerregen am Schlusse der Oper ist von Hrn. Schweizer angefertigt.

Preise der Plätze:

Erste Rangloge	1 fl.	Parterre = Gallerie	25 ß.
Logen Nr. 1 — 6	35 ß.	Parterre u. dritte Gallerie, Mitte	20 ß.
Logen Nr. 7 — 20	30 ß.	Dritte Gallerie, Seite	15 ß.
Sperrsitze	30 ß.	Vierte Gallerie	10 ß.

Anfang halb 7 Uhr. Ende vor 9 Uhr.

1850 program for Mozart's *Don Giovanni*, with new arrangements for dialogue and recitative by Wagner

By 1859, Zürich was rapidly losing its small-town character as it adjusted to the ebullient economic growth that had continued since the creation of the federal state in 1848. In their city survey of that year, J. J. Hottinger and G. von Escher proudly enumerated the signs of progress: a total of 1,510 dwellings (916 on the right bank of the Limmat and 694 on the left), including 228 public buildings, disposed along and connected by 57 streets and 66 narrower *Gassen*, which were illuminated or, in worst cases, made passable at night, by 440 gas lanterns and 42 more primitive *réverbères*. Congestion was relieved by 16 large public squares and 19 smaller ones, and the city was embellished by 40 public fountains, whose water was supplied by pipes, plus a number of pumps for local use. Two bridges for traffic now crossed the Limmat, as well as four pedestrian crossings, and there were 24 other bridges and walkways over the Fröschgraben, the Schanzengraben, and the Sihl Canal. The city had six churches and—since the body must be tended as well as the soul—very progressive health services, including the cantonal hospital, a lying-in hospital, and several asylums for the mentally defective, the indigent, and the aged. With the university and the Polytechnic Institute, the cantonal gymnasium and School of Industry, a veterinary college and a school for the blind, deaf and dumb and numerous other schools, Zürich was the leading educational center in Switzerland, and the existence of a large number of scientific and cultural societies whose interests ranged from archaeology to music afforded further proof of its cultural eminence, or at least of the intellectual energy of its citizens. As for industry and trade, while silk, cotton, and wool fabrication and export were of undiminished importance, there had been striking growth in the mechanical trades, particularly in machine tools, paper manufacturing, printing, publishing, and, most recently, the making of pianos, while both the coming of the railway and the growth of banking not only stimulated business activity in general but often led to the establishment of new corporate headquarters and affiliates in the city. The increase in the number of hotels, which now, in addition to the old Schwert on the lower Limmat bridge, the Baur *en ville*, and the new Bellevue on the lake, numbered well over a dozen, was a reflection of this enhanced commercial activity.

The population of the city proper, according to the census of 1850, numbered 17,040, among them 15,448 Protestants, 1,559 Catholics, and 33 Jews. Since the last figure is smaller than the number of Jews in the city at the end of the fourteenth century, it would seem to require some explanation. The simplest one, and probably the one closest to the truth, is that the Jews were never, for a combination of economic and socioreligious reasons, made welcome in Zürich, although it was by no means the most restrictive part of Switzerland in this regard. During negotiations for a new commercial treaty between the Eidgenossenschaft and the United States of America in 1857, the American envoy, Fay, complained about discrimination against American citizens of Jewish faith, pointing out that they were in some cases denied the right to do business or to take up residence. With respect to the treatment of Jews in general, Fay divided the Swiss cantons into three groups: the absolutely restrictive, which included Basel, Thurgau, and Schaffhausen; the moderately liberal, which included Zürich, and the absolutely nonrestrictive, which included Bern and Geneva. His demands that discrimination stop were still unsatisfied two years later, and the *Eidgenössische Zeitung* reported in September 1859 that he had said recently that he was becoming tired of the argument that, without restriction, Switzerland would be swamped by "low *Schacherjuden* from Alsace." It is interesting to note that Zürich was more liberal with respect to other outsiders, and that the 1850 population included 2,377 citizens of other cantons and 1,908 foreigners.

These figures give no very realistic picture of the actual size of the city in terms of population. Like other Swiss cities, Zürich was now pushing outward beyond its original borders, and if the new suburbs were included in the calculation (which is only fair, since many of their inhabitants worked in the city), its population was really in the neighborhood of 33,000.

These evidences of growth and the prosperity that accompanied them engendered an optimism and energy that found many expressions, not least of all in the annual *Sechseläuten* activities, which seemed to become more elaborate every year. This spring festival, whose origins probably went back to pre-Christian times, was managed and directed by Zürich's thirteen guilds, which made up for their loss of political and economic power by throwing themselves into preparations for the yearly parade and the ritualistic burning of the *Böög*, the spirit of winter, with unconstrained gusto. On the appointed day, which fell in late March or early April, the guilds marched in ancient uniforms or historical costumes, as did other societies and clubs, and there were brightly caparisoned bands, and male choruses, and columns of children with flags and flowers, and decorated floats that generally played on themes of the day, either local or foreign. In 1837, as we have seen, the expansion of the city had been such a theme; in 1849 the California gold rush had captured the imagination of the planners, and there were floats covered with miners in sombreros and with equipment for panning the precious metal, and in 1856 the high point of the parade was the appearance of gigantic locomotives in federal colors and covered with costumed figures intended to represent the lands of their imagined ultimate destinations—Laplanders in the case of the Nordbahn, for example, and Tatars in that of the Ostbahn.

This last extravaganza was the one witnessed by Gottfried Keller after his return from a long absence in Berlin and described by him in the letter to Ludmilla Assing quoted in the introduction to this volume. Another onlooker was Francesco De Sanctis, who was seeing the *Sechseläuten* festival for the first time and was moved to reflection upon this unexpected explosion of fantasy in what to him was a cold northern city. "It seemed to me," he wrote later, "as if all the peoples of the earth had arranged to meet in Zürich and, seeing them file before me in their bizarre modes and costumes, I laughed in my heart over this masquerade of the human race, conceived with such spirit and executed with such vivacity."

I

The cultural life of Zürich in the liberal era was a natural expression of the *Verbürgerlichung* and individualization of society that liberalism had effected by means of its successful struggle against the domination of society by aristocracy, church, and guild. It was predominantly middle class in nature, reflecting the traditions, tastes, and interests of the educated middle orders in society—bureaucrats, free professions, academicians, progressive businessmen, and the like—as well as their prejudices. Thus, it tended to be earnest and somewhat ritualistic, inclined to prefer the German mode to the Italian or French and the established to the new, and generally unadventurous (even its acceptance of Wagner was not, as we shall see, an exception to this). In matters of style it was given to the opulent and grandiose, and, in its domestic expressions, what Eric Hobsbaum has written of bourgeois style in general applied, namely, that "its objects, like the houses that contained them, were *solid*, a term used, characteristically, as the highest praise for a business enterprise. They were made to last, and they did. At the same time they must express the higher and spiritual aspirations of life through their beauty. . . . Beauty meant decoration . . . no picture without a gilded, a fretted, a chased, even a velvet-covered frame, no seat without upholstery or cover, no piece of textile without tassel, no piece of wood without some touch of the lathe, no surface without some cloth or object on it."

It was also, very largely, a male-dominated culture, for the emancipation of women was not far advanced in Zürich, and few of the leaders of the city's cultural establishment would have found anything objectionable in an advertisement that appeared in the press in May 1859, which read:

> Now in stock at Friedrich Schulthess in Zürich, a valuable book for grown-up daughters: *The Vocation of the Young Woman and her Situation as Loved One and Betrothed: With Excellent Rules Concerning Propriety, Dignity, Family Feeling, Order, Cleanliness, Independence, Friendship, Love, Marriage, Economic Efficiency: Rules about Good Tone and Behaviour in Society.* By Dr. Seidler. Fifth expanded edition. Price: 2 francs. We recommend this book, now in its fifth edition, to all young women, who will find in it their beautiful calling, to fulfill their natural and ethical vocation, to beautify family life, to appear attractive in society, as well as to prepare themselves to be worthy wives and governesses and good mistresses of the house *(Hausfrauen).*

Zürich historians have expressed pride over the fact that their university was pioneering in its open attitude toward women's education, but during the liberal period there was little sign of this. In the forties, Elise Sidler, daughter of the Landammann of Zug, and Josephine Stadlin, later a biographer of Pestalozzi, were permitted to attend lectures, but it was not until 1863 that a woman, Maria Kniaschina of Petersburg, was admitted as a regular student of medicine, and it was not until 1867 that another, Nadeschda Suslowa of Petersbug, who was married to a local politician, was granted a doctoral degree. The surge in women's university education came later, and most women students were for a long time foreigners.

Women were not admitted to any of the learned societies that played so pronounced a role in the city's cultural life, nor were they present at those banquets where Gottfried Keller pretended to be alarmed at the delicacies placed before him. Their role in society was so modest that Hermann Köchly, upon coming to Zürich from Dresden in 1850, felt that there would be little to occupy his wife in his new home, since "the Swiss, male and female, are above all completely unsociable house animals, although the former are quite friendly in pubs," and their part in culture was generally passive. There were, of course, some exceptions. One could not describe Charlotte Birch-Pfeiffer, who directed Zürich's theater from 1837 to 1843, as passive in any sense, nor does the word apply to those women who presided over the city's equivalent of salons in the fifties, Eliza Wille, Mathilde Wesendonck, and Emma Herwegh. But there were not many of these.

Perhaps the most characteristic feature of Zürich culture was its sense of didactic purpose. This derived partly from liberalism's central concern with the relationship of the individual to society and its faith in personal rather than ascriptive character, individual rather than corporate achievement, and progress and improvement (*Verbesserung*), but more perhaps from the assumption of the educated bourgeoisie in the nineteenth century that it was their mission to promote that vision of human perfectibility projected in Lessing's *Erziehung des Menschengeschlechts* and elaborated by Kant and Humboldt, Schelling and Hegel, Goethe and Schiller. *Bürgerliche* liberalism involved the belief that, just as legislative reform could advance the betterment of society by abolishing outworn institutions and eliminating social injustice and inequity, so could the forms and institutions of culture—schools and museums, arts and letters, theater and concert hall—promote the emancipation of people from ignorance and mental bondage by enlightening their minds and expanding their sensibilities. In liberal society the role of cultural activities was not merely to entertain; the role of the arts was no longer, as was true at an earlier time, to embellish aristocratic life or enhance symbol and liturgy in the church. Their function was to promote *Bildung*, to help form and develop the character of society's members. They were to serve as a medium in which, as formerly in the church, the individual citizen could find and profit from interpretations of life and human endeavor and edifying examples of moral virtue, civic courage, and the beautiful and sublime.

This view extended not only to theater and concert performances, the activities of learned societies and scientific institutes, and private entertainments of various kinds, but also to the public and communal festivals and competitions that added zest and variety to life in Zürich in the liberal era. Local and cantonal marksmanship contests, the so-called Wilhelm-Tell-Schießen, were important occasions to the liberals, who regarded them, as Gottfried Keller said in his story *The Little Banner of the Seven Upright Ones*, as a "school of morals for the young, the reward for a clean civic conscience and the fulfilled conscience of the citizen, and a rejuvenating bath for the old." The competitive aspects of these assemblies never obscured the political ones. When the Swiss Riflemen's Festival (*Eidgenössische Schützenfest*) met in Zürich in 1834, it was in the wake of the liberal defeat on the question of federal reform, and politicians who stood on both sides of that dispute harangued the 30,000 people who gathered in the Ägertenwiese in Wiedikon for the opening ceremonies with speeches that were so intemperate that the authorities feared a serious breach of public order. In contrast, when the national festival was held for a second time in Zürich in 1859, it was a celebration of freedom and independence and of the liberal achievement of the federal state. In order to preserve the communal energy and imagination for this great occasion, the city fathers decided not to hold the usual *Sechseläuten* activities in the spring of 1859 and mobilized all of the city's resources for the July festival, including the fading poetic talents of the poet Georg Herwegh, who hailed the marksmen who came with gleaming weapons and swinging banners from all the cantons and *Gauen* of Switzerland with a set of verses that perhaps showed more ardor than imagination.

Wetterumzogen brausen die Wogen;
Aber die Sterne, die sind dir gewogen!
Steure, du Schweizer, in Völkerorkan
Ruhig, wie Tell ihn gesteuert, den Kahn!

Tapfere Schützen werden sie schützen,
Kräftige Stutzen werden sie stützen,
Sichere Hand und sichere Blick
Werden behüten die Republik. . . .

Liebend umschlossen alle die Sprossen
Halte am Stamm die Eidgenossen!
Segnen sie alle, die Männer im Wehr,
Die von den Alpen und die vom Meer!

Segne, die ringen und mutig sich schwingen,
Ringende Geister und Herzen mit Schwingen!
Segnet das Spiel und den friedlichen Schuß,
Blitzende Sonne des Julius!

Doch wenn die Alten, die finstern Gewalten
Kommen, hier oben im Lichte zu walten—
Treffer im Himmel, zu unserem Heil
Lenke die Kugel, wie einst den Pfeil!

[Under threatening skies the waves rage,
But the stars are in your favor!
Man of Switzerland, steer your craft, like Tell,
Through the hurricane of the peoples!

Brave marksmen will protect it,
Powerful carbines will support it,
Firm hands and a steady gaze
Will protect the Republic. . . .

Bound in love, all the scions
Cling to the trunk of the Eidgenossen.
Bless them all, the men in arms,
Those from the Alps and those from the lakes!

Bless those who vie with each other and those
  who bravely swing the banners,
Contending spirits and hearts that swing!
Bless the games and the peaceful shot
And the shining son of July!

But if the old, the dark forces
Come to rule here above in the light—
Marksman in Heaven, for our sake
Guide the bullet as you once did the arrow!]

Communal singing and contests between male choruses were accorded an almost equal respect in liberal culture. The founder of this most popular form of musical activity was Hans Georg Nägeli of Wetzikon, a follower of Pestalozzi, who at the beginning of the century had begun to teach the art of choral singing in Zürich in the belief that it would be a means of mediating between the higher and lower cultures and propagating democratic ideas. Thanks to his influence, a Universal Musical Society was established in Zürich in 1812 and a Students Song Association in the Carolinum in 1818, and in 1826, after singers from Zürich had participated in a festival at Wädenswil, they formed a *Stadtsängerverein*, with Nägeli as president, which soon had over 200 members. Singing was an important part of the curriculum in the *Volksschulen*, and, after the liberals came to power in 1830, it received much attention in their educational reforms.

The tradition set by Nägeli inspired the foundation in Aarau in 1842 of the *Eidgenössische Sängerverein*, whose purpose, as described in its statutes, was "the development and exalting of folk singing, the inspiring of a deeper feeling for God, freedom, and fatherland, and the unity and fraternity of friends of art and the fatherland." The first song festival of the new organization was held in Zürich in 1843 and was impressive by any standard, with 1,200 singers participating, although paradoxically these did not include the Zürich *Stadtsängerverein*. That body, which had over the years become very conservative in membership, probably anticipated that the proceedings would be marked by liberal enthusiasm and propaganda for federal reform, as indeed they were.

Throughout the liberal period there was no sign of a waning

of enthusiasm for choral singing. In 1854, Zürich was host to the first cantonal song festival, and four years later it was once more the center of a national *Sängerfest*, this time even larger than of 1843, with choruses from all the cantons and from some of the German states coming to demonstrate their art and compete for prizes. Gottfried Keller was the laureate of the occasion, composing an "Opening Song" of unimpeachably patriotic sentiment:

> *Wir haben hoch im Bergrevier*
> *Den Tannenwald gehauen,*
> *Draus euch in rot und weißer Zier*
> *Das Wanderzelt zu bauen.*
> *Herein, was nun die Halle faßt,*
> *O Schweizerkind! Du deutscher Gast!*
> *Und wies im Bergwald kühn erklang,*
> *Laßt rauschen hier den Männersang! . . .*
>
> *Wie grüne Aun im Firnenschnee*
> *In alter Zeit verschwunden,*
> *So hat noch jedes Volk das Weh*
> *Des Endes auch empfunden;*
> *Doch trotzen wir den Untergang*
> *Noch langehin mit Sang und Klang!*
> *Noch halten wir aus eigner Hand*
> *Dich hoch empor, o Vaterland!*
>
> *[High in the mountain range*
> *We have cut the fir wood*
> *From which to build you*
> *Red- and white-decorated wayfarers' tents.*
> *Now enter, as many as the hall will hold,*
> *O child of Switzerland and you German guest!*
> *And as it rang bravely in the mountain forest,*
> *Let the sound of men singing thunder here! . . .*
>
> *As green meadows disappeared*
> *Long ago in the glacier,*
> *So still does every people sense*
> *The woe of last days.*
> *But we'll still defy extinction for a long time*
> *With song and harmony,*

And still in our own arms
We'll hold you high, O Fatherland!]

II

In liberal thinking about cultural affairs, the theater occupied an important place, and it is not surprising that, as we have seen, the building of Zürich's first permanent theater, the so-called Aktientheater, followed so soon upon the beginning of the liberals' ascendancy in the canton's politics. They were doubtless motivated by a desire to remove the ban upon theatrical performances that the church had been able to maintain even during the Enlightenment, a sign of obscurantism and intellectual myopia that was intolerable in the new dispensation. But even more important was their belief that the theater was an almost unequaled instrument of *Bildung*. Had not Friedrich Schiller himself defined it as a moral institution, as "the common channel through which the glow of wisdom flows from the intelligent, superior part of society and spreads itself in gentle streams throughout the whole state?" And were not these words virtually a summary of the liberal view of the very purpose of cultural institutions? If the radical liberals of the thirties were gratified by the opportunity to cock a snook at established religion, the bulk of the liberal party, radical and moderate alike, placed more importance on the educational opportunities provided by the establishment of a theater, and they supported it with enthusiasm.

This was hardly enough to guarantee success, and indeed the theater that moved into the old Barfüsser Church in 1834 had a rocky enough time in its first years, despite a series of brilliant guest appearances in 1835 by the Munich actor Ferdinand Esslair, who in his time enchanted both Goethe and Heine, and Seydelmann's long-remembered portrayals of Shylock, Franz Moor, Clavigo, Nathan, and Mephisto in 1836. Lack of consistency in overall performance and a number of amateurish productions were soon reflected in empty seats, and the theater seemed headed for serious trouble when Charlotte Birch-Pfeiffer became its director in 1837.

A native of Munich who had been admitted to the court

theater's company when she was thirteen, Charlotte Pfeiffer was playing tragic heroines at the age of twenty and touring Europe in such roles as Phaedra, Medea, Lady Macbeth, Mary Stuart, Countess Orsina, and Lady Milford. An actress of great sensibility and authority, she was handicapped by a rough, almost masculine voice and the lack of natural feminine grace, which she recognized and took into account when choosing her parts. After her marriage in 1825, her husband, a Dr. Birch from Copenhagen, discovered her talent as a playwright, and she soon developed a remarkable facility for turning out plays that were often heavily derivative from foreign novels but were ideally suited to middle-class prejudices, exciting, well-constructed, so that all of the problems were resolved before the final curtain, sentimental, invincibly moral, and always in the best of taste. To these gifts were added a thorough knowledge of the technology and economy of the theater and a good business head. This combination of talents recommended her to a theater board that was seriously worried about the future, and in 1837, after she had filled the theater to overflowing in a series of guest appearances as Lady Macbeth and Catherine the Great, in a now forgotten play, *The Favorites*, it offered her the directorship.

In her seven years in that position, Birch-Pfeiffer not only restored the theater to a sound financial condition but gave her public what enthusiasts later called the Golden Age of the Zürich theater. She was intelligent enough to realize that an unrelieved program of the classics would not for long satisfy Zürich theatergoers, and, if anything, she erred in the opposite direction, providing a variety of productions that included melodrama, historical and romantic pageants (including her own highly popular *Death of Huldrych Zwingli*), farces and *Singspiele*, classical tragedies and comedies, and opera (Mozart, Beethoven, Weber, Lortzing, Rossini, Bellini, Auber, Meyerbeer). She had a nose for new works, and Zürich was the first German stage to present Gutzkow's play *A White Sheet*, Scribe's *A Chain*, Bellini's opera *La Sonnambula*, and the highly popular *Postillon von Lonjumeau* of Adolphe Adam.

The respect that Birch-Pfeiffer won as a result of her skillful direction of the theater did not make her immune to pressures from the right after the conservative reaction of September 1839. The desire of the church and its allies for a system of censorship that would prevent the theater from corrupting public morals had been frustrated during the first five years of its existence, but when the reaction came so did demands for the banning of certain productions and the emendation of others. Spindler's *Waldmann* disappeared from the repertory, the police forced the excision of the friar's prayer from a production of *Wallenstein's Camp*, and when producing *Egmont*, Birch-Pfeiffer was forced to agree to the elimination of every passage that seemed remotely to suggest criticism of religion or of existing political conditions. The *Schweizerische Republikaner* expressed outrage over the treatment of the Goethe tragedy, writing on 6 December 1842:

> Hail to the country in which the ears of the multitude are not contaminated with such poison! What does Goethe matter? What does classic or artistic unity matter? What the understanding of the whole work? . . . What would Arnold of Brescia, what would the old burgomasters and councillors of Zürich, what would Waldmann and Zwingli have said of this mutilated *Egmont*?

Censorship was, however, a transient condition, and Birch-Pfeiffer's successors were not long forced to worry about it. Their principal difficulty was a financial one, for the theater from the beginning had been dependent exclusively upon private investment and subscription, and, in view of the mounting costs of the kind of productions that the public expected in the case of opera, these sources were never adequate. The government, however, saw no reason why it should support the theater, and in 1850—at a time when the city of Vienna was providing half a million Swiss francs a year for the Opera and the Burgtheater— pleaded its own limited resources as a reason for not doing so. Nor did it show any interest in Richard Wagner's proposal in 1851 for a revolutionary new kind of theater, which bore some marked resemblance to the utopian "art work of the future" that he was later, as we shall see, to elaborate on, but which, like all of his plans, called for heavy investment of public funds. It was not until 1856, and then only under the threat of a dissolution of the theater society, that the government approved a yearly subvention of 2,500 francs, and not until 1869 that this was doubled. The liberals did not allow their appreciation of the cultural significance of the theater to weaken their faith in the free enterprise system, and they would have found incredible the thought that in 1893 government support of the theater would be 20,000 francs a year.

The principal change in the theater after 1848 was a marked diminution of the number of sentimental melodramas, romances about knights and maidens in remote ages, and insubstantial farces and burlesques in the program and the gradual increase in the number of classical comedies and tragedies and serious dramas by modern writers. Kotzebue's plays, which figured heavily in Birch-Pfeiffer's *Spielplan* (thirty performances in seven years as opposed to five for the plays of Kleist), pieces like Clauren's *The Bridegroom of Mexico*, and Birch's own historical dramas tended to disappear completely. In contrast, Lessing, whose *Nathan the Wise* was never produced in the Birch era, now came into his own, as did Goethe and Shakespeare (*Hamlet* now superseding *Macbeth* in popularity), and, most of all, Schiller. Performances of *Wilhelm Tell*, which numbered only seven between 1834 and 1844, increased steadily decade by decade, reaching sixty-one in the eighties. This tendency toward greater seriousness strengthens Thomas Nipperdey's point that, leaving the aspect of entertainment aside, the theater became "a crystallization point in bourgeois life . . . a forum for the discussion of the meaning of life and the tensions of contemporary, and timeless, human destiny, a place of edification and, genuine or false, emotional shock, a place of pretension also, a temple of *Bildung* as well as a cultural institution, in which the young person, perhaps through attending *Wilhelm Tell*, in a sense completed the initiation rites of bourgeois culture." It may not be completely irrelevant in this respect to add that, in 1857, at the height of the Neuenburg crisis, a special performance of *Tell* was arranged at the request of General Dufour and his staff.

Enthusiasm for the theater was not expressed solely by sitting in the loges of the Aktientheater. In bourgeois society throughout the German-speaking area private groups organized for the purpose of reading plays aloud in clubs or in their homes, and in his novel *Problematical Natures*, Friedrich Spielhagen gives a satirical description of such a reading of *Wallenstein's Death*, emphasizing the competitiveness and petty jealousy that sometimes accompanied the distribution of roles. In Zürich several play-reading groups existed in the fifties, and one of them, in which the leading spirits were the former actress Karoline Bauer, now the wife of a Polish refugee Count Plater, and Eliza Wille-Sloman, the wife of the publicist Francois Wille, took the pastime with the utmost seriousness. This group alternated its meetings between the Wille estate at Mariafeld on the lake, Count Plater's home at Brölberg, and the city residences of the medical doctor Giesker, the jurist Dernburg, and the university professor Hermann Köchly, who had participated in a similar group in Dresden before his involvement in the rising of 1849 had forced him into exile. This company and invited guests read *Antigone, Coriolanus, Minna von Barnhelm, The Prince of Homburg*, and other standards of the classical repertory, as well as lighter pieces like Iffland's *Huntsmen*. They were successful in attracting even the reserved Theodor Mommsen into their circle, despite his sardonic opinion that "traffic in associations here is a virtual national plague and, before one knows it, one is involved in one of these *Kränzchen*, in which the flowers by no means all smell like roses."

Mommsen and Francois Wille had been associates on the liberal side in the revolutionary troubles in Hamburg in 1848, and he was a frequent guest at Eliza Wille's cultural *soirées* at Mariafeld, where his energetic hostess was soon enticing him to read aloud the works of the north German poet Klaus Groth. From there it was an easy step to the drama, and on one notable occasion at the Platers' he read the part of Octavius Caesar in *Antony and Cleopatra*, with Köchly as Antony and Karoline Bauer as the Egyptian queen. It was an appropriate role for the historian of Rome and filled with fine speeches, including the one over the dead Cleopatra:

> . . . *she looks like sleep,*
> *As she would catch another Antony*
> *In her strong toil of grace.*

It is amusing to speculate about what may have been passing through Mommsen's mind on this occasion. When he had first met Karoline Bauer at the Willes', she had shown great interest in his fiancée and, to his considerable irritation, asked whether she was a reading person or a *Hausfrau*.

III

Zürich was the home of numerous scientific and cultural societies, some of which, like the Music Society, the Quartet Association, and the Society of Artists, devoted themselves to the encouragement and the performance of the arts; others, like the Technical Society, the Architects' Union, and the Scientific Union, which was founded by professors of the university in 1855, fostered professional collaboration and publication of new research, while still others, like the Municipal Library Association, served to preserve and expand the record of the city's past and to accumulate other cultural and scientific materials.

Of the associations that concerned themselves with history, the most prestigious was the Antiquarian Society, which had been founded in 1832 on the initiative of the theologian and teacher of English Ferdinand Keller, as a result of a chance discovery on his part, during the felling and uprooting of some trees, of a number of Celtic burial mounds in Burghölzli in the community of Riesbach near Zürich. The mounds, which were similar to those on the Salisbury Plain in England, were so rich in artifacts that they suggested that wider searches would be rewarding, and the Antiquarian Society made such investigation and excavation its principal object. Nor was it disappointed in the results. The society attracted international attention when, on the basis of observations at Obermeilen in 1853 and 1854 and findings in the Bielersee, the Neuenburgsee, and the Pfäffikersee, Keller advanced his theory of a Stone and Bronze Age society of lake dwellers, living in pilework houses on the shores. As time passed the society's activities broadened to include researches into Roman remains, with excavations of settlements in east Switzerland and Roman Alpine roads, studies of heraldry, numismatics, and chronicles, publications on medieval history (like Keller's *History of the Islands of Ufenau and Lützelau in the Lake of Zürich* in 1843 and Georg von Wyss's *History of the Abbey of Zürich* in the years 1853–56), the preservation and study of the ruins of castles like Alt-Regensberg and Manegg, and the collection of ancient hymns, poems, and songs, like the poems of the Minnesinger Hadlaub and Swiss battle songs. With all of these activities, it is not surprising that the society's collections of artifacts and documents, which were housed in the Helmhaus in Zürich, as was the city library, and in the Predigerkirche, soon began to run out of room and could not be properly displayed. It was not until the eighties, however, that the building of the Swiss Landesmuseum relieved this problem.

It should be noted that, despite his fleering at the plague of associations, Theodor Mommsen did not hesitate to put his knowledge of ancient inscriptions and coins at the society's disposal when he was invited to do so, although he was characteristically sarcastic in referring to the fact. "Next winter I want to join the Antiquarian Society and see what they're pottering away at," he wrote to his brother Tycho in October 1852. "If you will lend me your Anglo-Saxon, I'll prove to those fellows that they're all Celts!"

Older than the Antiquarian Society was the Society for Natural Science (Naturforschende Gesellschaft in Zürich), which was founded in 1746 and whose declared purpose, entirely appropriate to the Zürich Aufklärung, was "the knowledge of nature, insofar as this serves the comfort, needs, and necessities of human society in general, but especially of our dear fatherland." Housed in the guild house Meisen until 1837 and, thereafter, in the Rüden, the society generally had a membership of about a hundred members, until the founding of the two universities and the growth of the local scientific community gradually increased this number. In the early years its principal interest was in practical researches for the improvement of the national economy, with particular reference to agriculture, and the giving of prizes for useful discoveries (new seeds, stocks, and tools, for example, and new techniques of planting) and other innovations. It early began to make statistical studies that would have relevance to the natural economy, and as early as 1756 was conducting censuses of population, supplementing these after 1780 with censuses of houses and households in Zürich. It took an early interest also in meteorological observations, and studies by David Breitinger in the 1770s and 1780s were largely influential in winning acceptance for the lightning rod in Zürich. After the turn of the century these studies were expanded, and in the 1840s the society built weather stations on the Uetliberg and the Rigi for wind and barometric observation. Hydrostatics also absorbed some of the society's energies, and in 1845, when the city was threatened with a recurrence of typhus and related epidemics, the society's studies of the city's water supply helped to keep these under control.

On 1 November 1846 the society celebrated its hundredth anniversary with a meeting in the large chamber of the Casino that was attended by three hundred members, state councillors and municipal officials, and guests. There were speeches of welcome and self-congratulation, but, true to the spirit of inquiry that had animated the society from the beginning, the greater part of the formal proceedings was given over to scientific papers: on progress in the natural sciences by Professor Schinz, on geognostic relations in Switzerland by Escher von der Linth, on steam electricity by Professor Mousson (with experiments on an Armstrong steam engine), and on the harmony of nature by Oswald Heer, a theologian turned natural scientist who was director of Zürich's Botanical Garden and already deep in the researches that would lead to his *Plants of the Swiss Tertiary Period* (1855–59) and win him world fame with his *The Ancient World of Switzerland* (1864). Those that survived this heavy bill of fare spent the evening hours, the record states, "in an intimate group, celebrating the beginning of a new era for our society with song and merriment."

This anniversary had important results, for in its wake the membership began to discuss the possibility of presenting a number of public lectures on scientific themes, and between February 1847 and March 1850 they actually gave eight such lectures, in their hall at the Rüden, on subjects like new planetary discoveries, the human eye, the galvanic current, and climatological conditions in the polar regions, often with accompanying illustrations and demonstrations. The response of the *Bildung*-conscious lay public to the lectures was so positive that members of the university faculty felt that the experiment should be carried further and broadened in scope, and they formed a Union of University Teachers (after the founding of the Polytechnikum called the General Union of Teachers of Zürich's Two Universities) for the purpose of planning and presenting popular scientific lectures.

This was the origin of the Rathaus Lectures, a feature of Zürich life for the next half century. During the fifties and sixties they attracted such large audiences that they had sometimes to be repeated, a circumstance that Mommsen noted with cynical amusement and which quite astonished Gottfried Keller when he returned to his native city from Berlin in 1855. In February of the following year Keller wrote to his friend Hermann Hettner:

Every Thursday there are academic lectures à la the Sing-akademie in Berlin in the largest hall in the city, to which man and wife shove in their many hundreds and then hold out for two hours without moving. [Gottfried] Semper gave a very nice and reflective lecture on the nature of decoration. [Friedrich Theodor] Vischer will give the concluding lecture on *Macbeth*. Aside from these, there are a lot of special cycles by single dignitaries, so that every evening one sees the servant girls running around with the big visiting lanterns to give external illumination to the inwardly enlightened ladies on their way home. To be sure, it is rumored that the demure and bigotted Zürcher ladies have discovered in these lectures a quite honorable and innocent rendezvous system and that thoughts are not always concentrated on what is being said.

To his amusement, Keller also discovered that some of the lecturers were becoming inordinately proud of their own lecture manner and critical of the speech and intonation of their rivals. The German professors, who, he said, were always "in each other's hair," were particularly prone to this, the Saxons and Prussians laughing at Vischer's Schwabian pronunciation. This infuriated Vischer, who was heard to say, after a lecture by a North German, "*That* is supposed to be proper German? When such a fellow says, instead of 'verloren,' 'vochlochen,' and instead of 'Liebe,' 'Lübhe'!"

The local newspapers followed the Rathaus Lectures with great respect, and it is possible from their columns to get a good idea of their number and variety—in January 1857, for example, there were lectures on coal, the Spartan kings, the relationship between state and society, and the German forest—but not of variations in quality, since the reviews, while always sizable and circumstantial, almost invariably concluded by saying that the audiences went home "richly nourished and fortified," or something of the sort. Other sources make it clear, however, that the intellectual level was high, that certain lectures—Jacob Burckhardt's on Agnes of Hungary in December 1855, for example, and Ludwig Ettmüller's on German mythology, the "White Women," and soothsaying in February 1859—had a remarkable resonance, and that certain lecturers were given a kind of star status by their auditors. This was true, for example, in the case of Friedrich Theodor Vischer, Gottfried Kinkel, and Hermann Köchly.

Vischer was a native of Württemberg and had been educated in the Stuttgart gymnasium, the cloister at Blaubeeren, and the University of Tübingen, where he studied philology, philosophy, and theology, taking his degree in 1830 and becoming a pastor in the village of Horrheim and, a little later, accepting a teaching position in the Maulbronn Cloister. He soon fell under the influence of Schelling and Hegel and, although he took his doctorate in theology in 1832, he followed it by a year's study in Göttingen and Berlin, in which he immersed himself in the works of Shakespeare and Goethe and soon turned his back on religious studies for good. He qualified for a teaching post at Tübingen with a dissertation on the sublime and the comic, which laid the foundation for his later work in aesthetics, and then wrote a number of literary studies that attracted considerable critical attention. His defense of David Friedrich Strauß, however, against attacks upon his *Life of Jesus* exposed him to the concentrated fire of the Protestant church and Württemberg pietism, and his inaugural lecture as professor at the University of Tübingen, which was a combative declaration of the independence of aesthetic judgment from considerations of religion and morals, led to charges in the press that he was endangering religion and the government. After lengthy hearings, the state ministry suspended his *venia legendi* for three years. When the revolution came in 1848, he was elected to the Frankfurt Assembly, where he was a member of the moderate left and, in its last days, an opponent of those who wished to rehabilitate its reputation by participating in the Baden revolution. After the restoration of order and the onset of reaction, he was subjected to new attacks and denunciations, from which neither the university authorities nor the ministry showed any disposition to protect him. In 1855, therefore, when the Polytechnic Institute in Zürich offered him a chair (without any apparent reservation concerning his Straußian connections), he accepted.

Vischer was not particularly happy in Zürich—his marriage was not a good one and his students were ill equipped to understand the subjects he professed—but he accomplished prodigies of work while there, finishing the last three volumes of his life work, *Aesthetics, or The Science of the Beautiful*, before 1857 and following it with a major work on Goethe's *Faust*, and his contributions to the Rathaus Lectures, on subjects like *Macbeth* and *Iphigenie*, were enormously successful. Why this was so it is difficult to say with any assurance, although there may be something to Georg Lukács's suggestion that it was because Vischer was the perfect barometer of bourgeois taste, his opinions and theories reflecting those of the *Bildungsbürgertum* who flocked to hear them. Karl Marx is said to have studied Vischer's *Aesthetics* with great care because he was fascinated by his elaboration of a system of aesthetics that bore absolutely no relation to the material circumstances of industrial society, so that the Beautiful and the Ugly, the Sublime and the Comic became mere abstract forms in a Hegelian dance of time. This enabled Vischer to ignore, Lukács argued, the true aesthetic problem of ugliness in the modern period, which was that of giving artistic reflection, reproduction, and form to capitalist reality, but this was eminently congenial to his middle-class audience, which did not believe that reality had anything to do with culture in any case. Similarly, Vischer's theory of tragedy, which was a watered-down version of Hegel's reflections on that subject and took the line that everything that happened was necessary and potentially productive of good, offered his hearers a comforting way of rationalizing the brutalities and injustices of society in the industrial age.

Gottfried Kinkel did not come to Zürich until 1866, but his life before then had been so full of incident, and his literary fame was so great, that his arrival was an event of major importance. Educated at the University of Bonn, where he studied theology, Kinkel began his career as a teacher of religion there and as an auxiliary pastor in Cologne, losing both positions in 1843, however, when he married Johanna Möckel, the divorced wife of a merchant whom he had rescued from drowning. He turned his attention to the history of art and culture and became professor of that subject at Bonn in 1846. He had great success both as a teacher, numbering among his disciples Karl Schurz and Jacob Burckhart, and as a writer of stories and poetry, his epic poem *Otto the Marksman* running through many editions. In 1848 he was a deputy in the lower house of the Prussian Parliament and, when the tide turned against the revolution, went to Baden and joined August Willich's proletarian Besançon Company in Mieroslawski's revolutionary army. During the retreat from the Neckar line he was wounded at Bruchsal and captured by the Prussians, subsequently being sentenced to life imprisonment in Spandau. His wife appealed to Karl Schurz, who had escaped from the encircled fortress at Rastatt and made his way to Zürich, and Schurz interrupted his studies there, went to Berlin, and engineered a daring rescue operation, going then with his old professor to England, where they were acclaimed as heroes. With the exception of a year's stay in the United States, Kinkel remained in London for more than fifteen years, teaching the German language and literature and writing a drama called *Nimrod*. He had many friends in London and was a prominent figure in exile political circles, to the great irritation of Karl Marx, who accused him and his wife of moral posturing and virtually broke off relations with the poet Ferdinand Freiligrath because he refused to agree with Marx's caustic evaluation and actually, when Johanna Möckel died, wrote a poem that was read at her graveside.

Kinkel was only fifty-one years old when he took up his professorship of art at the Polytechnikum, and he threw himself into his new responsibilities with great energy. He taught a wide variety of courses in art and literature, including the lectures on Shakespeare that Vischer had given before returning to Tübingen in 1866; he was the founder of Zürich's collection of copper engravings, after Basel's, the first public collection in Switzerland, and he was active in the Antiquarian Society and other associations. And, from the beginning, he was in great demand as a lecturer, for the eloquence and spirit that had once charmed Schurz and Burckhardt had not waned with the years. The content of his lectures was less important than the personality of the lecturer. Kinkel, indeed, became a revered figure in the city on the Limmat, his funeral procession in 1882 being one of the largest in Zürich's history.

Personality was also the strong suit of Hermann Köchly, one of the most frequent of the lecturers in the Rathaus series and perhaps the most widely admired. A philologist by training, Köchly had been a senior teacher in the Kreuzschule in Dresden in the years before the revolution. In 1848, as a member of the second chamber of Parliament, he found himself involved against his will in the radical movement, for, when the King dissolved Parliament in April 1849, he was elected a member of the three-man Security Council of the chamber, which in turn nominated the provisional government that was the author of the troubles that followed. In the May rising he tried to remain detached, refusing to fight on the barricades and, after the repression began, retiring to his home, where he stayed until friends warned him that he was in deadly danger. In a state of mixed terror and incomprehension, he made his way to Berlin and Hamburg and finally to Brussels, where he was joined by his wife and learned that his name was on an official wanted circular along with those of Karl Todt, a member of the provisional government, and Richard Wagner and Gottfried Semper, who, as we shall see in due course, had also been involved in the rising. Köchly was not the most sophisticated or courageous of men, and he was scared nearly witless when he learned that the wireless telegraph now facilitated the apprehension of fugitives. From this state of moral collapse he was saved by a letter from his friend Zschetzsche, who taught in the Fröbel Institute in Zürich and had some influence in the Educational Council there. Zschetzsche urged him to apply for the university position left vacant by Caspar von Orelli's retirement, adding that anyone who could revive philological studies in Zürich would have a promising future. Köchly followed that advice and, although the *Eidgenössische Zeitung*, which was working in the interest of one of Orelli's students, opposed his appointment on the grounds that he was not Swiss and was a political refugee, the *Neue Zürcher Zeitung* supported him on precisely the same grounds, as "a foreigner, like so many other adornments of our university, [and] a fugitive, like so many other honorable men of the most diverse political parties." This and his friend's influence in the right places won the post for him.

Köchly was never a scholar of the first order. Long after it had been discredited, he clung to the theory that *The Iliad* had no single author but was the result of the stringing together of older narrative poems, and when Wilhelm Rüstow worked with him on a bilingual edition of Greek war poets and a history of the Greek art of war from the most ancient times to the age of Pyrrhus, he claimed that Köchly's factual knowledge was often inaccurate and his understanding of ancient warfare so deficient that Rüstow had to build scale models of catapults and other devices in order to make clear the meaning of certain texts. (In justice to Köchly it has to be said that, in his view, Rüstow suffered from the fact that he was a trained practitioner of modern war and was always reading things into the ancient texts that were not there.) Theodor Mommsen, after hearing Köchly's Rathaus lecture on Demosthenes, said rather grudgingly that he had "a marked talent for saying things, if not in the finest way, at least emphatically and clearly," but then spoiled the compliment by adding, "I always regret that I really cannot respect him. . . ." Mommsen's later statement to Otto Hahn, that "there is nobody here who understands the classics in the slightest degree, except perhaps Köchly. You will crucify yourself, but we're so badly off here that he has very often been a support for me," in no way represented a change of heart. For his part Köchly tried hard to be friendly with the North German scholar, whom Georg von Wyss once described as "a sharpened knife that one must take proper care not to grasp clumsily." He had immense respect for Mommsen's learning, and it must have taken some courage on his part, in a lecture on the occasion of the university's jubilee in 1858, to defend the Roman statesman Cato against the somewhat frivolous attack on him in the now departed Mommsen's *Roman History*.

As a public lecturer, however, Köchly was without a peer. While he was still a teacher in Dresden, he had won local fame with a lecture series on modern German poets, delivered in a style that was clear and ingratiating, taking the audience into the speaker's confidence and persuading them to adopt his point of view. In Zürich he developed this further, never hesitating to use exaggeration, dramatic effects, and appeals to the emotions when they served his purposes. He always found it easier to speak to a mixed audience than a scholarly one—in one of his appearances at the Antiquarian Society he became so violent and polemical when opinions contrary to his own were mentioned that the meeting broke off in disorder—and such audiences always reacted most positively to his effects. According to reliable eyewitnesses, the people who filled the Rathaus to hear him talk about Demosthenes or, in 1854–55 (a long-remembered series of nine lectures), about *The Iliad* and *The Odyssey* or, in later years, about the Greek poets were left in a condition of intellectual excitement and spiritual exaltation.

And yet there is some evidence of a growing tension between them and the man who was always described in the press as "one of the most beloved teachers in the university." Köchly was an unconditional believer in what Hölderlin had called "the devastating glory of the Greeks." He stood for that belief in the absolute cultural preeminence of Greece that is so congenial to the German soul but is perhaps less so to the Swiss, particularly when it is used in argument as a foil against modernity. And the fact was that Köchly was prone to using it in that fashion. Increasingly, he viewed changes in the society of which he was a part as threats to his cultural ideals. His lecture series on Homer in the winter of 1854–55 ended with an expression of fear lest the rapid advance of the natural sciences and the growth of materialism should progressively destroy the influence of the classics. He was far from enthusiastic about the coming of the Polytechnic Institute to Zürich and, as we have seen, was not charitable in his view of its mission in his speech on the occasion of the university's jubilee in 1858. Gradually, in his defense of the classics and humanistic studies in general, he became a bit of a common scold, a tendency that reached an extreme when, as a member of the Board of Overseers of the Cantonal Gymnasium in 1859–60, he undertook to challenge Alfred Escher's plans for modernizing the curriculum, digging his heels in in an attempt to save the compulsory Greek requirement and being roundly defeated. His resultant bitterness probably prompted his decision to return to Germany in 1864, but the incident has perhaps a deeper significance, indicating that Alfred Escher sensed and reacted to the cultural values of the Zürich *Bildungsbürgertum* much more accurately than Köchly could possibly do. It was Escher, after all, more than any single individual, who had brought the Polytechnikum to the city that he loved, and Escher never doubted that, while the educated elite of its citizens had a passion for *Bildung* and a strong desire to become cultivated human beings, they saw no reason why this should force them to deny themselves the material comforts that scientific progress made possible.

IV

The liberal period was, as we have seen, filled with festivals of one kind or another, but certainly the one that was most clearly a celebration of the *Bildungsbürgertum* and its cultural values was the hundredth anniversary of the birth of Friedrich Schiller in November 1859. The occasion received ceremonial attention from governments and private associations throughout the German-speaking world, as well as in the United States, but its observance in Zürich was certainly as elaborate as in most other capitals, and considerably more so than in Berlin, where the president of police forbade the planned procession of the guilds and the factory workers in Schiller's honor. In the city on the Limmat the program extended over two days, beginning on 10 November with a prologue delivered by the poet Georg Herwegh in the Aktientheater and ending with an address by Friedrich Theodor Vischer in St. Peter's Church. In between there were productions of Heinrich Laube's *Die Karlsschüler*, a play about Schiller's youth, and Schiller's *The Robbers* and *Wilhelm Tell*, a performance of Beethoven's Ninth Symphony, and a theatrical presentation of "The Song of the Bell" with *tableaux vivants*. Surely, the *Eidgenössische Zeitung* wrote, "Zürich will occupy a high position among the festival centers."

Yet there were some curious dissonances in the ceremonies. Gerhard Storz has pointed out that, in the German states, the *Schiller-Feier* of 1859 was a tacit reconciliation between those who had fought for constitutional change in 1848 and the establishment that had opposed and defeated them, a reconciliation effected with the aid of the nationalistic feeling that had been inspired by Napoleon III's intervention in Piedmont's war against Austria. Francesco De Sanctis refused to have anything to do with the festivities because he felt that they were intended to transform "the lovable dreamer of our acquaintance [into] an Austrian political and diplomatic figure," and the Swiss, to whom Schiller was primarily the poet of freedom and the author of *Tell*, may have felt less than happy about the note of German nationalism that flavored much of the public rhetoric during the two-day program.

This perhaps explains the stormy applause that greeted Herwegh's "Prologue" and the praise accorded it in the postfestival discussion. By any objective standards this was hardly a distinguished achievement. It was so stuffed with Schiller quotations—from *The Maid of Orleans*, *Tell*, *Wallenstein*, "The Song of the Bell," and poems like "The Votive Tablets" and "The Invincible Fleet"—that it was hardly a poem in its own right. But it at least provided Herwegh's audience with an opportunity to demonstrate their cultivation by recognizing the citations for what they were, and, aside from that, Herwegh's emphasis was squarely upon Schiller's contributions to the cause of freedom. Recalling the poet's first expression of his own love of liberty, the stormy *Robbers*, he cried to the packed theater:

Ihr, junge Herzen, haltet fest das Echte
In eures Dichters erstem Jugendschwung—
Ach, nur zu frühe vor dem Rausch der Knechte
Lernt in uns schweigen die Begeisterung.
Bleibt jung! Bleibt jung! Bleibt jung!

[You, young hearts, hold fast to the substance
Of your poet's first youthful fling—
Ah, all to soon the drunkenness of slaves
Teaches us to mute our inspiration.
Stay young! Stay young! Stay young!]

There was no talk of truces with the established powers in the lines of the aging freedom fighter of the forties.

Die Freiheit ist die Flut der Weltgeschichte,
Und manche Woge sehn wir, die sich hebt.
Wir sehen auch, es schwindet das Vertrauen
Auf jeden ird'schen Herrscherstab;
Drum wollen wir auf jene Krone bauen,
Die er der Menschheit wiedergab.

[Freedom is the floodtide of world history,
And we are seeing many a wave rising now.
And we're also seeing the vanishing of confidence
In any earthly scepter.
Therefore, we wish to rely upon that crown
That he gave back to humanity.]

This could not help but appeal to the democratic prejudices of a Swiss audience, which could also respond with gratification to a later passage in Herwegh's "Prologue," in which, loosely citing *Tell*, he cried:

"Das Reich der Freiheit hat dir Gott gegründet,"
O Schweiz, nur dir allein!
Sein Wort hat überall gezündet;
Das Reich der Freien, es muß größer sein.
Deutschland und Schweiz! Wie uns ein Strom, der
  Rhein,
So hält ein Geistesstrom uns heut zusammen,
Und wie wir glühen von denselben Flammen,

Sei unser Gruß dem, der sie angefacht,
Demselben Genius von uns gebracht!

["God has founded for you the realm of freedom."
O Switzerland, for you alone!
His word has lighted flames everywhere;
The realm of the free must become larger.
Germany and Switzerland! As one stream, the Rhine,
So one spiritual stream holds us now together,
And, as we glow from the same flames,
Let our greeting be sent to him,
The genius who kindled them.]

In contrast, Vischer's speech in St. Peter's Church, while much admired, must have encountered some reservations when he criticized Schiller's cosmopolitanism, for example, saying, "The thought of freedom, when it becomes completely dominant, overlooks the fact that we all must have a fatherland, regardless of whether it is free or not," and again when he credited Schiller's inspiration for the victory over Napoleon, adding, "and when we again have to struggle for fatherland, morality, law, and truth, his song will float upon our lips, his flaming word will be our battle cry!" In this passage Vischer was already slipping into the attitude that he was to adopt after his return to Germany, when he cast off the liberalism of his early maturity and accepted Bismarck's war against Austria as a tragic necessity and the victory over France as the fulfillment of German destiny.

No one in St. Peter's Church in November 1859 could have foreseen anything of the sort, but some may have felt that this kind of tub-thumping was hardly appropriate to the occasion. But they could not have been disturbed for long. The bulk of Vischer's discourse dealt with Schiller's progress from the ebullience of youth to the maturity of his last plays, with his friendship with Goethe, and with their creation of an ideal of beauty to sustain humanity in troubled times. In the abstract, somewhat flocculent style that often overcame him in the course of his aesthetic reflections, Vischer assured his audience in Schiller's name that human beings should "be educated to inner harmony with themselves" before they grappled with the problems of the world, that "in the beautiful and in art one should seek the road to goodness and justice," and that "it was only worth the effort to be free when freedom bore the fruit of purely harmonious *Bildung.''* The logic of the argument was not always easy to follow, but the tone was elevated and all of the right symbolic words were used, and Vischer's listeners were left comforted and flattered and confirmed in their cultural prejudices.

Chapter 7

ART AND REVOLUTION: RICHARD WAGNER AND GOTTFRIED SEMPER

♦

Along with the political storms that blew up at the end of the last century, a new fermentation began simultaneously in art. Politics and art have always gone hand in hand. —GOTTFRIED SEMPER, *Kleine Schriften* (1884)

And this devil, this mad need without need, this need of need—this need of luxury, which is luxury itself—rules the world; it is the soul of this industry, which kills the human being in order to use him as a machine; the soul of our State, which declares the human being to be without honor in order to restore him to grace as a subject; the soul of our deistic science, which throws the human being to an absurd god, the efflux of all this intellectual luxury, for his consumption; it is—ah!—the soul, the condition of our—Art!

Who now will effect our salvation from this most calamitous condition? —RICHARD WAGNER, *Das Kunstwerk der Zukunft* (1850)

Richard Wagner

Gottfried Semper

A judge of Zürich's contribution to the major cultural developments of the middle years of the nineteenth century would, if he wished to be disparaging, doubtless describe it as modest at best, pointing out that, with the exception of Gottfried Keller and Oswald Heer, the canton possessed no distinguished native artists or scientists and that its greatest cultural achievements were all the work of visitors. Such a view would be neither charitable nor fair. Theodor Mommsen's *Roman History* and Friedrich Theodor Vischer's *Aesthetics* would doubtless have been written even if their authors had never set foot in the city on the Limmat, but it is impossible to believe that they would have been written in quite the same way. Is it reasonable to suppose that Mommsen's later work was wholly unaffected by the research that he did on native antiquities and inscriptions while he was in Zürich, or that Vischer's work profited in no way from the long conversations that he had, about Dante, Petrarch, Leopardi, the Hegelian philosophy, and other subjects, with Francesco De Sanctis during their walks along the quays? To believe so would be to attribute to both men extraordinary qualities of detachment, self-absorption, and, indeed, intellectual insensitivity, and unless one is willing to make such attribution one is compelled to admit that Zürich should be granted some share in their accomplishments.

This is even clearer in the case of Richard Wagner and that of Gottfried Semper. The musician who left Zürich in 1858, in the hope that the propitious time had arrived for him to conquer the Parisian stage, was a far different person from the disheveled and weary political refugee who came knocking on the door of Alexander Müller's house in the Rennweg on the night of 29 May 1849, after a headlong flight from the Saxon police. Zürich gave Wagner a refuge in which he could write his theoretical works and return from politics to music. It introduced him, through the agency of Georg Herwegh, to the work of Schopenhauer, an intellectual encounter that profoundly affected him and may, as Friedrich Nietzsche believed, have quenched what was left of his revolutionary ardor. It provided him with the romantic inspiration for what has been considered his most perfect work, *Tristan und Isolde*. It nurtured his growth and challenged his creative imagination.

As for Semper, his call to the Polytechnic Institute in 1855 probably saved him from long years of further frustration by granting him the opportunity to give expression to those powers that had been unrealized, because unencouraged, in London. He responded with some of his greatest architectural achievements, in the creation of which he was inspired not only by his vision of an art appropriate to the modern age but also by the beauty of the city that his creations were to adorn.

I

In Wagner's case as in Semper's, the road to Zürich began during the May rising in Dresden in 1849, in which both of them were deeply involved. This was a fact that Wagner later found it expedient to depreciate, and the reader of his autobiography is left with the impression that he was caught up in the sweep of events against his will, in much the same way as Hermann Köchly. Given the extent of his other activities and preoccupations, it is, indeed, not easy to believe that he had either time or energy for politics. Since the premieres of his operas *Rienzi* and *Der fliegende Holländer* in October 1842 and January 1843 and his appointment as Royal *Hofkapellmeister* in February of the latter year, his activity both as composer and conductor had been extraordinary. In 1844 he began work on *Tannhäuser* and in the following year made sketches for *Die Meistersinger von Nürnberg* and *Lohengrin*; in October 1845 he conducted the premiere of *Tannhäuser* and almost immediately began the composition of *Lohengrin*; in the theater in these years he directed productions of Gluck, Mozart, Weber, Lortzing, Auber, Bellini, Spontini, and Meyerbeer; in July 1845, as director of the Dresden male chorus *Liedertafel*, he produced a grandiose song festival in the Frauenkirche, and he had a spectacular success in April 1846 when he conducted Beethoven's Ninth Symphony in the Old Opera House next to the Zwinger. Yet, despite these exertions, at no time did his restless temperament detach itself from

the political agitations of this troubled decade. He had almost
daily discussions with his friend and musical director August
Röckel, who poured into his willing ear the doctrines of Proudhon and Weitling and Feuerbach and Stirner, which Wagner
found all the more congenial for having been spared the trouble
of reading them. He was a member of the Monday Club at the
Engel restaurant, a group of artists and intellectuals who debated
the issues of the day and speculated about the changes that
seemed to impend, and in 1848, when Michael Bakunin came
from Leipzig to Dresden, he became fast friends with this passionate and original mind, who is generally considered to be the
founder of the modern anarchist movement.

Wagner's views were influenced but not formed by what he
heard from these people. In politics he had—as Margot Asquith
once said of Winston Churchill—a "noisy mind," thinking being
to him only a brief prelude, indeed, an incitation, to action,
which was often ill considered and inconsistent. During the
March days of 1848 he was an enthusiastic supporter of the
essentially meaningless concessions that the Saxon King made
in an attempt to stop the agitations for liberal reform, but two
months later he published a "Greeting from Saxony to the People
of Vienna," in which he talked ominously of violence to come,
and in June 1848 he made a violent speech to the Vaterlandsverein, a society dedicated to the founding of a republic, in which
he called for the abolition of the aristocracy, the arming of the
people, and the establishment of a state in which the King would
be the first republican. Frederick August II showed no desire to
follow his bidding and, in April 1849, after Frederick William IV
of Prussia refused the imperial title offered him by the Frankfurt
Parliament, aligned himself with that sovereign and relied on
him for support against his own parliamentarians. When this
happened Wagner moved further to the left and wrote a series
of flaming hymns to revolution that were heavily Bakuninian
in coloration.

Ten years older than Wagner and more solidly established
in Dresden than the mercurial composer, Gottfried Semper was
no less deeply engaged in the politics of his time. Called to
Dresden in 1834 as professor of architecture and director of the
Academy of Fine Arts, he gained the respect of his fellow citizens
with two buildings that were to be city landmarks as long as

they existed. These were the Dresden synagogue, built in the years 1838–40 after the city's Jews had been granted the right to form a religious community, a building of simple elegance, cubic in form, with a superimposed cupola and decorated on the outside with Roman pilasters and friezes and on the inside with orientalized ornaments very sparingly used, which was burned down by the Nazis on Reichskrystallnacht in November 1938, and the building that made him world-famous, the Royal Court Theater, or New Opera House, built in the years 1838–41 and destroyed by fire in 1869.

Semper was a more consequent politician than Wagner, for he was a convinced republican from the beginning of the political turmoil in Saxony and probably had been ever since 1830, when, as a student of Franz Christian Gau in Paris, he had been profoundly influenced and exhilarated by the revolution of July. Always of a combative nature, he had a keen interest in modern warfare and strategy and, during his study of mathematics as a young man, had thought for a time of putting this to practical use in a military career. In 1848, when the duchy of Holstein rose in revolution against the overlordship of Denmark, he sent his brother in Altona plans for the defense of the duchy and a highly detailed description of how the city could be secured against occupation, supplying a street-by-street analysis of the crucial points and those of greatest vulnerability. Not unnaturally his thoughts turned in the same direction as matters came to a head in Dresden. A leading member of the Vaterlandsverein, he was a deputy in the Parliament that the King dissolved in April 1849. He also had close connections with two organizations that came into being during the constitutional struggle in the spring of 1849, the Sharpshooters Company of the Communal Guard and the Academic Legion, which was led by one of his students, the architect Gustav Heine.

The question concerning the degree to which the politics of Wagner and Semper were motivated by their artistic objectives and frustrations is difficult to answer. Semper, who from the moment of his arrival in Dresden had shown a strong dislike for the prevailing romanticism of its architecture, had drawn up a plan for the construction of a classical forum on the left bank of the Elbe in which the Zwinger, the Opera, and the planned museum and art gallery would be given space enough to show the beauty of their lines and decorations instead of being huddled together. This had been defeated by the purse-proud estates, and it may be that, in accordance with his often expressed view that politics and art go hand in hand, Semper believed that a republican regime would prove to be more enlightened. But this cannot be proved by anything he said in 1849. Wagner, on the other hand, quite clearly hoped that political change might improve the condition of the arts and relieve his own financial difficulties. In a letter to his wife written after the failure of the revolution, he explained his behavior by writing, "In a state of the most intense dissatisfaction with my position and almost with my art . . . deeply in debt, so that with my ordinary earnings it would have taken me long years and mortifying sacrifices to satisfy my creditors, I broke with this world, stopped being an artist . . . and became . . . only a revolutionary, that is, I sought in a completely transformed world the basis for new artistic creations of my intellect," and later still, in the interesting *Communication to My Friends* of 1851, he insisted that his role in "the political world of appearance" was always "artistic in nature." But these statements do not fully explain his actions in 1849. It is also true that Wagner became a revolutionary because the dramatic events in the Saxon capital appealed to his romantic nature and his habit of wishing to dominate any situation in which he found himself.

On 30 April 1849, tired of his Parliament's demands that he give his support to the Frankfurt constitution, King Frederick August threw down the gauntlet by dissolving it. The Communal Guard and its radical auxiliaries responded by mobilizing, and on 3 May, amid rumors that Prussian troops were advancing on the city, fighting broke out between them and regular units of the Saxon Army, with twenty-five casualties as a result of a muddled firefight at the Armory. The flight of the King the next day led to a brief cease-fire, during which the city assembly elected a provisional government, composed of Government Councillor Karl Todt, the Freiberg Judge Otto Leonhard Heubner, and Samuel Eduard Tzchirner, a lawyer from Bautzen. They immediately took an oath to support the Frankfurt constitution and set about building defenses against the expected arrival of the Prussians.

During the cease-fire Wagner for the first time clearly exposed himself to charges of treasonable behavior by distributing handbills to the loyal Saxon units, urging them to make common cause with the Communal Guard. These efforts were fruitless, and Wagner then went to the Rathaus, where he placed himself at the disposal of the provisional government, helping maintain liaison between it and fighting units and, for much of the time, observing troop movements inside and outside the city from the tower of the Kreuzkirche, the highest point in the city, from which he dropped messages to those below by tying them to loose tiles. It was from this vantage point that, on 6 May, as the Prussian advance into the city began, he watched the burning of the Old Opera House, a consequence perhaps of Bakunin's theory that fire was the best strategic defense, a theory to which, he later complained, the Germans were strangely resistant. The sharpshooters who shared the Kreuzkirche with Wagner were exultant at the sight, and one of them, perhaps remembering that the composer had conducted Beethoven's Ninth Symphony in the house only a few weeks earlier, laughed, *"Herr Kapell-meister, der Götterfunke hat gezündet!"* (Herr Kapellmeister, the spark of the gods is lit!)

In the actual fighting that took place in the city, and which eventually caused the death of roughly 300 persons, only thirty-one of whom were Prussians or Saxon regulars, Semper played a more direct part. Troubled at first by the conflict between his position in the Royal Academy and his political beliefs, he soon decided in favor of the latter, later writing to a friend that "when the rising started, my republican convictions would not be gain-said." He ranged himself alongside his comrades in the Sharp-shooters Company, which took up its position behind the main barricade that had been built in the Wilsdruffer Gasse. The con-dition of this obstacle so offended his professional instincts that he complained to the provisional government of its inadequacy, and he was authorized to correct its flaws and those of the other inner-city defenses. This he did with such effect that a Prussian officer later said that the Dresden barricades were "of a quality perhaps never seen in any previous street fight," being impreg-nable to direct assault and vulnerable only when taken from the rear. In addition to performing this vital service, Semper helped stiffen the wavering morale of Professor Franke's Technical Le-gion during the fighting of 6 May and commanded the barricade on Waisenhaus Street until 9 May, covering the rebel retreat.

That retreat became inevitable when Prussian columns be-

gan to penetrate the city's inner districts on the morning of 6
May. Fire upon the Kreuzkirche tower was soon so heavy that
Wagner abandoned his post and went to the Rathaus. Here he
found signs of discouragement as reports came of Prussian cap-
ture of the outer barricades, and he learned that Karl Todt had
already left for Frankfurt to urge the National Assembly to mediate, surely, at this late date, a measure of desperation. Wagner
himself does not seem to have been despondent. On the morning
of 7 May he accompanied his wife, Minna, to Chemnitz, where
her sister lived, but, after haranguing the local Communal Guard
to seize their guns and join the fight for freedom in Dresden, he
returned to the capital himself on the eighth. During his absence
the rebels, under the leadership of Heubner and Bakunin, had
been conducting a dogged street-by-street defense against the
more numerous and better-armed Prussians, but they were now
all but exhausted. Bakunin suggested blowing up the Rathaus as
a last demonstration of defiance and a means of gaining time.
His Saxon comrades, more logical than he, saw no point in this,
and on the ninth abandoned their city to the enemy. Wagner
accompanied members of the provisional government and *Freischärler* to Freiberg, where Heubner made an impassioned plea
for continued resistance from the balcony of the Rathaus, and
Wagner completed the burning of his bridges by embracing him
to the cheers of the crowd. The composer was still confident
that the cause was not lost, but there was no spirit of resistance
left in Freiberg or in Chemnitz, which was their next stop, and
where, indeed, the police were on the watch for Heubner and
his companions. It was clear now that the only alternatives were
trial for treason or flight, and Wagner did not hesitate to choose
the latter. His brother-in-law took him by carriage to Altenburg,
whence he made his way to Weimar, and then, with many stops,
including a visit to Eisenach to visit the Wartburg, to the Bodensee, which he crossed on 28 May and from Rorschach traveled
by coach to Zürich.

Semper's journey to Zürich was even more circuitous and
took much longer. When resistance came to an end in Dresden
on 9 May, he managed to escape from the city and, with the aid
of a friend, Karl-Wilhelm Devrient, to reach the town of
Zwickau. Here he learned, as Wagner had done earlier, that war-
rants had been issued by the Saxon government for their arrest,

and that his life was in danger if he returned to Saxony or any part of Germany under Prussian control. He made his way, therefore, to Baden, where the fight to defend the national constitution was reaching its critical point, with the Prussians poised to repeat the action that they had just completed in Dresden. Some of Semper's fellow refugees were joining the Badenese cause—his friend and fellow member of the Vaterlandsverein, Adolf von Trützschler, was to die for it—and he was urged, when he reached Karlsruhe, to do the same. He declined the invitation, writing on 30 May 1849, "If I were twenty years younger, didn't have a wife and six children and was rich, you would hear more from me." He asked the same friend to whom he wrote these words to go to his wife and collect his working papers and send them on to Paris, where he hoped to find employment. This proved to be an illusion and, after much fruitless inquiry after positions in Belgium, Greece, and Switzerland (his Dresden friend Köchly discouraged him from pursuing opportunities in Geneva, telling him that the only successful architects there were speculators in land), he was on the point of sailing for the United States when a letter from a Dr. Emil Braun held out vague promises of prospects in England. He decided to follow these up, went to London in September 1850, and remained there until the call from Zürich came five years later.

II

As soon as he arrived in Zürich, Wagner went directly to the home of Alexander Müller in the Rennweg and, knocking on the door, cried, "Be quick and open up! It is I, Richard Wagner!" and then, as Müller complied, blurted, "Alexander, you have to keep me by you. I'm safe here. I've had to flee from Dresden and leave my wife and everything I own behind!" He had not seen Müller since 1833, when they had spent long evenings playing music and drinking beer together in Würzburg, but it never occurred to him that his plea would be unsuccessful, and he was right. Müller, now a music teacher and the leader of a choral group, not only put his home at Wagner's disposal but introduced him to friends who proved willing to give him both moral and financial support, of which he was sorely in need, since he had no fixed income and was dependent largely on funds advanced to him by Franz Liszt in Weimar.

Among these new acquaintances the most helpful was Dr. Jakob Sulzer, who had forsaken a career in philology to enter liberal politics, where he soon won the confidence of Alfred Escher and was appointed to the position of *Staatsschreiber*, an important post whose incumbent not only administered the work of the state chancery and served as secretary of the Department of Political Affairs but was charged with keeping the protocols of the Governing Council and maintaining liaison with federal agencies and other cantonal governments. A man of inquiring mind and more than usual intellectual curiosity, Sulzer was perhaps intrigued more by the mixture of genius and political naivité in Wagner's character than, as the composer supposed, by his knowledge of German mythology. However that may be, he did not hesitate to supply Wagner's most pressing needs: papers that would enable him to travel to Paris (which he did in August in another fruitless attempt to arrange for a production of one of his operas there) and to return safely, later the removal of his name from the list of political refugees who had to be kept under police surveillance, and a residential permit. In addition Sulzer turned his own home into a kind of forum in which Wagner could expound his opinions and theories to a group of congenial listeners, which included Müller, the second cantonal secretary Franz Hagenbuch, the music teacher Wilhelm Baumgartner, the professor of literature Ludwig Ettmüller, and the lawyer Bernhard Spyri, editor of the *Eidgenossische Zeitung*, who became one of Wagner's most enthusiastic public supporters. (Spyri's wife, Johanna, later the author of *Heidi* and other books for children, was immune to her husband's enthusiasm, finding the Venusberg parts of *Tannhäuser* "repulsive" and "redolent of sulphur.") This was the group that in August heard Wagner read the text of his projected musical drama *Siegfried's Death*, an occasion on which so much inspiration flowed from the poetry and the abundance of wine from the Sulzer estate in Winterthur that, as the composer remembered later, the aged Ettmüller had to be taken home, while the other guests diverted themselves by removing their host's front doors from their hinges.

It was in this early stage of his time in Zürich that Wagner decided to give literary form to his philosophy of art. In the memoirs that he dictated to his wife, Cosima, twenty years later, he said:

> The peculiar outlawed state in which I found myself affected me with increasing inner agitation. I was often alarmed at the excessive exaltation of my whole being, which disposed me, continually and toward anybody at all, to let myself go in the most curious paradoxes. Soon after my arrival in Zürich, I set about making notes about the nature of things as they had taken shape under the pressure of my experience as an artist and the influence of the political agitations of the time. Since I had no alternative whatsoever to trying, with my literary talents, such as they were, to earn a living, I conceived the idea of submitting a series of articles to an important French journal, perhaps the then still existing *National*, in which I wanted to speak out, with my revolutionary conviction, about modern art and its relationship to society.

Out of this resolution came hundreds of pages of prose. Some of them were self-serving, like the proposal for a reform of the Zürich theater that has been mentioned earlier; others had no apparent *raison d'écrire*, like the essay *Art and Climate*, which argued that, in the present age, climate had no effect on art, and among them was the notorious essay *Jewishness in Music*, a particularly nasty combination of resentment at the failure of the world to recognize Wagner's genius and that violent anti-Semitism to which he was so often prone. But they also included three essays on aesthetics, which, despite the frequent turgidness of the author's style and his sovereign indifference to inherent contradictions, deserve some brief comment, if only to suggest the discrepancy between their author's revolutionary theories and his future practice. These were *Art and the Revolution*, in which Wagner sought to supply a historical-philosophical basis for his aesthetic theory, *The Artwork of the Future*, which expounded the theory itself, with particular reference to the total work of art (*Gesamtkunstwerk*) that was to be the art of the future, and *Opera and Drama*, which explained the reasons why opera had failed to meet the test of great art and must be superseded by the musical drama.

It is impossible not to be impressed by the effrontery of

Richard Wagner, living in middle-class comfort in Alfred Escher's Zürich, under the protection of Jakob Escher and on subventions sent to him by Franz Liszt, while he wrote *Art and the
Revolution*, in which the main targets were bankers, cotton manufacturers, and artists who were content to work under the conditions of bourgeois society. But spoiling the Egyptians was ever
a specialty of his, and, drawing upon the aesthetic ideas of German idealism and remembered fragments of Proudhon and
Feuerbach, he proceeded, with great vigor and confidence, to
compare the glory of art in the classical age of Athens with its
degenerate forms in the present. In Greece—and this was in
marked contrast to the situation in modern Europe—art was an
expression of the common life and values of a race of free men
and thus was a public activity, inspired by the religion of Apollo
and finding its highest form in Aeschylean tragedy. But Greek
classical culture bore within itself the seeds of its own decay,
the institution of slavery, and that "fateful axle of all world
destiny" not only brought the Greek world to its disastrous end
but destroyed its religious and artistic ideals. The former were
superseded by Christianity, whose principal doctrine, "to yield
patiently to a miserable existence here for the sake of a better
life beyond," was appropriate to a general proliferation of slavery,
while the ideal of a united homogeneous art form gave way to
the atomization of the arts and the loss of their public character.
These evils perpetuated themselves throughout the ages. In modern bourgeois society all men are slaves to capital and are taught
daily by bankers and factory owners that the end of existence
lies in laboring for one's daily bread. Even the artist, as culture
has been commercialized, has been taught the same lesson; in
a society in which art has, like everything else, become a com-
modity with a price, the artist has become alienated from his
own social function and reduced to being a mere entertainer of
jaded moneygrubbers who are incapable of appreciating beauty,
nobility, or tragedy.

> *That is the art that fills the whole of the contemporary
> civilized world!* Its real essence is industry, its moral *goal,
> the acquisition of money*, its aesthetic claim, *the entertain-
> ment of the bored*. Out of the heart of our modern society,
> out of the center of its circular motion, large-scale specu-
> lation in gold, our art sucks its elixir of life, borrows for itself

a heartless grace from the remnants of medieval feudal convention, and then reaches down—with an artificial Christian spirit, not even scorning the poor man's mite—to the depths of the proletariat, debilitating, demoralizing, dehumanizing everywhere where the poison of its life's blood is poured.

That is why true art, which was conservative in classical Greece, where it represented the life and spirit of the whole community, must be revolutionary in the modern age. For only revolution will make the highest form of art possible once more. The task of the present is more difficult than that which the Greeks achieved. "If the Greek work of art comprised the spirit of one beautiful nation, so should the art of the future embrace the spirit of free humanity beyond all limitations of nationality. In it national essence will be only a decoration, a charm of individual diversity, not a restrictive barrier."

Art and the Revolution indicated that Wagner was still as much the revolutionary as he had been when he was colloguing with Bakunin in Dresden, and that he hoped for, and indeed expected, a resumption of revolutionary activity in the near future, and on the widest scale. The same spirit animated *The Artwork of the Future,* also written in 1849. Dedicated to Ludwig Feuerbach, this essay begins and ends with an invocation of the revolution of humanity, which is described this time as necessary to free mankind from culture—which has alienated it from nature (a Feuerbachian gloss)—as well as from luxury and fashion, the "artificial charm that awakes an unnatural need," which are the industrial system's instruments for keeping human beings in servitude. Only when these are swept away, as well as the state, which gives legitimacy to the power of wealth in bourgeois society, will the art of the future emerge. This Wagner in the bulk of the essay describes as the union of the art forms of dance, poetry, and music by means of rhythm, harmony, and melody into the *Gesamtkunstwerk* that will be the art of the future, performed in revolutionary new theaters that no longer reflect social stratification in their seating arrangements and are free to the public, by actors who are drawn from the local population and belong to a free association of free artists. Thus, the revolution will have effected, for both society and art, the "absorption of egoism in communism."

The third and most ambitious of the Zürich essays was *Opera and Drama*, written in 1850–51 and devoted in large part to a critique of opera from the time of Gluck to the present, with resounding attacks on Rossini (for his frivolity) and Meyerbeer (for his penchant for "effect without cause"), followed by a fascinating discussion of what Wagner considered to be the proper relationship between music and drama. It is in the latter, which cannot be treated here in any detail, that Wagner is often at his most political. Thus, in his chapter on the nature of dramatic writing, he argues that the most important task of the dramatist is to recognize the immanence of myth in the human consciousness because "the unique feature of myth is that it is always true and that its content, even when most deeply repressed, is inexhaustible for all times." It is up to him to reinterpret myth in ways that illuminate contemporary conditions and to give it comprehensible dramatic form. As an illustration of how this can be done, Wagner retells the Oedipus myth, interpreting it as a struggle between the state, in the person of Creon, and human individuality in the person of Antigone. Gratuitously, he adds:

> *To organize society* on the basis of this individuality *is the task of the future.* . . . *To bring the unconscious of human nature to consciousness in society*, and in this consciousness to know nothing but the common necessity of expressing *the free self-determination of the individual in all of the functions of society*, amounts to—*destroying the State.* For the State's role in society was to deny the free self-determination of the individual—it lived from his death.

Exactly who or what was going to precipitate the revolution of humanity that he desired Wagner never made clear. Despite the superficial similarities that his system bore to those of Hegel and Marx, it had none of their dialectical or analytical rigor and failed even to explain why the slaves—a term very loosely employed in Wagner's treatises—should consider the cultural utopia that he held out to them sufficiently attractive to make them seek to change their present condition by violent means. This is all the more puzzling when we consider Wagner's contempt for the intellect and taste of the masses, or *Pöbel* as he was wont to call them. We must suppose that he believed that the revo-

lution would just somehow turn up, although, like Mr. Micaw-
ber, he was not at liberty to say in what direction. When it didn't
he became peevish and turned away from politics completely.

This is what happened at the end of 1851. As late as July of
that year, his faith was still in fairly good repair, and he was
writing to his Dresden friend, the young sculptor Gustav Adolf
Kietz, "I long for the revolution with passion, and only the hope
of experiencing and participating in it gives me real courage to
face life." In December, after Louis Napoleon's *coup d'état* had
succeeded in destroying the French Republic without precipi-
tating a general rising, Wagner's tune had changed. "My whole
politics," he wrote to Kietz's brother Ernst Benedikt, "is from
now on nothing but the bloodiest hatred for our whole civilization, scorn for everything that issues from it, and longing for
nature. . . . The mentality of slaves is rooted in every part of
us. . . . In the whole of Europe I like the dogs better than these
dog-like humans!"

It is doubtful whether this was very deeply felt. Life in Zürich was so pleasant that the composer admitted in the spring
of 1851 that he was becoming "*ganz eingeschweizert.*" For one
thing, he was much in demand as a conductor, which is not
surprising since, unlike most of the conductors of his time, he
was no mere human metronome but rather a vital and exciting
presence on the podium and, in addition, possessed the extraordinary ability to coax out of second-rate orchestras performances
that astonished the musicians themselves. Talent like this was
badly needed in Zürich, where lack of coordination between the
Aktientheater and the Musical Society (*Allgemeine Musikge-
sellschaft*) had prevented an intelligent development of the community's musical resources or the appointment of musical
directors capable of conducting symphonic or operatic music.
Wagner's reputation had preceded him, he was soon being asked
for advice, and in January 1850, after repeated invitations, had
given his first concert in the hall of the Casino. The program
was unconventional (the overture to *Wilhelm Tell*, some horn
and guitar solos, a group of songs, and Beethoven's Seventh Symphony), the orchestra was composed of about twenty-five professionals who had been hired by the Musical Society for the winter,
supplemented by enthusiastic amateurs from the city, and one
of the soloists was over eighty years old, but the evening was a
decided success, and was hailed as such by the *Eidgenössische*

Zeitung on the following day, and it led to new invitations and new triumphs. The next three years saw frequent performances under Wagner's baton: from October to December 1850 two performances each of Weber's *Freischütz* and Boieldieu's opera *Die weisse Dame* and single performances of Bellini's *Norma* (which he criticized in *Opera and Drama* as a chief example of the purely modish opera, which existed only to gratify the vanity of singers), *Don Giovanni* and *Die Zauberflöte*; in March 1851, *Don Giovanni* again and concerts devoted to the music of Weber and Beethoven; in 1852 several Beethoven programs (Georg Herwegh, who was not particularly musical, declared that his performances of the Egmont Overture and the Eighth Symphony were "divine"), the overture to *Tannhäuser* (for which the Musical Society had to mobilize twenty violins, six violas, five cellos, and four bass violins from Winterthur, Schaffhausen, St. Gallen, Aarau, and Lenzburg to supplement the local musicians), and, on 25 April, the first Zürich performance of *Der fliegende Holländer*, which was repeated three times in the following week.

The crowning point of all this activity came in May 1853, when, after another extensive importation of talent, which this time brought musicians from as far away as Lausanne, Freiburg, Stuttgart, and Wiesbaden, Wagner arranged and conducted a festival program that included the overture to *Rienzi* and extensive excerpts from *Der fliegende Holländer*, *Tannhäuser*, and *Lohengrin*. This program, which was repeated three times, was preceded by three evening lectures on the plots and music of the three latter operas. The *Neue Züricher Zeitung*, unconsciously anticipating something that Nietzsche was to say in *The Wagner Case* in 1888, expressed the view, after the third performance, that Wagner's music could be everything but gay and that "something eerie is always mixed with his merriment; in its bluest heaven a cloud hangs, and one knows that there is a thunderbolt in it that is about to rush down upon a ship." Neither orchestra nor audience was troubled by such presentiments. One of the musicians recited a poem in the composer's honor, and women presented him with a laurel wreath and a silver cup. There was a torchlight procession to Wagner's home in the Zeltweg, where the City Chorus and members of the Gesangverein Harmonie serenaded him with songs and speeches and made him an honorary member of their associations.

All of this was gratifying to Wagner's ego and possibly contributed to the diminution of his revolutionary ardor. In July
1853, Franz Liszt visited him and wrote later to his mistress,
the Princess Sayn-Wittgenstein, that the man who had fulmi-
nated so furiously against luxury in his writings obviously had
no objection to it in his own way of life and that, in his manner
and dress, there were no signs of democratic conviction. Indeed,
Wagner had told him that *"depuis son séjour ici il avait com-
plètement rompu avec le parti des réfugiés et s'était même fait
bien voir et bien venir auprès des gros bonnets de la bourgeoisie
et de l'aristocratie du canton."* Liszt added, *"Ses rapports avec
les musiciens sont ceux d'un grand général qui n'aurait qu'une
douzaine de marchands de chandelle à discipliner."*

Meanwhile, his circle of acquaintances had expanded. He
still saw a great deal of Sulzer, despite some strain caused at the
end of 1851 when Wagner, whose painful intestinal problems
had been relieved by a stay at the Wasserheilanstalt at Albis-
brunn, was seized by a virtual hydromania and wanted to convert
all his friends. He usually met Sulzer and Hagenbach and Spyri
at the Café Orsini, a frequent haunt of his in his early Zürich
years, although he also frequented the Guildhouse Zimmerleu-
ten, where Baumgarten and other musicians could be found, and
the Guildhouse Saffran, where university professors foregath-
ered. His wife Minna liked to entertain, so that, in their home
in Enge, named Villa Rienzi, and later in their apartment in the
Zeltweg, there were lively gatherings in which old Dresden
friends appeared, like Lieutenant Hermann Müller, once the
lover of the opera singer Wilhelmine Schröder-Devrient, who
was now making his way in the cantonal military service, Professor Hermann Köchly, and the lawyer Herbert Marschall von
Bieberstein, who was to introduce Wagner to Otto and Mathilde
Wesendonck, and in which Wagner sometimes made music with
the dilettante clarionettist Konrad Ott-Imhoff, one of the directors of the Musical Society, and with the hornist Bär.

Still another circle of friends was opened to him in May
1852, when Georg Herwegh took him for the first time to the
home of Francois and Eliza Wille at Mariafeld. Like Herwegh,
Wille had a very limited interest in music, but he was a cultivated man who liked to talk with Wagner and Herwegh about
politics and philosophy and literature, and soon the three men
had formed an intimate inner core within the wider society that

Eliza Wille brought to Mariafeld—people like Professor Ludwig of the university, whose lectures on physiology Herwegh was attending, and the ancient Ettmüller, who instructed Wagner about the mysteries and charm of the Edda, and the group that periodically assembled to read plays. It was at Mariafeld that Wagner—again through the agency of Herwegh—first encountered the work of Schopenauer and, with the surprise felt by Molière's M. Jourdain in a somewhat analogous case, discovered that he had been thinking in his terms all along without knowing it. His obsession with the philosopher, which lasted until the end of his life, as Cosima Wagner's *Diaries* attest, ended all talk about water cures and, indeed, about politics, and the walls of Mariafeld now reverberated with endless discussions of the will, and its manifestation in its highest form in sexual love, and the necessity of renunciation and ascesis, all of which astonished the practical-minded Eliza Wille, who could not understand how a man like Wagner, who was so obviously intent on both worldly and amatory success, could talk so much of self-denial.

The discovery of Schopenhauer may have been the decisive factor in completing the extinction of revolutionary political purpose in Wagner's work and in marking the beginning of its bourgeoisification. This is not to say that he abandoned his ideas of revolutionizing art, and objective judges were now willing to admit that the arguments advanced in *Opera and Drama* were by no means as fanciful as they had once been labeled. During the visit of Franz Liszt and Princess Carolyne von Sayn-Wittgenstein and her daughter Marie in October and November 1856—an occasion that caused considerable excitement in a society that was not too republican to be titillated by aristocratic impropriety—the new Hotel Baur au Lac was the scene of a grand celebration of Liszt's forty-fifth birthday. This was attended by the leaders of the city's intellectual and artistic community, who heard an improvised performance of the first act of *Die Walküre*, with Liszt at the piano, Wagner's neighbor Emilie Heim, wife of the director Ignaz Heim, singing the part of Sieglinde, and Wagner as both Siegmund and Hunding. Afterward, the *Neue Zürcher Zeitung* wrote:

> With this tone poem, Richard Wagner's effort to reform the field of musical drama by the presentation of a new art form is revealed in the clearest fashion. His much-scorned idea of

the artwork of the future was no artistic-philosophical illusion; it has become an actuality and will have an epoch-making influence upon the whole musical world.

On the other hand, the political content of the work now shriveled and disappeared. The great Ring cycle had been conceived in a mood of revolutionary exuberance, with a young Siegfried who was an anarchistic world-renewer, but it seemed to lose its way while its author became accustomed to the social pleasures of Zürich and, after Schopenhauer had come along to provide him, as he once confessed to Roeckel, "with reasoned conceptions to correspond to [his] intuitive principles," it was never quite the same again, the hero losing stature and vitality and falling under the shadow of a Wagner-like Wotan, who was disappointed in his political expectations and welcomed self-immolation.

Auf geb ich mein Werk;	*[I give up my work;*
nur eines will ich noch:	*I want only one thing more:*
das Ende,	*the end,*
das Ende!	*the end!]*

Tristan und Isolde, which among all of Wagner's works was the most intimately Zürichean in provenance and inspiration, had no politics at all. Wagner once wrote that it was "partly the earnest mood in which Schopenhauer had put me and which now called urgently for an ecstatic expression of its basic elements that gave me the idea for a Tristan und Isolde," and Thomas Mann was not alone in pointing out that the achieved work was an extended elaboration of the reflection on the metaphysics of sexual love in The World as Will and Idea. Yet the music drama was inspired to an even greater degree by Wagner's passion for Mathilde Wesendonck, the twenty-six-year-old wife of a Rhineland merchant and partner in a New York silk firm who had settled in Zürich in 1852 and—as his investments prospered during the great boom that set in in the following year—became a local Maecenas and supporter of worthy causes. One of the latter was Richard Wagner. Otto Wesendonck was helpful in financing his concerts in 1853 and, a year later, undertook to extricate the composer from his financial difficulties, which were daunting, by assuming his debts and advancing him a quarterly stipend against prospective royalties from *Tannhäuser* and *Lohengrin*. In addition, he offered the Wagners, at a nominal rent, a small wooden house on the estate that he had bought in Enge, where he built an imposing villa for his own use, and Wagner and his wife, Minna, moved into the "asylum on the green hill" in April of that year.

Wesendonck may later have felt like echoing King Mark and crying out:

Dünkte zu wenig	*[Seemed too little*
dich mein Dank,	*to you my thanks*
daß, was du mir erworben,	*when what you won for me,*
Ruhm und Reich,	*fame and fortune,*
ich zu Erb' und Eigen dir gab?	*I gave you as inheritance of*
	your own?]

As early as 1854, when he was composing the second act of *Die Walküre*, Wagner had become infatuated with Wesendonck's wife and was referring to her as his *Seelenfreundin*. His feelings became stronger as he embarked upon the work that was intended, he wrote to Franz Liszt, to compensate for the fact that he had "never in his life enjoyed the real happiness of love" and so wanted to "erect a monument to this most beautiful of dreams in which, from beginning to end, this love will sate itself." *Tristan und Isolde*, the text of which Wagner read for the first time in September 1857 at Villa Wesendonck to a group of friends that included his wife, Minna, his host's wife, and the young Cosima von Bülow—whom Martin Gregor-Dellin in a fine passage describes as "the mystic trio of norns who held the invisible thread that soon broke"—was the product of Wagner's domestic arrangements and an expression of his erotic preoccupations; it was also the agency that brought this fruitful period of his life to an end. The interpenetration of the mythic and the real was too palpable to be tolerated by the persons playing the secondary roles, and Wagner had to leave his comfortable *Asyl* in Enge and resume his travels.

Nor did this shattering private drama revive Wagner's revolutionary instincts, as his later work makes clear. *Die Meistersinger von Nürnberg*, which was written in 1862, was a brilliant reconstruction of an imaginary medieval past, which ended with a burst of nationalism that foreshadowed the jingoistic attitudes that Wagner was to strike in 1871, although it too was heavily colored by Schopenhauerian pessimism, as in the *Wahn* monologue of Hans Sachs. *Parsifal* was again a disquisition on eros, which this time was forced to yield to agape, although Wagner was inclined to attribute this deviation to his favorite philosopher also, telling Cosima that he was indebted to Schopenhauer (an atheist!) for having "opened up Christianity" to him.

There was a time when Wagner had dreamed of a revolutionary theater, and on 29 September 1850 he had written his close friend Theodor Uhlig to say that, if Uhlig would only find him 10,000 thaler, he would build *"a rude theater with boards and beams according to my plan"* in a beautiful meadow near the city, bring the best singers available, wherever they might be, to Zürich for six weeks, recruit an orchestra, and then use all the newspapers in Europe to invite people, particularly young people, to attend, at no cost to themselves, a festival at which his music drama *Der junge Siegfried* would be presented in three performances, "and *after the third the theater will be pulled down and my score burned.*" Nothing much was left of such plans now except for the pleas for money. The planned theater in Munich in the sixties and the completed one at Bayreuth a decade later differed in no essential respect from the conventional model, and the audiences who filled the latter, paying their way to do so, were for the most part drawn from that *Bildungsbürgertum* that wanted edification rather than political inspiration from the theater.

Indeed, Wagner's late work showed a remarkable accommodation to bourgeois taste: the texts of each of the musical dramas appealing to subconscious memories and predispositions—the Ring, a druidical puppet show that assumed profundity from its author's insistence that fate was pulling all the strings; *Tristan und Isolde,* as Nietzsche wickedly suggested, a Flaubertian family drama made respectable by its mythological trappings; *Die Meistersinger* a historical pageant in the manner of Charlotte Birch-Pfeiffer, and *Parsifal* a German *Märchen* suffused with religiosity—while the music, like the furnishing of the bourgeois home, was overrich and overpowering, in Nietzsche's words again, "a heavy drapery, something voluntarily barbaric and ceremonial, a flaunting of esoteric and dignified jewelry and lace."

III

In *The Artwork of the Future*, Wagner had some highly uncomplimentary things to say about contemporary architecture, accusing it of being prey both to the "stupidest kind of utilitarianism" and to the most chaotic forms of eclecticism, which, because of the dictatorship of fashion and the desire for luxury, brought "all the national architectural styles in the world together in incoherent motley forms." This would not be corrected, he added, until the egoistic and atomized forms of art were fused together in the common artwork of the future and *"people obsessed with utility became the artistic people of the future."* Only then would "architecture be freed from the bonds of servitude, from the curse of sterility, and become the freest, inexhaustibly richest artistic activity." Meanwhile, however, there was at least one man who deplored its grievous state and sought to lay the foundations for the architecture of the future. That was Gottfried Semper, and from the very beginning of his stay in Zürich, Wagner urged that the man who had been his comrade in the May rising in Dresden be brought to the city on the Limmat.

This proved to be impossible until the foundation of the Polytechnic Institute opened up a position that was more attractive than the appointment that Semper had held since 1852 in the London Department of Practical Art. At the end of 1854, at the urging of Jakob Sulzer and Herbert Marschall von Bieberstein, Johann Peter Kern, the president of the Swiss School Council, invited Semper to come to Zürich as director of the School of Architecture at the Polytechnikum, and Semper—not without some doubts concerning whether Swiss mountains might not make architecture on the grand scale impossible—accepted.

The seventeen years that Semper spent in Zürich saw him at the height of his creative powers, which found expression not only in such masterpieces as the Stadthaus in Winterthur and the main building of the Polytechnikum (1858–64) but also in the Zürich observatory and his contributions to the new railroad station and to the reconstruction of the Kratzquartier between the upper Bahnhofstraße and the Limmat. The Polytechnical building above all—a Neo-Renaissance palace located high above the Limmat on its right side, with proportions generous enough to accommodate the much-expanded student body of the future and a magnificence of decoration that could not fail to impress them—left a permanent impression upon the city's profile, and a not inappropriate one, since it provided visitors with a highly visible indication of the importance that its citizens attributed to education. Semper's own skills as an educator were not the least of his contributions to Zürich, for his students admired him and perpetuated his principles, to the considerable advantage of city architecture in Switzerland in general.

Semper was a lifelong democrat and, since he was also a man of irascible, uncontrolled, and often wounding temperament, a highly contentious one. His home life was stormy, since his wife, who died in 1859 after bearing him six children, did not take his politics seriously and let him know this, and his social life—in his *Stammlokal*, the Guildhouse Saffran, and in the Wille and Wesendonck households, where he was always a welcome guest—was no less so. His relations with Wagner in particular, while basically friendly, were marked with frequent altercations that startled onlookers by their intensity and, at least on Semper's side, their fury. In his memoirs Wagner tells us that, when they first met in Dresden, Semper had been reading the text of *Tannhäuser* and told its author that he had only contempt for such stuff; indeed, for a long time he seemed to regard Wagner as representing a medieval catholicizing tendency that was repugnant to him. In Zürich the violence of their quarrels was in no way diminished. He loathed Schopenhauer, whose doctrines he believed to be destructive of both political conviction and art, and was unimpressed by Wagner's rejoinder, "My works say the opposite!" In 1859, when Wagner returned briefly to Zürich, there was a particularly tempestuous evening at the Villa Wesendonck. Referring to the recent hostilities in Italy, Semper maintained that Austria's surrender represented a defeat for the German national principle, whereas Napoleon III stood for the force of Assyrian despotism, inimical both to freedom and art. He expressed these views so unconditionally that Gottfried Keller, who was present but had been silent in the discussion, was moved to mild expostulation, whereupon Semper rounded on Wagner, who had introduced him to the household, and, in what the composer later called a state of "real desperation," accused him of having led him into an enemy ambush.

The relationship between Semper's democratic views and his architectural work is interesting, although difficult to elucidate without some reference to his written work. In the world of art the basis of Semper's reputation was laid in 1834 with his *Preliminary Observations Concerning Painted Architecture and Sculpture Among the Ancients.* A contribution to an ongoing debate over the significance of polychromy in ancient art, this work was also a political statement, for Semper argued that art is an expression of the needs and the social relations of an age and that the glories of Greek art were the result of a demand for freedom and political self-expression after a long period of domestic tyranny and foreign invasion. A similar tendency, he argued, was now becoming evident in Germany, "an approximation to the times of the ancients," as the former dominance of church and absolutism collapsed before the forces of freedom released by the French Revolution. Art would go hand in hand with politics; monuments to militarism and princely egoism would give way to an architecture that reflected the values of free peoples and took for its models not the cathedrals of the Middle Ages but the temples and forums of the classical age.

The failure of the revolutions of 1848–49 did not change his political convictions. In London he was a member for a time of a group of German exiles that included Karl Marx, Friedrich Engels, Arnold Ruge, and Gottfried Kinkel. Inevitably, this was soon riddled with intrigue and contention between those who placed their faith in the proletariat and those who, like Semper, continued to believe in bourgeois democracy. The dispute was not without effect upon Semper's theoretical essays. He continued to believe that artistic change was not the result of anything immanent in art itself but was due to social conditions external to it, and particularly to political change and revolution. But like Wagner (and unlike Marx), he never seriously analyzed the socioeconomic foundations of change, a fact apparent in his work *Four Elements of Architecture (1850),* and in time he came to place his faith in the reformative tendencies of capitalism.

Thus, in *Science, Industry and Art* (1859), while answering the question why no new forms of art were appearing by writing that artists had not been able to master the new materials and scientific and technical advances of the industrial age because the influence of capital had made them part of the production process and subordinated their work to profitmaking rather than artistic purpose—"Everything is calculated and tailored for the market"—he expressed the belief that this was a passing phase.

The times would demand new artistic forms, and the capitalistic system of production would rise to the challenge by overcoming regionalism, destroying the heavy hand of tradition, dissolving parochial stereotypes, and invalidating romanticism, thus opening the way to a truly modern and cosmopolitan art. The similarity with Marx's own thinking is apparent, although once more the process described is not carried to its logical conclusion, since Semper believed the changes envisaged would be compatible with a bourgeois democratic system.

There was, in short, no real revolution in Semper's theories of art. As Heinz Quitsch has written, he was an essentially bourgeois thinker who did not see that the bourgeoisie were not likely to produce the big ideas that would effect the artistic revolution he desired. There were moments when some appreciation of this touched his thoughts. In 1864, in the introduction to his two-volume work on style, he asked himself whether the apparent decline of art in his own time was not a "sign of a general decay that was the result of deeper lying social causes," but he left the question hanging and continued to believe that change would come, perhaps, in the case of architecture, generated by technological innovation and the appearance of new materials of construction and hastened by a broadening of popular influence on art. To this latter end, Semper argued, the artist must seek to improve the taste of the masses by building museums and holding exhibitions.

As Wagner was primarily a musician, Semper was primarily an architect, passionately interested in his creations, which took precedence over his writings and, indeed, his politics. It should not be surprising, then, that there were contradictions between theory and practice in what he did—that the democrat, building for princely patrons and, in the case of Zürich, for a community whose taste in public architecture was determined by bankers and merchant princes like Alfred Escher, would make concessions to their preference for monumentality and decoration, that new construction materials, like iron and glass, that did not accord easily with the grand style would be neglected or disguised or given a subordinate and invisible role in his buildings, and that the eclecticism that both Wagner and he had condemned in their writings would assert itself in his work in rich combinations of Classic, Romanesque, Gothic, Byzantine, Moorish, and Renaissance elements.

Significant in this respect also was Semper's gradual change from emphasizing the basic structure in his architecture, as in the case of the Dresden synagogue, to emphasizing the facade, which is notable in the Winterthur City Hall and the plans for the new Rathausplatz in the Kratzquartier in Zürich, more emphatic in the New Opera House in Dresden, and clearest of all in his designs for the expansion of the Hofburg in Vienna. In an interesting article on the contradictions in Semper's creative life, Klaus Zoege von Manteuffel has written that it is not by chance that this transition from *Körperarchitektur* to *Fassadenarchitektur*, this stylistic division between core and decorative exterior, took place at a time when Karl Marx was formulating his theory of basis and superstructure, and that there was a parallel between the denial of the esthetic qualities of the new building materials and the banning of technology to a lower and invisible sphere and the inability of the upper classes of society to assimilate the social realities of the time or to recognize the existence, let alone the misery, of the fourth estate. He writes:

> How deep and unbridgeable the gulf in the nineteenth century was is made clear in the life and work of a man like Gottfried Semper, who had a real political and social conscience but became a collaborator in the building of this magnificent superstructure world with its fragile foundations, or, if one will, this world floating above material reality.

Semper left Zürich in 1871, perhaps feeling that there were no more opportunities there for the kind of architecture that would challenge his talents, and accepted the post of Imperial and Royal Superior Building Councillor (*K. und K. Oberbaurat*) in Vienna. Here his facade architecture attained its most complete form in his designs for the massive coulisses of the Hofburg, whose construction he did not live to complete. It is a crowning irony in the life of this dedicated democrat that Adolf Hitler, an admirer of his architecture, celebrated the *Anschluß* in March 1938 from the niche of the imperial rotunda in this last of Semper's creations. This did not prevent his party comrades from destroying the first of them, the Dresden Synagogue, eight months later.

IV

When Richard Wagner left Zürich in 1858, it is doubtful that those who mourned his going were numerous, for his constant requests for money and his improvidence when he received it had long exasperated his benefactors, and the complications of his love life had become an embarrassment to those who had befriended him. Even Gottfried Keller, who had seen a good deal of him and found him an attractive companion, does not seem to have felt much regret over his departure. Keller greatly admired Wagner's literary powers and, while harboring some reservations about the idea of a *Gesamtkunstwerk*, which he found threatening to the autonomy of literature, regarded Wagner's Nibelungen saga as "a treasure house of original national poetry" and a work that was "full of ancient-tragic spirit." On the other hand, he had no great confidence in the composer's moral integrity—"a very gifted person," he wrote to Ferdinand Freiligrath in April 1857, "but also something of a *faiseur* and charlatan"—and he was put off by Wagner's eccentric behavior during the visit of Liszt and Princess Sayn-Wittgenstein in the same year, which showed him, he thought, to be "hotheaded and obstinate."

It was quite different in the case of Semper, who had a host of friends whose lives were diminished by his going. Here again Keller is our best witness. He had a warm affection for the architect, whom he described on one occasion as "a man who is as learned and as theoretically well-educated as he is an artist of genius, and personally a true example of the pure and simple artistic temperament" and again as "a childish hypochondriacal being who has nevertheless worked himself up into being a splendid and much loved teacher, a further sign of his deep and many-sided *ingenium*." They were often together, in September 1869, for example, when the news arrived of the burning of Semper's Hoftheater in Dresden, moving the architect to a fit of uncontrollable weeping. There is no doubt that Keller missed Semper when he went away and thought of him often. Indeed, in May 1880, a year after Semper's death, Keller told of having dreamed that his friend, covered with dust and shabbily clothed, came slipping into his room, followed by the shadowy figures of many Zürich men and women from the Rindermarkt, whom Keller had once known but had long forgotten. When asked whether he had not died, Semper answered, "Indeed, but he had taken leave, for in the place where he had been since then, it was insupportable." Then he had silently left the room again, followed by the rabble at his heels. In the doorway he paused and said, "Don't go there, Herr Keller! Bad business there!"

Whatever this may tell us about Keller's private demons, it seems to point to his private belief that, given the chance, Semper would come back, not to Dresden or London or Vienna, but to Zürich.

Chapter 8

THE ITALIAN CONNECTION: EMMA HERWEGH AND HER CIRCLE

◆

*I see nothing before me at all but war and revolution in
every direction. . . . My head is really burning and my
pulse flying. A girl is a stupid useless thing in such times,
and yet how conditions can steel her and strengthen her!
I feel that I would develop in such a stormy time.*
　　　　　　　—EMMA HERWEGH, Diary, 17 July 1842

*. . . a clever woman, for all of the learned swashbucklers
and Brutuses praise her.*
　　　　　　　—GOTTFRIED KELLER to Lina Duncker,
　　　　　　　8 March 1857

Emma Siegmund, shortly before her marriage to
Georg Herwegh (portrait by Friederike Auguste Miethe)

In view of what has already been said about the degree to which mid-century culture and society was male-dominated, it should come as no surprise that few, if any, women in Zürich had any active interest in politics. In the annals of Swiss liberalism there are no Mary Wollstonecrafts or George Sands or Bettina von Arnims, women who combined literary careers with a strong commitment to humane and progressive causes and whose expressed opinions often challenged those of the establishment. Not even the wives of Zürich's political leaders are memorable in this regard, for although they must have been aware of, and indeed compelled to listen to, their husbands' views, they made no contributions of their own, either positive or negative, that appear in the historical record.

Emma Herwegh was the striking exception to this general rule. Even during her privileged youth in Berlin, she had a strongly developed political instinct, which gained strength from her marriage to the radical poet Georg Herwegh in 1843, from their life together in Paris, and, most of all, from their joint intervention in the Badenese insurrection of April 1848. Her lifelong dedication to lost causes dated from that debacle and from her subsequent friendship with Felice Orsini, who aroused her interest and involved her in the fight for Italian liberation. After she came to Zürich in 1852, the Herwegh home became a haven for veterans of the forlorn defense of the Roman Republic, as well as for those who still yearned to reverse the recent verdict in Germany. Mikhail Bakunin, who was a witness at her wedding, Friedrich Wilhelm Rüstow, whom she persuaded to join Garibaldi in 1860, and Ferdinand Lassalle, who became her friend in the last years before his untimely death, believed that she possessed more revolutionary energy than her husband, which was doubtless true, although she never wavered in her devotion to the man whose poems had enraptured young Germans in the forties. In Zürich she had many admirers and was recognized even by those who disliked her as a formidable presence.

I

Born in 1817, Emma Herwegh was the youngest daughter of the Berlin silk merchant and court purveyor Johann Gottfried Siegmund, an assimilated Jew of Protestant observance. Siegmund was liberal in politics and had a strong interest in cultural activities. He paid careful attention to the education of his children, and Emma received instruction in painting and drawing from Professor Holberg, the director of the Berlin Academy, in piano from Ludwig Bayer, one of Felix Mendelssohn-Bartholdy's teachers, and in history from the liberal scholar and politician Max Duncker, in addition to a thorough acquaintance with the German classics and extensive training in modern languages. It is possible, however, that her formal education was no more important than the informal one that she acquired from the company she met in her home, which was always open to foreign visitors, particularly French businessmen and writers, students from Switzerland (including, on at least one occasion, the young Jacob Burckhardt, who had come to Berlin in 1839 in order to study with Leopold von Ranke), a not inconsiderable number of Polish intellectuals, as well as local artists like the actresses Klara Stich and, before she went to Zürich, Charlotte Birch-Pfeiffer. Her conversations with such people protected her against parochialism and local patriotism, and the diary that she began to keep in 1839, and which is now in the Dichtermuseum in Liesthal near Basel, reveals the development of a critical attitude in politics that was not usual in one of her years.

Perhaps her admiration for Gotthold Ephraim Lessing, whose "energy, creative spirit, and depth of intellectual comprehension" she praised in one of its early entries, protected her against the unreasonable expectations that affected the liberal community when Frederick William IV ascended the throne of Prussia in 1840. On 18 October 1840, when the ceremony of homage took place in Berlin, she and a friend had seats on the platform, but the king's spread-eagle oratory and his call for the audience to join him in a sacred oath to "maintain Prussia as it is . . . and as it must remain if it is not to perish," elicited from her only the diary notation "Boredom above all." A year earlier, after a heated discussion in which one of her father's guests had accused her of a lack of Prussian patriotism, she had written, "That I place no particular value upon being a Prussian should irritate no one. Is it not much more elevating to take as one's home the whole Reich, as far as the German tongue and German thought reaches?" Like others of her generation, she was more interested in the unachieved German nation than in Prussian particularism, and by extension her sympathies went out to peoples who combined national self-determination with freedom, like the Swiss, of whom she had a somewhat idealized conception ("O Switzerland!" she wrote in the spring of 1841, "how I long for your Alps, your lakes, and your free, God-breathing air!"), and to others, like the Poles, whose aspirations for freedom and nationhood were blocked by the reactionary powers Prussia, Russia, and Austria. In September 1842, after a friend had taken her target-shooting, she wrote that she had been in good form and that "if the Russian government, complete with Nicholas, had stood before her target, then, *piff paff!*, and those types would have been blown up and the white Lithuanian eagle would be soaring high in the air." It is clear that she was skeptical about Prussia's ability to reform itself, let alone to give freedom to its Polish subjects, her interest in whom led her to visit Posen in the spring of 1842.

The diary is rich in entries that make it clear that she was often lonely and frustrated by the realization that she possessed powers that were unfulfilled, and that she longed for an opportunity to escape from what she once called her "useless, destructive apathy." She sought relief from these moods in violent exercise ("Friday I mounted my horse and rode more madly than ever, for I had a lot to ride out of me"), in Schleiermacher's views about religion, and in poetry, and it was in the last of these that she found it, for she came upon Herwegh. In October 1841 his *Poems of One Who Is Alive* fell into her hands, and she was soon writing of her gratitude to "the noble German singer" whose "brazen songs like a solemn organ chord had sung Sunday into [her] heart" Her mind singing with strophes like

Junge Herzen, unverzagt! *[Young hearts, unafraid!*
Bald erscheint der neue Täufer, *Soon the new baptist comes,*
Der Messias, der die Käufer *The Messiah who will drive*
Und Verkäufer aus dem   *The buyers and sellers from*
 Tempel jagt.   *the temple.]*

and

Gib uns den Mann, der den Panier	*[Give us the man who will seize*
Der neuen Zeit erfasse,	*The banner of the new age,*
Und durch Europa brechen wir	*And through Europe we will break*
Der Freiheit eine Gasse.	*A road to freedom.]*

she stopped reading Schleiermacher and began to study histories of the French Revolution. She was soon a confirmed republican with an avid interest in the possibilities of radical change and, in the summer of 1842, after a discussion of these things at the home of Max and Lina Duncker, she resolved to write to Herwegh about her views and perplexities.

The poet was beginning that extraordinary tour of Germany in which he was hailed as a conquering hero from one end of the land to the other, and in November he was in Berlin to see the King. That visit, in which Herwegh played a rather too insistent Posa to Frederick William's Philip, ended badly, indeed, with Herwegh's permanent expulsion from Prussian territory. But before that happened he had visited Emma Siegmund, and a week had hardly passed before they were engaged to be married. For the impecunious Herwegh, whose trip to Germany was designed in part to seek money for the founding of a new journal, it was a good match, but there is no reason to doubt that he was impressed by Emma's intelligence, charm, and spirit and was sincere when he told his friends that she could "give us all worthy lectures on the subject of freedom." As for Emma, she was deliriously happy. "So *free* a man I have *never* seen," she wrote, "let alone one so untouched by any trace of egoism, regarding himself only as a tool for the execution of a great idea!" "Now heart," she added in self-admonishment,

> *show that you can love*
> *And have no care, whatever your destiny,*
> *And whether it lead to heaven or to hell.*

The couple were married in March 1843. There were preliminary difficulties. Herwegh, who had fled to Switzerland in 1840 to escape military service in Württemberg and who had subsequently been associated with the radical circle of Adolf

August Follen and Julius Fröbel in Zürich, returned there after the ignominious end of his German tour and applied for the right of permanent residence. Largely at the insistence of J. K. Bluntschli, the conservative government that had taken power in September 1839 refused the request because of Herwegh's association with people like Bakunin and the communist Weitling and gave him four days to leave the canton. If this was an omen, it did not daunt Herwegh's bride. Bakunin, who had met her in Leipzig in 1842 and liked her immediately, wrote to her in February that her future existence was in all probability not going to be tranquil, but that tranquillity was the worst misfortune that could befall one. *"L'amour réuni à une large et continuelle action,"* he continued, *"voilà le seul et unique vertu, car tout le reste n'est que néant et mensonge."* Emma entirely agreed.

Despite the momentary hitch, the marriage was formalized in Baden in the canton of Aargau, and the newlyweds then moved, by easy stages, to Paris. Here they had an extensive circle of acquaintances that included artists like Hugo, Béranger, Turgenev, and Heine but was largely dominated by representatives of the radical left in politics. After his German trip Herwegh had at least temporarily lost his faith in the possibility of a liberal revolution and considered himself, and was considered by others (even for a time by Karl Marx), to be a communist. He saw his poetic function now as one of arousing the masses to a violent protest against their conditions, and this was the purpose of poems like "Poor Jacob" and "The Sick Lise" in the second volume of his *Gedichte*. Emma was enthusiastic about the new emphasis. "If the impression [made by a poem] remains only an impression," she had written to Herwegh on the eve of their wedding, "then the devil take all literature! . . . Only from the masses of the proletariat can we now expect an Easter." She probably felt this more strongly than her husband, whose communism did not in fact run very deep. He was becoming used to the commodious apartment in the Rue Barbet, where his wife's wealth allowed him to live in idle luxury—it was not an accident that he and Richard Wagner found so much in common when they met later in Zürich that they they swore intimate friendship and became *Duzbrüder*—and when the second volume of his poems fell stillborn from the presses, he became disenchanted with both poetry and politics and absorbed himself in dilettantish studies of biology and natural philosophy.

His wife refused to believe that this was more than a temporary aberration. In October and November 1847, when she returned to Berlin for a visit and saw the Dunckers and other old liberal friends, she wrote to Herwegh that none of them had any comprehension of, or desire for, the freedom for which he was striving and that "people like you and me could not honorably participate" in the liberal charade. She was surrounded by people "with not a spark of the holy flame, without a drop of blood that has not been watered down, philistines, egoists, old women with and without trousers, and yet I do not know what I would not give to see you among them for one day—but on a tribune in the public square." During her visit Berlin was engrossed in the question of the future fate of Ludwik Mierowslawski and other Polish patriots who had, a year earlier, planned a national rising in Posen but been betrayed, arrested, and imprisoned in Moabit with death sentences hanging over them. This was a cause that touched Emma Herwegh very nearly, and with that mixture of effrontery and charm that always characterized her, she went to the prison and persuaded its director to let her see and talk with the prisoners, although such visits were strictly forbidden. This gesture may have brought some psychological comfort to the Poles—Mieroslawski declared, "*Que je suis content de vous voir, Madame, laissez vous regarder, il y a un an que je n'ai vu une femme*"—but it did not bring any material alleviation of their fate. That had to wait upon the March events of 1848. Even so, it is clear that Emma regarded her action as a necessary one, a demonstration, as she said in a different context, that "I am your wife," and it is significant that before leaving Berlin she presented a copy of Herwegh's poems to the prison director.

Her faith in her husband's basic political instincts were more than justified in the spring of 1848. As thrones began to topple in Germany, he became president of a new German Democratic Society in Paris, negotiated with the revolutionary government of France for financial and military support, and set off as the head of a hastily improvised legion of ex-soldiers, professional revolutionaries, and German, French, and Polish volunteers to carry the message of freedom and the republic across the Rhine. He did not go alone, for, in Heine's words,

Als Amazone ritt neben ihm	[Beside him rode an
Die Gattin mit der langen	amazon,
Nase;	The wife with the long
Sie trug auf dem Hut eine kecke	nose,
Feder,	With a saucy feather in
Im schönem Auge blitzte	her hat,
Ekstase.	And ecstasy shining in her
	eyes.]

Corvin-Wiersbitski, who became the effective military leader of the expedition, had a more accurate description. When the column crossed the Rhine, he wrote, Herwegh's wife "wore black cloth trousers and a black silk blouse with a leather belt, in which were stuck two small pistols and a dagger. . . . As head-covering, Frau Herwegh wore a broad-rimmed, black hat without cockade or feather. Her blond-brown hair was ordered like a man's." She was eager now to do what she had written in one of her letters to her husband, namely, "to show what two people can do who are sworn to the same flag: that no human strength is too puny to set the great wheel rolling, and the movement has giant strength, or arouses giant strength in women too."

This ill-starred adventure was not as harebrained as conservative opinion made it out to be after its collapse. Herwegh was not, to be sure, the ideal leader for such an enterprise: the power of his rhetoric was greater than his attention to detail, and his despotic nature could not tolerate criticism. But no one could fault his courage, and if he failed in the end, this was due less to his own deficiencies than it was to inadequate support from the French, particularly with respect to guns and ammunition, to petty jealousies and professional incompetence on the part of his military commanders, the former Prussian lieutenants Bornstedt and Löwenfels, who had to be superseded by Corvin, and to the curious disinclination of the German revolutionaries on the other side of the Rhine to accept the Paris Legion as an ally.

There is no doubt that Herwegh's column might have made a positive contribution to the revolutionary cause if they had effected a timely junction with the republican columns of Friedrich Hecker, Gustav Struve, and Franz Sigel in southern Baden. This was prevented by Hecker's reluctance to alienate local opinion by inviting into Germany the French anarchists who, he had been told, constituted the bulk of Herwegh's forces. With a complete indifference to the risks involved, Emma Herwegh made two trips into Baden in an attempt to coordinate plans with Hecker, first traveling, presumably in normal attire, by train and post to Mannheim, Basel, and Schaffhausen, before finding him in the neighborhood of Donaueschingen, where he gave her vague assurances that he would send information about a juncture of their forces soon, and then again, four days later, when she tracked him down in Kandern and worked out a rather imprecise plan for the legion to cross the Rhine at Großkembs and join Hecker's forces in a joint drive on Freiburg. Jubilantly, Emma carried this news back to Straßburg, and the legion moved out. By the time it had crossed the river, however, Hecker's forces had been surprised and defeated at Kandern, and the troops led by Struve and Sigel were being decisively repulsed before Freiburg. Herwegh's tiny army had no alternative now but to try to avoid battle until it could cross the Rhine again and take refuge in Switzerland, and this, under Corvin's leadership, it had almost succeeded in doing when it was cut off at Niederdossenbach by a superior force of Württemberg infantry.

About this short encounter there were many malicious legends, most of them telling of Herwegh's cowardice under fire and his wife's efforts to protect him at the risk of her own life. Corvin, who was in a position to know, would have none of these. During the legion's retreat he had learned to admire Emma's courage, watching her "endure the unaccustomed exertions without grumbling, bravely facing the danger, of which she was fully conscious." Much of the time she and her husband traveled by carriage, and it was behind the dashboard of this that Herwegh was supposed to have crept when the shooting started at Niederdossenbach, while his wife sought to shield him with her body. In reality, the carriage had no dashboard, and the Herweghs worked feverishly during the fight to make new cartridges for a legion that had shrunk to less than 500 men and had only 250 guns, only half of which fired efficiently, and fewer than four cartridges per gun. The fight did not last long. Despite courageous resistance, and a gallant but costly flanking movement by the former Prussian Lieutenant Reinhard von Schimmelpfennig's *Sensenmänner*, a detachment armed only with scythes mounted on pikes, the legion was forced to fly in disorder, its members making their escape as best they could. The Württembergers were intent above all on capturing "Herwegh and his accursed wife," against whom there was an extraordinary local animus, and, judging from the brutal treatment accorded other legionnaires who were apprehended, they would, if caught, have been summarily executed. But they found refuge in a farmer's cottage, where they donned the clothes of agricultural workers, Herwegh shaving off his beard, and after some close calls they managed to cross the Rheinfelden bridge into Switzerland by mingling with crowds who were going to market.

II

Despite the derision of Herwegh's enemies, the adventure had been an honorable one, dedicated to a noble cause and carried out at grave personal risk. There is little doubt that Emma Herwegh regarded it later as the high point of her marriage. It was a pity that it was followed so quickly by what was without doubt its lowest. When the couple returned to Paris they found themselves compelled to retrench their expensive style of living. Johann Gottfried Siegmund had been investing for some time in building property in the west end of Berlin. The upheaval of 1848 caused a precipitous fall in values, and he fared so badly in consequence that he was forced to reduce his support for his daughter to little more than subsistence. The luxurious trappings of the Paris apartment had to be sold, which further depressed Herwegh's spirits, already lacerated by the defeat in Baden. He began to spend his evenings in the comfortable flat of the Russian exile Alexander Herzen near the Madeleine, leaving Emma at home. The two men became fast friends, but so did Herwegh and Herzen's wife, Natalie, a neurotically romantic woman who felt a strong compulsion to relieve the poet's melancholy. Fearing police surveillance, Herzen, in June 1849, took his wife to Geneva; Herwegh followed, again leaving Emma behind, and by September, Natalie and he were lovers. The course of the affair, which dragged on for two and a half years and ended badly, with Natalie dead and Herzen and Herwegh slanging each other in the public prints, is described in E. H. Carr's *The Romantic Exiles*, with an admirable psychological insight into Herzen's remarkable myopia, Herwegh's self-indulgence, and Natalie Herzen's ability to convince herself that she was only doing what George Sand's heroines were admired for doing. Carr's sympathy is reserved for Emma Herwegh, who knew of the affair long before Herzen did but tolerated it because she was confident that her husband's dependence upon her would not permit it to last indefinitely. At the cost of much personal humiliation, she was in the end proved to be right, and Carr is entirely correct in writing that her "infinite patience, toleration, and self-effacement" deserve "more than the cold contempt which Herzen pours on her in *My Past and Thoughts*."

During the last part of 1851 and the first half of 1852, while Herwegh was in Zürich, alternately drafting hysterical letters to his wife and Herzen and introducing the works of Schopenhauer to Richard Wagner, Emma and the children were in Nice, living near the Herzens but no longer in intimate communication with either of them. Her closest friends in this unhappy period of her life were professional revolutionaries of one stripe or another, particularly the German naturalist Karl Vogt, a Pole named Chojecki, who was generally called Charles Edmond, and the Italian *carbonaro* Felice Orsini. A veteran of the lost battle for the Roman Republic, Orsini was now an agent for Mazzini's Central Committee for European Democracy, although, until such time as his chief had devised new plans for insurrection, he was pretending to be engaged in the manufacture of hemp. He admired Emma's unquenchable revolutionary spirit and was amused by her romantic extravagance, both traits that were seriously lacking in his own wife, Assunta, who hated politics and longed for a life of bourgeois conformity. They had long talks together about lost battles and future hopes, talks that gained in intimacy because of Emma's fluency in Orsini's native tongue and her ready sympathy for the cause of Italian freedom, but there is no convincing evidence that their pleasure in each other's company ripened into a *Liebesverhältnis*, as the catalogue of the Herwegh Museum in Liesthal states. Emma was too devoted to her husband to think of imitating his behavior. In the summer of 1852, when the Herwegh-Herzen affair had become a European *cause célèbre*, Orsini begged Emma to abandon "that brigand George," Karl Vogt urged her to go back to her parents in Berlin, and Charles Edmond invited her to divorce Herwegh and marry him. She refused all three suggestions with indignation, gathered up her children and belongings, and rejoined her husband in Zürich.

III

Their reconciliation was not difficult. Emma was ready to forget the affair with Natalie, and Herwegh was happy to be able to rely once more upon her encouragement and guidance, for he was, in these years, more and more a man of vast and unfocused projects and of failing energy: Eliza Wille said that he reminded her of "a foot asleep." Emma never relinquished the hope that she could bring him back to political activity, and to the extent that her own strong personality was a magnet, drawing like-minded people to their home, she succeeded. With the friends Herwegh had made during their separation, she was cordial without being intimate. She was never a member of the Mariafeld circle—she regarded Eliza Wille as an intriguer who reveled in the opportunities for gossip provided by the Wagner-Wesendonck affair and once referred to her as *"cette nature épileptique par excellence"*—and Herwegh's own visits to Mariafeld seem to have diminished after her arrival. Wagner she did not like and once explained her antipathy by calling him an *"égoïste sans coeur qui se démine comme une femme hystérique,"* apparently not realizing that she was unconsciously describing her own husband. She had a great facility for keeping the composer off balance—when he asked her once whether they were not intimate friends, she answered, *"Dites des ennemis intimes, ce sera plus exact"*—and for pricking his inflated self-esteem. During the visit of Franz Liszt and Princess Carolyne Sayn-Wittgenstein to Zürich in 1853, Wagner was chagrined to discover that Emma Herwegh was the person that the princess wished to see and that Liszt was visibly touched by Emma's recollection of a concert of his that she had heard in Hamburg in 1841. After the illustrious pair had left, the princess sent Emma a medallion bearing Liszt's image, and the two women carried on a lively correspondence for some years.

Emma took greater pleasure in her acquaintance with the physiologist Jakob Moleschott, with Gottfried Keller, with whom she shared a common esteem for the philosopher Ludwig Feuerbach, and, after he came to Zürich in 1855, with the architect Gottfried Semper, of all "the 'eminent' men here," she told Princess Wittgenstein, the one with whom she sympathized most deeply, "a true artistic temperament without any trace of vanity." But it was with the group that she fondly called "my Italians"—De Boni, Imbriani, De Sanctis, Agneni, Cironi, Malegari, Marcato—that she, and often Herwegh as well, sat up till two o'clock in the morning, talking about the state of European politics. These discussions were contentious in the extreme, for while several members of the group, like Pietro Cironi, were ardent Mazzinians, Filippo De Boni, who had served as the short-lived Roman Republic's envoy to Bern in 1849, was at heart a follower of Gioberti and was savagely referred to by the anti-clerical Vittorio Imbriani as Emma's *"prete spretato"* (defrocked priest). Imbriani, whom one historian has called a "tempestuous D'Artagnan," was a notorious duelist, with indeterminate political views, which allowed him to be contemptuous of almost everyone in the group except Emma. Francesco De Sanctis had been on the barricades in Naples in 1848, but his republicanism was tempered by a certain respect for the royal house of Piedmont, which put him at odds with De Boni, who had a bitter hatred for the Piedmontese. What prevented the group from flying into fragments was the personality of Emma Herwegh, whose power over these desperadoes Gottfried Keller found both amusing and impressive. Imbriani frankly adored her and continued corresponding with her until 1877, although by that time he had become a hypochondriacal ultra, whereas her political stance never changed. He could never understand, he wrote in July 1864, how she could have stayed for so many years in Zürich without having died of boredom or becoming stupid.

> How can one endure that absolute lack of moral and intellectual life? How can one take any interest in the cantonal politics of Switzerland, in those microscopic passions that smack always of petty wrangling, that remind one of the isolated warfare that takes place in a drop of water between the volvoce, the vibrio, and other gigantic beasts of the same kind.

Affection for her must also have played a part in the offer of a professorship in the University of Naples that De Sanctis, when he was Minister of Education, made to Herwegh in 1861, an opportunity that came to nothing when the government fell from office and the ministerial portfolios were changed.

Symptomatic of Emma's growing enthusiasm for Italy (but

also, no doubt, of her vulnerability to the local culture's zeal for self-improvement) was her decision, shortly after her arrival in Zürich, to form a group that would read the Italian classics in the original. She recruited Jakob Moleschott and his wife and Semper's daughter Lisbeth, taught them the language, "surrendering herself," as Moleschott later wrote, "to its rebirth in freedom with emotion and willingness to sacrifice," and then led them through the *Inferno* and *I Promessi Sposi* and Petrarch and Tasso. The group practiced the language on its walks through the markets, which must have added to the gaiety of the Zürich scene.

All of this Italianity made it appropriate, if not inevitable, that Felice Orsini should come back into Emma's life. In truth he had never entirely disappeared from it, for in August 1853, when he had been commissioned by Mazzini to be the commander in chief of a national insurrection in central Italy, he wrote and asked her to send some manifestos in German that might shake the loyalty of Austrian garrisons in Modena. He never got a chance to use these, for he and the pitifully small number of recruits who responded to his call were arrested by Piedmontese troops before they had begun their march, and as a result he was expelled from the country and put on a ship for England. From London he sent Emma doleful letters filled with worries about his wife Assunta, comments on the coldness and lack of education of English women, and laments that he was doing nothing for his country, until suddenly, in June 1854, he wrote jubilantly, "Read this and speak to no one! I go now to my fate!" In fact, he was simply embarking upon another of Mazzini's forlorn enterprises, which this time led him, under the name of Tito Celsi, to a series of ill-planned landings on Ligurian beaches, much scrambling on mountain paths to meetings that were betrayed, several close calls with government troops, and finally a desperate escape through the Grison Alps, which brought him on the last day of August to Emma Herwegh in Zürich.

Orsini was pretty fed up with Mazzini by this time and, in the three weeks of concealment in the Herwegh home, debated whether he should not enlist in the Russian Army, which was now fighting in the Crimea, or any other force (except the Piedmontese or the French) that would give him a chance to fight as a regimental officer commanding regular troops with a defined objective. Emma talked him out of this piece of self-indulgence, and Pietro Cironi, who, according to Michael St. John Packe, had fallen in love with Emma and wanted to get rid of Orsini, suggested that he go to Milan, whence signals were still coming to Mazzini, and discover what was left of the revolutionary organization there. This prospect was dangerous enough to appeal to Orsini's quixotic temperament, and he set forth carrying an old passport of Herwegh's that Emma, who had been struck by Orsini's likeness to the photograph in it, had altered in such way as to describe the bearer as Giorgio Hernagh, Swiss watchmaker. It was not, unfortunately, to protect him for long. The chief result of his activities in Milan, and later in Vienna, was to alert police spies and informers. Oblivious to this, he spent a good deal of time in cafés writing a series of letters to Emma signed Dr. De Balossis, in which he talked about the importance of his mission, his continued concern for his family, and his gratitude for Emma's support. "As for the friendship between us," he wrote on 8 November 1854, "it appeared truer, on my side also, in Zürich than it had been even in Nice. There my mind was inflamed by my imagination. Now it is my heart that I listen to, without passion and without exaggeration, and it speaks to me only of true friendship, of true esteem, and I feel that for you." It was a friendship that was now to be exposed to considerable strain, for in mid-December, having happily traveled from Vienna to Budapest and then into Transylvania, Orsini was arrested in an inn in Hermannstadt, sent to Vienna for interrogation, and, his attempts to obscure the truth proving fruitless, charged with high treason and imprisoned in the fortress of Mantua.

Knowing that there was a good chance that, sooner or later, execution awaited him, Orsini began immediately to think of the possibility of escape and applied to the prison governor for permission to write to Emma Herwegh, claiming that he was without money for food and tobacco and that she, as the godmother of his daughter, was his only relative, his wife having separated from him. The fact that this request was granted, after a superficial checking of church records in Nice, and the further fact that the name Herwegh aroused no sense of recognition and its similarity to the name Hernagh no suspicion, does not speak well for the Austrian police system. Within two months Emma Herwegh received three letters from Mantua that were puzzling in their triviality until her husband realized that there was invisible writing in lemon juice between the lines. From that time on, until March of the following year, she was the recipient of a stream of requests for money, details about Orsini's arrest, descriptions of the internal arrangements of the fortress of San Giorgio, messages for Mazzini, and plans for escape.

She must have enjoyed herself hugely during these months, feeling her hand once more on the great wheel of history. To be sure, Orsini was a demanding correspondent. Not only did he request a good deal of money, which had to be assembled from various revolutionary committees and groups, but he had bizarre ideas concerning the materials needed to facilitate his liberation. For a time he was convinced that the best method would be to drug all of the guards with opium, and he asked that a greatcoat be sent to him with the drug concealed in its buttons. In London, Mazzini had such a paletot made and, when it failed to arrive, Emma procured another in Zürich and prepared the buttons herself, but when it was tried at a Twelfth Night party in the prison that was attended by all the turnkeys and soldiers of the guard, the drug had little effect. In the end Orsini fell back on literature, more precisely on the works of the French physicist and astronomer Dominique François Arago, which, after his request for them had been approved by the prison authorities, Emma dispatched to him, along with invoices from Zürich booksellers but with metal saws concealed in their bindings. With these Orsini laboriously severed the bars in his cell's windows and, at 2 A.M. on the morning of 30 March 1856, after many anguished delays, lowered himself down the prison wall, fell heavily into the moat, injuring his leg, and then, by a series of happy accidents, was extricated by friendly strangers and spirited off to a nearby village, where friends came and carried him out of Austrian territory. On 11 April, Emma received a message reading, "*Carissima Emma. Sono libero da 12 giorni da 2 in luogo non austriaca,*" and a week later he was concealed once more in her house in Zürich.

It was the last time. Orsini really did go now to his fate, and in circumstances beyond any help that Emma Herwegh could give him. On 21 May he left Zürich for London, where he was soon involved in the preparations for the *attentat* upon Emperor Napoleon III that took place before the Paris Opera House on 14 January 1858. For this he was tried and, because eight persons had died in the explosion of the bombs, executed.

Emma was in labor at the time, giving birth to her third child, Marcel. Through the good offices of Orsini's lawyer, Jules Favre, she was able to send him a letter before his death, and her presence was otherwise felt, for in his summation for the defense, Favre recalled her part in the escape from Mantua. "A woman did not want him to die!" he cried. "With that delicacy, with that abnegation, with that sagacity of which only warmhearted women are capable, she saw that he obtained the instruments of his liberation." But that was impossible this time.

IV

Without wavering in her devotion to her husband, Emma Herwegh always attracted to her side stronger men than he, and she encouraged them partly because she admired their energy and partly, one must suppose, because she hoped that that their example might draw Herwegh away from the world of contemplation and back into that of action. Orsini was not the last to serve as such a model. He was in a sense succeeded by Friedrich Wilhelm Rüstow, a close friend of the Herweghs since 1852, who now became, by a kind of conversion, one of Emma's Italians.

Rüstow was the descendant of Pomeranian forebears and the son of the commander of a Prussian infantry company in the wars of 1806 and 1813. Fascinated at an early age by military affairs, he had broken off his legal studies at the University of Heidelberg to join the Prussian Army as a *Gardepionier* in 1838. Two years later, after attending artillery and engineering school, he received his officer's commission. From the beginning he was a prolific writer on technical and administrative subjects, with pronounced ideas of his own about the necessity of basic reform of the Prussian military constitution, and as time passed his views became steadily more democratic and nationalistic. He was soon in trouble with his superiors because of his book *The War of the Future, A Few Words to the Young Generation*, which was written in 1848 and which argued for the raising of a people's army, and his appeal to the Prussian National Assembly to support democratic officers and to prevent the army from becoming a tool of reaction involved him in a series of hearings and courts-martial. After the defiant publication of his *The German Military State Before and During the Revolution* in 1850, which attacked the standing army for being the inveterate foe of liberty and for having suppressed legitimate democratic aspirations during the recent fighting, he was charged with high treason and sentenced to the loss of his commission and fortress detention for a period of thirty-one and a half years, with ten further years of police surveillance. Rüstow actually served six months of this horrendous sentence in the fortress at Posen, but in July 1850, as he was about to be transferred to another prison, he escaped and, dressed as a woman and with two companions, made his way by carriage and train to Switzerland.

Rüstow settled in Zürich, where he earned his living by his pen and, after 1852, by his work as *privat dozent* for military studies at the university. With the classical philologist Hermann Köchly, he collaborated on a bilingual edition of Greek military writers, a history of the Greek military system, and a highly successful edition, with commentary, of Caesar's *Gallic War*. He became a Swiss citizen in 1853 and shortly thereafter established contact with the new federal army, lecturing to its officers and writing technical and historical studies, including a handbook on tactics, a history of the infantry, and treatises on general staff functions, as well as accounts of the Crimean and Italian wars.

This hectic literary activity was apparently not enough to satisfy what Gustav Mayer called the "desperado" side of Rüstow's nature. He often took part in the emotional discussions of Emma's intimate circle, and, in May 1860, when Garibaldi began his campaign in Sicily, it was perhaps not surprising that he proved susceptible to her suggestion—or, as her son has written, her demand—that he put his talents at the disposal of the Italian patriot. Filippo De Boni made the necessary arrangements, and Rüstow went to Genoa in June, where he became chief of staff of a division and was asked by Mazzini to plan an attack upon the Papal States. This was canceled because of urgent needs in the south, and Rüstow joined Garibaldi in Sicily, where he served as his chief of staff and later, in the fighting at Salerno, Naples, and on the Volturno line, as commander of the Milan Brigade. He was a competent and audacious leader, having three horses shot from under him on the Volturno front, but the campaign was over all too quickly, and Garibaldi's willingness to hand the fruits of victory over to the Piedmontese, whom Rüstow regarded as the Prussians of Italy, left him without an occupation, and he returned to Zürich in a restless and discontented mood.

The conflict between the Prussian King and his Parliament, which was coming to a head in 1861, led him to the belief that there might soon be an opportunity to reverse the verdict of 1848–49, and he began to devise expansive plans for indulging it. He was particularly interested in persuading the National Union, a liberal organization in Germany that was working for national unification, to begin to recruit a national army, which might be based on the popular *Turnverein* movement and could serve to counteract Prussian militarism. Emma Herwegh encouraged him in this and, indeed, seems to have corresponded with his closest German supporter, a member of the *Turnverein* in Koburg named Ludwig Schweigert, for Schweigert wrote her a number of letters, in rather excited prose, to assure her that what Rüstow and he were planning was "in harmony with [her] ideas, with [her] patriotic and sound political wishes," that when the time for action came he wanted to be at Rüstow's side, "to fight, conquer, or die with him," and, somewhat gratuitously, that he regarded her as *"ein kreuzbraves Weibchen"* and a *"Mordsweiberl."*

This wholly impractical plan—impractical because the leaders of the National Union steadfastly ignored it—acquired a new dimension in September 1861, when the German socialist Ferdinand Lassalle, accompanied by Countess Sophie von Hatzfeldt, whose liberty and fortune he had saved from her husband in a notorious divorce case, came to Zürich. During their visit the Herweghs arranged a large party at the Swan in their honor. The guest list included Ludmilla Assing, the niece of Karl August Varnhagen von Ense, a long-term friend of both the Lassalles and the Herweghs, the Russian nihilist Lydia Idaroff, Colonel Rüstow, wearing his red Garibaldi shirt, a good number of what would today be called the radical chic of the town, and the novelist Gottfried Keller. Keller had just been appointed cantonal *Staatsschreiber* and was to begin his service the next day. For whatever reason—celebration, apprehension, regret—he drank incautiously and, as he did so, became steadily more morose and disapproving of the company, in which the women were now drinking champagne freely and smoking Havana cigars. When the guests called for Lassalle to show his skills as *magnétiseur*, and he began to dangle a gold watch above Herwegh's head, Keller's patience reached its limits, and shouting, "That's too much for me, you riffraff, you crooks!" he seized a chair, tried to brain the guest of honor, and had to be forcibly ejected.

The Lassalle visit had a more important result than to make Keller oversleep on his first day in his new post. It gave birth to a grandiose projection in which Rüstow's *Turnverein* plan, Lassalle's political ambitions, Emma Herwegh's Mazzinian connections, and perhaps her hope that Herwegh and she might yet wipe out the memory of Niederdossenbach by a new invasion of Germany all played their part. This called for an attack upon Austria by a mixed Italian-German force under Garibaldi's command, with other columns operating from the Slav lands, and perhaps from Switzerland, which would then spread to Germany and give Lassalle an opportunity to play tribune in a popular rising against reaction. Immediately after the party in the Swan, Lassalle and Sophie von Hatzfeldt, accompanied by Lydia Idaroff and Rüstow, set off in high good humor for Italy, Lassalle sending almost daily letters to the Herweghs to inform them of new ideas that had occurred to him and to report on the progress he was making in learning Italian. Unfortunately, nothing very tangible emerged from all of this, or from a visit that Lassalle paid to Garibaldi on Caprera in November, except that Rüstow, who was estranged from his wife, fell hopelessly in love with the countess, which rather complicated relations between the conspirators. The grand design received its death blow in August 1862, when Garibaldi made his rash attempt to take Rome and was defeated and captured at Aspromonte.

For Emma Herwegh there was a crumb of comfort in the general disappointment, and that was that her husband showed some sign of reviving political interest. After Aspromonte he wrote the poem called "Εσσεταιἠμαρ" (The Day Will Come), with the defiant lines:

> *And if at Aspromonte*
> *The cowards could betray him,*
> *If, wounded like Achilles,*
> *The universally loved one lies*
> *Wan and silent on his bed, so be it!*
> *Achilles fell, but so did Troy.*
> *The day will come!*

which Lassalle liked so much that he had it printed in the paper *Berliner Reform*. Subsequently, in April 1863, when Lassalle asked him to aid in the effort to establish the Universal German Workers Association by writing an "inspired and inspiring poem" and also to become the representative of the ADAV for Switzerland, Herwegh agreed to do both, to Emma's great satisfaction. She had taken up Lassalle's cause as enthusiastically as she had the schemes of Orsini and Rüstow and, during a trip to Berlin in November 1863, where she experienced the excitement engendered by Lassalle's speeches and witnessed the banning of his meetings and his own arrest, she wrote to Herwegh, "I regret that as a woman I cannot have myself inscribed as a member, for, if I could, I should do so in this very minute!" Herwegh's poem, she reported proudly, had been widely distributed, despite police attempts to confiscate it. This was the *Bundeslied*, "The Song of Union for the Universal German Workers Association," which Shlomo Na'aman has called "the most effective piece of social poetry since Heine's 'The Weavers,' " a song whose stirring lines,

Mann der Arbeit, aufgewacht!	[*Man of labor, awaken!*
Und erkenne deine Macht!	*And recognize your power!*
Alle Räder stehen still,	*All wheels stand still,*
Wenn dein starker Arm	*When your strong arm*
es will,	*wills it,]*

set to music by Hans von Bülow, were to be sung by generations of German proletarians.

The heady excitement that Emma Herwegh felt in November 1863 did not last long. Lassalle threw his life away in a duel in August 1864, a loss that Marx attributed to his having spent too much time with "military adventurers and *révolutionnaires en gants jaunes* in Switzerland." Rüstow, who was his second, was never forgiven by Sophie von Hatzfeldt for having, as she thought, encouraged Lassalle to fight, and he became an embittered, lonely man, who, despite his valuable work for the Swiss Army's general staff, suffered from a sense of unfulfillment and took his own life in 1878. Long before then it had become clear that Europe had changed and that its climate was no longer congenial to *Eisenfresser* like Bakunin and Orsini and Rüstow and the others upon whom Emma Herwegh had doted. She was left to face the hard reality that in the new world of power and money that had been ushered in by the wars of 1866 and the 1870s there would be no more romantic revolutions and that the rhetoric that had informed her husband's songs now seemed faintly comic. The poet understood this rather sooner than his wife and accommodated himself apathetically to the shadowy existence of the once famous. Emma fought against the truth and against the material deprivation that accompanied it. In October 1865 she wrote to Ludwig Feuerbach, their longtime friend, that they were in dire straits, with no property left except Herwegh's books, upon which they had already borrowed 7,000 francs. She implored him to help her find someone who might advance them enough to bring a little security to "a noble and rare nature who is being pitifully destroyed in the petty struggle of daily misery."

It was not the first of such letters, and it would not be the last. Poverty forced the Herweghs to leave Zürich in 1866 and, since the poet had now been granted an amnesty, they settled in Baden-Baden, where Herwegh died in 1875. By that time— although it may seem unkind to say so—Emma had, out of sheer necessity, developed sponging into a fine art. When the young Frank Wedekind met her in Paris in 1897, he was excited to meet a woman who had been a legend in her time, but he warned his mother that Frau Herwegh was now using the methods that she had once employed to maintain her husband's well-being in behalf of a son who was capable of supporting himself, and that if she received any requests for a loan, she should refuse to honor them.

Chapter 9

THE CIVIC CONSCIENCE: GOTTFRIED KELLER AND JACOB BURCKHARDT

♦

*I maintain that, even when a citizen does not agree with
the existing political system, it is nevertheless his duty,
to the best of his ability, to work with others so that the
welfare of the state may be increased and damage be
spared it.*

—LUDWIG MEYER VON KNONAU (1841)

*The life of the occident is struggle. And, as an individual,
even the historian cannot detach himself from that of his
locality; as a person in his temporality, he must desire
and represent something definite, but in his scholarship
he must reserve for himself the higher view.*

—JACOB BURCKHARDT, *Gesamtausgabe*,
Bd. VII, 36A, S. 374.

Gottfried Keller

When he wrote his political memoirs in 1841, Ludwig Meyer von Knonau, who had been a member of the Regeneration government that was driven from office in September 1839, ended them by appealing to his fellow citizens to remember their duties to the commonwealth of which they were a part, to serve it by faithfully executing their military and electoral obligations, to select as their leaders men who were not ambitious for personal power or advantage, to watch over the education of youth, "this instrument for inculcating civic virtues and useful civic energy," and to guard against the divisiveness that was caused by social privilege, religious obscurantism, and party strife. "Be mindful," he concluded, "of the shameful decline of many a free state destroyed by such discord, and do not forget that the world's ridicule and the curses of their most remote descendants pursue those whose egoism is responsible for it."

Civic virtue was, of course, neither the invention nor the exclusive property of the liberal party that dominated Zürich's political life in the middle of the nineteenth century. Indeed, there are grounds for regarding it as a general characteristic of Swiss politics, with deep historical roots, a necessary condition of national existence in a world dominated by great powers, and Karl Schmid has written persuasively of the psychological importance of the fact that, in a small and vulnerable nation, "concern for the commonwealth has remained something that is indivisible and unparted. It is not to be parceled out, and the individual cannot emancipate himself from it." But certainly the liberals, in their struggle against the old aristocratic elite, against French domination, and, later, against parties that seemed willing to make concessions to foreign powers for their own advantage, were more explicit in their invocation of the principle than had been true in the past and, when they were in power, used the schools and popular festivals to exalt it as a patriotic obligation of the individual. Their ranks, moreover, were well filled with persons whose social conscience impelled them to serve the state at not inconsiderable personal sacrifice. Paul Usteri, Jonas Furrer, and Alfred Escher were the most distinguished, but not the only, liberal leaders who paid heavily for their recognition of their civic duties in terms of health, wealth, and civilian career, and their dedication to the commonwealth could be, and often was, held up as a model and a guide.

It is clear that in any nation civic virtue is something its citizens will exemplify in varying degrees. One of the characteristics of modern society is the existence of large numbers of what Alfred Weber has called "free-floating intellectuals," persons whose loyalties to class, community, and nation are apt to be looser than those of other citizens and who are less susceptible to appeals to civic duty. In Switzerland in the nineteenth century, as we shall see in the next chapter, some of the country's leading writers found it difficult to identify with the land of their birth because of what they regarded as its insignificance in world politics and its tendency to materialism and philistinism. There were others—one thinks of Pestalozzi and Jeremias Gotthelf, whose novels can almost be regarded as, among other things, catechisms of social obligation—whose recognition of their country's frailties enhanced their loyalty to it. The problem can be illustrated by a consideration of the careers of Gottfried Keller and Jacob Burckhardt. The novelist not only recognized his duty to the commonwealth of which he was a citizen but sacrificed fifteen years of his productive life to its service. The historian, after years of denying any ties to his native canton, finally returned to it from Zürich and dedicated his total energies in the last phase of his life, if not to the *polis*, then to his surrogate for it, the University of Basel.

I

The two men had much in common. Born within a year of each other (Burckhardt in May 1818, Keller in July 1819), both witnessed the intercantonal strife of the years 1845–47 and the creation of the federal state in their early manhood, were critical observers of the crisis of liberalism in their years of maturity, and died (Keller in 1890, Burckhardt in 1897) in the decade in which Europe began to slide toward the holocaust that would threaten Switzerland's very existence. Both men went through life without the solace of religion—Keller's Christianity fell victim to the influence of Ludwig Feuerbach in Heidelberg in 1848; Burckhardt, while never formally leaving the church, had little contact with it after 1844—or marriage, both suffering traumatically unrequited passions in the 1850s and resigning themselves to bachelor existences in which their erotic energy was largely diverted to highly mannered letters to female correspondents and, in Keller's case, to the creation of some of the most entrancing portraits of women in German literature. Each of them, as a young man, aspired to a career (Keller as a painter, Burckhardt as a poet) that he later abandoned to pursue his life work. These similarities are perhaps trivial. Certainly they are less important than the differences in the social circumstances in which the two men were born and in their reactions to the political storms that affected their country in the years in which they grew to maturity.

The future novelist was the son of Johann Rudolf Keller of the city of Zürich, an energetic man who left his native land after his father's death, learned the trade of wood turning, wandered through most of Germany and Austria in the years 1812–16, and then returned to marry the daughter of the pastor in nearby Glattfelden and set himself up as a master carpenter and house builder. A man who had seen much and responded positively to the currents of change moving over the continent, J. R. Keller played an active part in the life of his community. He had a strong interest in popular education and was one of the supervisors of the School for the Disadvantaged (*Armenschule*); he participated with enthusiasm in reading clubs intended to raise the cultural level of the working and lower middle classes, and he was a charter member of a benevolent society for the protection of the widows and orphans of the membership. He kept himself informed about international politics and was a supporter of the Greeks in their struggle for independence, and in national politics he was a unitarian and once wrote a newspaper article pointing out the disadvantages that untrammeled cantonal sovereignty brought to Switzerland in its trade relations with the neighboring national states. He was a proud member of his local *Schützenverein*, and one of his son's strongest memories of his father was of him wearing the green marksman's uniform.

Johann Rudolf Keller died in 1824, six years before the

triumph of the liberal principles that he exemplified in his own life. His early passing deprived his son of guidance that might have prevented the abrupt termination of his formal education. After attending the *Armenschule* in Zürich, he was admitted, in 1833, to the cantonal School of Industry. It was a time when the controversy over the new liberal government's School Law and its decision to level the city's fortifications was at its height, and when it was fashionable for students to pose as aristocrats and, often with the encouragement of their parents, to make life miserable for their liberal teachers. Gottfried Keller became involved in such a demonstration, unwittingly lending his voice to an attack upon principles that his own father had held very dear, and although his role was not a major one, he was expelled from the school.

This event effectively barred his way to a career in business or one of the professions, and he resolved, without much reflection, to become a painter. His first experiments were made while living with his mother's relatives in Glattfelden, and he also had some instruction in Zürich, but nothing that he learned prepared him to meet the challenges that he encountered when he tried to establish himself as a landscape painter in Munich in 1840. After two years of poverty and failure, which were later to form the basis of some of the most harrowing chapters of his novel *Green Henry*, he was forced to admit that his talents did not measure up to his ambitions.

During these years of frustration his political ideas had gradually taken shape. As a youth in Zürich he had frequented the homes of former friends of his father who were ardent radicals and, like the old men in his later story, "The Little Banner of the Seven Upright Ones," faithful readers of Ludwig Snell's *Schweizerische Republikaner*. Under their influence, he was a defiant "Strauß" in the confessional struggle that led to the reactionary coup of September 1839, and when he went to Munich one of his first requests of his mother was that she ask his father's friend, the cabinetmaker Schaufelberger, to send him occasional copies of the *Republikaner* and the Winterthur *Landbote* so that he could remain informed of the course of politics at home. She responded by sending him the *Landbote*'s account of the gathering in the Unterstraß of the Zürich contingent to the Bassersdorf Assembly, the first public protest against the consequences of the September *Putsch* and an event that was regarded as the rebirth of the liberal party, writing "This will probably give you marvelous radical enjoyment." In the Munich artists colony, Keller was a member of the Swiss Society, an organization that conducted itself like a student corporation, with much beer drinking and dueling, but also subscribed to the *Neue Zürcher Zeitung*, the *Aargauer Zeitung*, and other papers and held debates on subjects of current interest. Keller was a frequent participant in these, and indeed read his first political essay before the society.

This was prompted by a discussion in the German press of a perennial theme: whether Switzerland had a national identity of its own or was not merely an unnatural construct of provinces that were essentially part of France, Germany, and Italy. In Keller's essay, which was designed to appear in the society's *Wochenblatt* but proved to be too long for publication, he indignantly repudiated the second suggestion. "The national character of the Swiss," he wrote, "derives not from its ancient ancestry, nor from the saga of the land, nor from anything material, but from the love of freedom and independence; it derives from the extraordinary devotion to a fatherland that is small but beautiful and dear; it derives from the homesickness that befalls them in foreign lands, no matter how beautiful they may be." There is no doubt that Keller himself suffered from that homesickness. In his autobiographical novel, *Green Henry*, he later described how, night after night, during his darkest hours in Munich, his hero's mind was touched with dreams of longing for his homeland, dreams in which Switzerland assumed fantastic and even threatening forms, and it is interesting to note that when Green Henry returned home in the novel, his recognition of his belongingness was expressed in the same terms that the young Keller used in his defense of Swiss national identity in 1841, namely, beauty and freedom. Green Henry sees

> the rich molding of my native land, in plains and sheets of water calm and flat, in the mountains steeply and boldly jagged, at my feet the blossoming earth, and near the sky a marvelous wild region, all incessantly changing, and hiding many well-populated valleys and electoral districts. With the thoughtlessness of youth or childhood, I considered the

beauty of the country to be a historical and political merit, in a sense a patriotic achievement of the people and synonymous with freedom itself.

His dreams of becoming a painter shattered, Keller returned to Zürich in the winter of 1842. It was a sad and lonely time for him, and he found relief from his troubles in political discussions with the master craftsmen who had been his father's old friends and in poetry, for in the course of his reading he had come upon the political poems of Anastasius Grün and Georg Herwegh, and these inspired emulation. In the summer of 1843 he sent a sheaf of political verse to his former teacher in the School of Industry, Dr. Julius Fröbel, and Fröbel, a man of radical views who was soon to become editor of the *Schweizerische Republikaner*, not only encouraged him to continue writing but introduced him to the group of German writers and publicists who met in the home of August Adolf Follen. Here he met the poets Hoffmann von Fallersleben and Ferdinand Freiligrath, who proved to be useful and friendly critics of his work, and became intimate with the publicist Wilhelm Schulz, who had been a friend of Georg Büchner and whose economic and military ideas interested and influenced Karl Marx, his wife, Caroline, and other German refugees from Metternich's *Demagogenverfolgung* of the 1830s. These new relationships confirmed him in his political liberalism, while his continued contact with his father's old circle, whose ideas were grounded in the ideals and aspirations and the unalloyed patriotism of the Swiss common people, protected him from the cosmopolitanism and the extreme radicalism of some members of the group around Follen and Fröbel. He had no sympathy for communism, for example, and thus was not as outraged as they were when the Great Council expelled Wilhelm Weitling from Zürich in 1843.

Keller's liberalism was as simple and uncomplicated as his father's and was based on the assumption that liberalism was a requirement of good citizenship, since civic conscience was a matter of social sympathy, which was most frequently found on the liberal side of the political spectrum. Keller would have had no hesitation about subscribing to Leonhard Frank's later dictum that "left is where the heart is." In his excellent study of the novelist's political ideas, Hans Max Kriesi has suggested that the essence of Keller's own political views are summed up in Frau Regel Amrain's naive view that

> The man who is liberal [*freisinnig*] trusts the good in himself and the world and recognizes manfully that there is nothing that he can do but stand up for it, whereas illiberalism or conservatism is based on faintheartedness and narrow-mindedness. These qualities are hard to reconcile with true manliness. Over a thousand years ago, the time began when men were considered perfect heroes and knights only when they were at the same time perfect Christians, for at that time it was in Christianity that one found humanity and enlightenment. Today one can say that, however brave and resolute one may be, if he finds it impossible to be liberal, he is not a complete man.

During the years when he was a member of the Follen circle, Keller won his spurs as a poet, in 1844 alone writing an impressive number of works that have survived the passage of time and the change of poetic fashion. These included hymns to nature like "The Still of the Night" and "Under the Stars," which show the influence of Lenau and Freiligrath but have their own individual voice, and the sonnets "Nationality" and "Eidgenossenschaft," in which he returned to the theme of his Munich essay, comparing Swiss nationality in the latter poem with a diamond that has evolved over time:

> *Zu unzerstörlich alldurchdrungner Einheit,*
> *Zu ungetrübter, strahlenheller Reinheit,*
> *Gefestigt von unsichtbaren Banden.*

> *[To indestructibly all-pervasive oneness,*
> *To unclouded, gleaming clarity,*
> *Strengthened by invisible bonds.]*

Much of what he wrote was polemical in nature, for he was greatly excited by the confessional differences aroused by the question of the Aargau convents and Luzern's invitation to the Society of Jesus to take over its teaching seminar. Anti-Jesuit verse poured from his pen, some, like the 1844 "In a Swiss Armory," of considerable poetic merit, others, like "The Luzern and Wallis Refugees" and the "Jesuit Song" quoted in an earlier chapter, being distinguished only by their energy and facility in rhymes. That they expressed Keller's deep concern over the threat that militant Catholicism posed for the country he loved, there is, however, no doubt, and the poet was so far carried away by this feeling that he participated in the two free corps expeditions launched against Luzern from Zürich.

Keller was later to regard this part of his life with amused irony, and he not only excluded most of his political verse from collected editions of his poems but, in "Frau Regel Amrain and Her Youngster" in the first series of his Seldwyla stories, questioned whether the free corps activities were not merely a deplorable reversion to the intercantonal violence of the Middle Ages. Even in the days that followed the defeat of the second expedition against Luzern, he seems to have regarded it as a tragic mistake and to have realized that, if a solution to the confessional strife was to be found, it could only be done by the setting of a clear policy and the mobilization of popular will behind it by legally constituted government. The deliberate course of the Zürich government in the crisis that finally led to the Sonderbund war and the resultant creation of the federal state aroused his unqualified enthusiasm, and he wrote in his diary at the end of 1847 that the courage, determination, and patience shown by the liberal leaders during the recent events had helped transform him from "a vague revolutionary and *Freischärler à tout prix*" to an admirer of the political qualities that had given Zürich a position of moral leadership in the movement to create a more perfect union.

Keller's politics in these years were doubtless muddled and inconsistent, but they were at least always inspired by a recognition of his national identity and by a desire to serve his country's best interests as he saw them. In his contemporary Jacob Burckhardt, this sense of civic responsibility was not highly developed.

II

Born in Basel on 25 May 1818, Burckhardt was the fourth of seven children. His father, a descendant of a family that had come to Basel from the southern Schwarzwald in the sixteenth century, was elder and, later, first preacher in the cathedral; his mother's family was also German in origin, a Hans von Schorndorf (her family name) having immigrated from Württemberg in the fifteenth century. She died when her son Jacob was twelve years old, an event that must have had as traumatic effects as Keller's loss of his father and may have contributed to the melancholy cast of Burckhardt's temperament and his sense of the fragility and instability of human affairs. It does not seem, however, to have affected his schoolwork for the worse, and he graduated from the gymnasium in 1836 with an excellent record and enrolled as a student of philosophy in the University of Basel, subsequently changing his mind and going to Neuenburg, where he remained for nine months, acquiring a thorough mastery of the French language and an easy relationship with French culture and thought that was to remain with him for the rest of his life. After his return to Basel in the spring of 1837, he yielded to a request of his father's and took four semesters of theology at the university, but in 1839 he put these studies aside and went to Berlin to pursue the study of political history and the history of art.

That this was to be a turning point in his life is clear from a letter to a friend in January 1840 in which he confessed, "When I had heard the first lectures of Ranke, Droysen, and Boeckh, my eyes opened wide. I realized that, up till now, like the knights with their ladies in *Don Quixote*, I had loved scholarship by hearsay, and now it stood in its gigantic dimensions before me, and I had to cast my eyes down. Now I am firmly resolved to dedicate my life to it, perhaps to the detriment of domestic happiness." From the rich talents in the philosophical faculty of the university, it was Leopold von Ranke whom he chose as his principal professor, working in his seminars and winning his approbation with his first historical essays, on Charles Martell and the famous Archbishop of Cologne, Konrad von Hochstaden. There is no doubt that this apprenticeship was a fruitful one and that it was to Ranke that Burckardt owed his respect for sources and his methodological rigor, but as time passed a certain disenchantment set in, caused by what he considered to be Ranke's excessive emphasis upon political history, deficiencies of character that revealed themselves in a tendency to worldliness and social snobbery, and a habit of distancing himself from his students that led Burckhardt to write to a friend that "one never

knows how one stands with this *Satyrikus*." In the art historian
Franz Kugler he found a more congenial and, in the end, a more
inspiring teacher, and with him he forged a professional tie that
was to outlast the older man's lifetime.

Aside from the intellectual and cultural side of Berlin,
Burckhardt found little in the city to attract him. But he spent
the summer semester of 1841 in Bonn, prefacing it with a journey
down the Rhine, and this experience was overpowering. In April
1841 he wrote to his sister Louise, "I am like Saul, the son of
Kis, who went out to look for asses that had strayed and found
a king's crown. I should like to go down on my knees before this
sacred German earth and thank God that I speak the German
tongue! I owe Germany *everything*: my best teachers have been
German; I was suckled on the motherly breast of German culture
and scholarship; from this earth I shall always derive my best
qualities—and now this people, this marvelous German youth,
and this land, this garden of God! . . . My love my life long—
that is all that I can offer this wonderful country . . . !" This
reaction was not unique, and there had been other young men
before Burckhardt from whom the romantic beauties of the
Rhineland had elicited sentimental outpourings of this kind.
Even so, the surrender was so complete that it cannot simply be
passed over, particularly since it does not stand alone in the
correspondence of these years. In December 1841, Burckhardt
wrote to Gottfried Kinkel, with whom he had become friendly
during his Bonn semester, of "our great, common German fatherland, which I first scorned and rejected, as almost all of my Swiss
fellow countrymen are wont to do." Now that it had drawn
him to its heart, he added, and lavished its riches upon him, he
would spend the rest of his life, "showing the Swiss that they
are Germans."

This was a proposition, of course, that Gottfried Keller, at
roughly the same time, was indignantly repudiating, and it in-
dicates that, at least at this stage of Burckhardt's life, he had
none of the deep consciousness of being Swiss that bound the
future novelist to his country and his home canton. It is significant that, while he was in Berlin, Burckhardt came to avoid his
fellow countryman, whereas Keller, when not painting, sought
fellowship and recreation in the Swiss Society of Munich. In
Keller's *Green Henry* the hero's chosen friends outside the society are a Dane and a Norwegian, like him subjects of small

countries with strong feelings of independence, outsiders who viewed the German scene with interest but detachment, knowing that in the end they were going home. With his talk about the motherly breast of Germany, it is clear enough that Burckhardt did not want to be an outsider, and that going home did not appeal much to him either.

He did return, however, in the fall of 1843, after rounding out his German studies with a month in Paris, but he was not very happy when he did so. After four years in the great world, Basel was, as he wrote Kinkel, unbearable. He was granted the right to lecture at the university, but this oldest of Switzerland's *Hochschulen* had fallen on evil days; student enrollment was falling, and there was talk of having to curtail operations or even shut the institution down, and Burckhardt's prospects were hardly promising. The cultural life of the city did not commend itself to one who had gloried in the museums and theaters of Berlin and Paris. "O Kräwinkel, my fatherland!" Burckhardt sighed, and, again, in a letter to Kinkel in November 1843: "How a city like this goes to the dogs without stimulating elements of life from outside! There are learned people here, but they have really made themselves as hard as stone to foreign influence. It is not good in our times when such a little hole in the corner remains wholly given over to its own individuality. —*Sapienti sat*, or I'll be committing high treason again."

Partly out of a feeling of *noblesse oblige* (his family, after all, was a prominent one), partly out of boredom, partly to be able to earn some money that would facilitate his escape, Burckhardt turned to political journalism, in June 1844 becoming the editor of the *Basler Zeitung*. Ever since 1833, when the attempt of the conservative Basel city government to suppress the liberal movement in the Basel countryside had threatened to embroil the whole Eidgenossenschaft, the political atmosphere in Basel had been tense, with constant rumors of new conspiracies and *Putsches*. Burckhardt had never shown any interest in politics and, shortly after his return from abroad, had written to Kinkel, "I scorn all parties because I know them all." Now, however, he told his Bonn friend that he had taken on the editorial function "principally in order gradually to kill off the contemptible sympathy that reigns here for all absolutism (for example, the Russian) and at the same time to take a stand against the bawling radicalism [*Brüllradikalismus*] of the Swiss, the latter being ex-

actly as disgusting to me as the former." From the start he seems
to have been more interested in the second of these tasks than
in the first, and in any case he soon discovered that it was harder
to educate reactionaries than he had imagined. On the other
hand, when he decided that the true function of his paper was
"to oppose the false impure liberal party in behalf of the impulses
of the population itself," he found that he was cheered on most
enthusiastically by supporters of the Jesuits, which offended his
religious prejudices. It became harder and harder for him to de-
lineate a coherent position for the paper, and as the *Freischar-
enzeit* began he gave up the effort.

A month after the second free corps assault upon Luzern,
Burckhardt announced that the emotional atmosphere of Switzerland had become so frightful and brutal that he had made up
his mind to expatriate himself as soon as possible, and his letters
for the next year were filled with premonitions of impending
disaster and mob rule. His friends in Germany, he wrote, thought
of agitation in the abstract, but he had looked into "its wild and
drunken eyes"; two-thirds of the prisoners in Luzern, he added,
were "a rabble that one would not want to meet in the woods
of an evening if one were alone." Nor was what happened in
Luzern the end of the story, for the leaders of the "mobile anarchy" clearly intended to carry their violence from canton to
canton until all public order had been destroyed. What one was
witnessing was a general process of disintegration rather than a
disputed cause in which one could engage oneself.

> How gladly would one join in a struggle that was sanctioned
> by clear federal law and was for a great national interest. But
> we are a hodgepodge of fragments of three nations; every-
> thing is patched together *a priori*; what is there to inspire
> one about that? It is dreadful!

In the circumstances, what was a peace-loving man to do but
flee a situation in which the everlasting agitation and the per-
nicious and all-pervasive spirit of party left no room for privacy
and made work impossible? "Criticize me in God's name as a
bad citizen!" he wrote to his friend Eduard Schauenburg, "but I
have given up all political activity forever. I can retire with
decency. I have never had a special, personal complaint. The
whole business is alien to me." And, cheered by the prospect of

imminent departure, he wrote to another friend in February 1846, "O my dear fellow, the cause of freedom and the state have not lost much in me. With people like me, one constructs no state at all."

Two months later he was receiving his mail at the Café Greco in the Via Condotti. In view of the passionate nature of his earlier professions of love of Germany, it may seem surprising that he sought his escape not there but in Italy, but Fritz Kaphahn is probably correct in suggesting that his decision was also an expression of his abhorrence of politics. What was happening in Switzerland, he must have sensed, would soon affect the German states too. North of the Alps the spirit of the times was increasingly one of change and impermanence, as nationalities struggled for self-expression and individuals sought after power and money, and human affairs would for a long time be dominated by the shifting tides of political fortune. But Burckhardt scorned the transitory and was little interested in the new; he was "tired of modernity," he wrote to Hermann Schauenburg, and wanted to "escape them all, the radicals, the communists, the industrialists, the overeducated, the fastidious, the imitative and the abstract, the absolutists, the philosophers, the sophists, the state fanatics, the idealists, the -ists and -ers of every kind." He was searching for the permanent, the perennial, the eternal. In turning his face toward Rome, he was abandoning politics for history.

III

Keller would have reacted to the views of his Basel compatriot, had he known of them, with irritation and contempt. To the intimations of change that could be sensed all across the continent in 1847 and 1848, he responded with enthusiasm, and after the fall of Louis Philippe and Guizot in February 1848 he went daily to the reading room of the Zürich Museum to learn of the progress of Europe's liberation from absolutism and militarism. He did not believe that victory would be sudden or without setbacks, but the success of liberalism in Switzerland encouraged him to think that its triumph elsewhere was inevitable—"In two years we shall be in 1850. What all can not be ripe by then and ready for the great turning in our histories!"—if men of goodwill did what they could to advance the cause. In his *Dream Book* he wrote in May 1848, "My heart trembles with joy when I think that I am a part of this time. . . . Woe to anyone who does not tie his own fate to that of the public community, for he will not only find no peace, but in addition will lose his foothold and be delivered to the scorn of the people, like a weed that is trampled on the way. The great throngs of the indifferent ones and those without conviction must be dissolved. . . . No, there must be no private persons anymore!" This was, of course, more a reflection of attitude than a principle of action, for Keller's days as an active revolutionary were behind him. But it was his deeply held belief that the individual could not separate himself from the problems and aspirations of the society to which he belonged, and as he became a professional writer this was a theme that occurred frequently in his works.

It was some time before the world was to know anything of this, for Keller's recognition of his calling came slowly. In the fall of 1848—probably at the urging of Alfred Escher, in whose chancery Keller had worked for a time as a volunteer and who had concluded that he had talents worth nurturing—the Zürich Great Council had given Keller financial support for two semesters of study at the University of Heidelberg. It was during his sojourn there that he witnessed the Prussian defeat of the revolutionary forces of the Palatinate and Baden on the Neckar, an event that put an end to the bright hopes of March 1848 and which he commemorated in two moving poems, "Four Seasons" and "The Boatsman on the Neckar." It was in Heidelberg also that he had his encounter with Ludwig Feuerbach, whose influence destroyed what was left of his allegiance to formal Christianity and probably contributed to the melancholy realism that was to pervade his fictional work.

That work began to emerge slowly when he went on from Heidelberg to Berlin, a transfer, he assured his friend Freiligrath, that had nothing to do with politics. It was not his intention to imitate his namesake Ludwig Keller, who, after the overthrow of September 1839, had foresworn his radical politics, gone to the Prussian capital, and become one of the supports of Frederick William IV's throne. On the contrary, it was the fame of Berlin's theater that attracted him, for he hoped now to make himself a dramatist. But, although his Zürich sponsors were very patient, allowing the philologist Ferdinand Hitzig to persuade them to renew his grant with very little to justify their doing so, nothing came of this ambition either, and at long last he turned to storytelling, significantly to a cycle of novellas about the social mores and the ambitions and contentions of the inhabitants of an imaginary but archetypical Swiss community and an autobiographical novel about the education in social responsibility of a failed artist. The latter work was *Green Henry*, the first volume of which appeared in 1853; the former was *The People of Seldwyla*, the first volume of which saw publication a year after his return to Zürich in 1855.

Meanwhile, Burckhardt's alienation from politics seemed, if anything, to deepen. His stay in Italy was shorter than he had expected (although long enough to give a decisive direction to his later work), for a month after his arrival in Rome he received a letter from Franz Kugler asking him to accept a position in the Berlin Academy of Art and to take responsibility for the preparation of the second edition of Kugler's *Handbook of Art History* and his *History of Painting*. In view of the professional recognition that this would bring, Burckhardt found it impossible to decline the invitation, and after six months of furious work in Italian museums and galleries, he went to Berlin in September 1846 and remained there for a year. It was a time of mounting political excitement, but its principal effect upon Burckhardt's life was to bring the cooling and, in the end, the termination of most of the friendships that he had made during his first trip to Germany. His old friends were, almost to a man, supporters of liberal revolution, which he viewed with mounting apprehension, and, as was to be true throughout his life, he could not tolerate such differences of principle for long. Not even his friendship with Gottfried Kinkel survived. As early as December 1846 he was writing to Kinkel, with a brutal forthrightness that was in sharp contrast to the intimate *Schwärmerei* of their earlier correspondence, to say that a recently published revolutionary poem of his, which he described in scathing terms as both silly and boastful, had virtually ended the possibility of his getting an appointment in Berlin for which Burckhardt had supported him, and from that time on their relations deteriorated steadily until they lapsed into silence. In August 1848, Burckhardt wrote a mutual friend that Kinkel was bound to come to a bad end, since he lacked the balance and reflectiveness that even a republican needed, and in September 1849, after Kinkel had been captured by the Prussians during the collapse of the Badenese revolution and sentenced to life imprisonment in Moabit, Burckhardt, with no apparent sympathy, wrote to the same correspondent, "Kinkel's fate I have been expecting since 1847; one couldn't talk with him anymore; . . . sooner or later he had to run his head, if not into this wall, then into another."

Burckhardt returned to Rome in September 1847, but his sense of impending disaster prevented this second sojourn from being as idyllic as the first and, although he worked energetically, he was not sorry to return home in May, when the reverberations of the events in Paris and Vienna began to be felt throughout the peninsula. It is perhaps not surprising that the principal product of the five years that he now spent in his native city, the brilliant volume of cultural history called *The Age of Constantine the Great*, should have been colored by his deep pessimism about his own society. In his description of the crisis that confronted the Roman Empire in the third century, and of the fanaticism and sectarianism, the credulousness of the upper classes and the mass violence that characterized it, it is not difficult to read references to the crisis that confronted bourgeois society and established authority in his own time. That he felt the connection himself is indicated by his letter to Hermann Schauenburg in September 1849, at about the time he had committed himself to the project, in which he wrote, "For the future I have absolutely no hopes. It is possible that we will be granted a couple of halfway tolerable decades, genre Roman imperial times."

He was no happier in Basel now than he had been in 1845, and his discontent was deepened by an unsuccessful love affair that found some reflection in two slim volumes of valedictory verse, *Holidays, an Autumn Miscellany* (1849) and, in the local dialect, *A Handful of Songs [E Hampfeli Lieder]* (1853), which also marked the end of his poetic ambitions. He returned to Italy for the studies that produced, in 1854, the first of his works in the history of art, the brilliant *Cicerone*, which Gottfried Keller was later to pronounce a masterpiece and to use as a means of accompanying his friends in spirit, if not in person, when they traveled in Italy. After that, it was believed, at least by his friends, that he would receive the chair in history at Basel as soon as the incumbent, who was ill, retired, but Burckhardt seems to have received no assurances on this score from the authorities, and it was probably his growing resentment over this lack of official recognition that led him to apply for the professorship in art history at the new Polytechnicum in Zurich. His candidacy won immediate approval, and he moved to the city on the Limmat for the beginning of the winter semester of 1855.

IV

Compared with the somnolence of his native city, Zürich was a beehive of activity, but Burckhardt remained as detached as possible from its social and cultural whirl, burying himself, when he was not lecturing, in the local libraries' rich holdings on Italian literature in the fifteenth and sixteenth centuries. He had come to Zürich, he wrote to Paul Heyse, because he felt that he could be virtually incognito there and have an opportunity, as Goethe once said, to " 'roll up [his] sleeves, spit happily in [his] hands,' and undertake something worthwhile." This he certainly accomplished, for *The Civilization of the Italian Renaissance*, although not published until 1860, was essentially a product of his Zürich years. On the other hand, he was far from being solitary or unapproachable. He was a member of the Antiquarian Society and spoke frequently before that body, and in the prestigious Rathaus Lectures he gave highly regarded lectures on the character of Queen Agnes of Hungary and on the cloister church of St. Troud. He had a few close friends, some of whom he met at the guildhouse Schmieden in the Marktgasse in the evenings, and it may have been a sign that his conservative prejudices were becoming less intransigent that these were members of the exile community whose political views were hardly conformable to his own. He was, to be sure, discriminating about this: he had little sympathy for the three Dresden exiles, Wagner, Köchly, and Semper, and saw little of them, and with his chosen friends De Sanctis, Dufraisse, and De Boni, he seems to have avoided politics. He was drawn to De Sanctis by the Neapolitan's intimate knowledge of the Italian literature of the thirteenth century, and from his animated discussions of Dante, Petrarch, and Poliziano he learned much that influenced his own work before De Sanctis's veneration of Hegel (whom Burckhardt detested) and his willingness to sacrifice his walks with Burckhardt to the more exciting task of giving Italian lessons to Mathilde Wesendonck brought their intimacy to an end. His friendship with Marc Dufraisse, a member of the extreme left of the French National Assembly who had been expelled after Louis Napoleon's *coup d'état*, and with Emma Herwegh's friend Filippo de Boni was based on the fact that both combined sympathetic personalities with scholarly gifts of the first order, Dufraisse later becoming a distinguished legal scholar and De Boni having been the editor of Gioberti's *Del primato morale e civile degli Italiani*, the theme of which accorded with one of the major theses of Burckhardt's *Civilization*.

Two months after Burckhardt began his teaching duties, Gottfried Keller came back to Zürich from his long absence in Berlin, and it was not long before the two men met, probably at the guildhouse Schmieden, for one of Keller's letters talks of "drinking a *Schöppchen* now and then in the evening" with Friedrich Theodor Vischer, the philologist Ferdinand Hitzig, Burckhardt, and, less frequently, Gottfried Semper. Despite a sadly not untypical example of Keller's more berserk tendencies at one of these gatherings—during the discussion of the work of a writer whom he detested he became so enraged that he smashed all the china and had to be taken home—the two men were drawn together in mutual esteem, and Keller's name was, with that of Filippo De Boni, on the small list of friends for whom Burckhardt had free tickets set aside for the last of his Rathaus lectures.

What might have become a firm friendship came to an end in 1858, when Burckhardt went back to Basel. His scholarly reputation was well established, he felt that it was now time to put an end to his years of wandering, and he finally accepted the professorship in history that he had in effect turned down in 1855. He was to hold it for thirty-five years, combining it after 1874 with the professorship of art history, and during that long period he stoutly resisted invitations to accept chairs in other universities or even to give lectures at them. It would be an exaggeration to describe this as a reconciliation with his native city or a belated recognition of its charms. He still detested its politics, which he said was dominated by the doctinaire radicalism of "MM. Homais and their consorts" and the demagogery of self-appointed leaders of the masses, and he laughed helplessly over its cultural backwardness, writing to Paul Heyse, with respect to its low theatrical standards, that "our good people are indifferent to such tomfoolery. Only scandal attracts attention." And yet, in his view, things were no better elsewhere, for the crisis of the age was a general one, and that being so there was some advantage to living in a small place. "The little state exists," he was to write in his reflections on history, "so that there is a spot on the globe where the greatest possible quota of state subjects are citizens in the full sense." Or, in Karl Schmid's interpretation of this cryptic statement, the small state is an Archimedean point outside the world of great affairs where (the phrase is Burckhardt's from a letter to Eduard Schauenburg in December 1869) "every breath can find its employment."

What this involved for Burckhardt was the conscious dedication of all his energies not to Basel as such but to its university. "I for my person," he wrote in November 1876, "have long since simplified my field of vision in such a way that I bring every question absolutely into connection with the University of Basel and always say only: Does this or that serve it? Or does it not?" On the other hand, the university was not, in any sense, an ivory tower but an institution whose gates were open to the world. In contrast to the generality of European universities, the University of Basel, whose financial resources did not allow it to compete with its greater rivals or to buy the scientific equipment and set up the laboratories that would have made that possible, was less a center for scholarship and professional training than a *Bildungsuniversität*, a center of humanistic studies, which existed primarily to form and cultivate character. To Burckhardt, who believed that the age needed less specialized knowledge and more perspective and balanced judgment, the qualities that humane studies—and particularly history, with the vicarious experience that was its stock in trade—provided, this was profoundly attractive, and so was the freedom that the university granted him. He no longer was expected to go on publishing works of scholarship or to train professional historians. He could do what he wanted to do, which was to teach history, and he could do so in such a way that his students grew used to viewing their world in historical terms and that each of them, as he once said, "could make that part of the past that appealed particularly to him his own, quite independently, and could find pleasure in doing so."

This is what Burckhardt did for the rest of his life. Nor did he confine his teaching to university classrooms. On the contrary, he wrote to Eduard Schauenburg in December 1869:

> I have already given two evening lectures *coram publico* this winter, and I still have three Saturdays before me, the 4th, the 11th, and the 18th. It is a kind of duty of honor for those of us teachers who were born in Basel to preach before great mixed auditoriums. . . . Every winter we guarantee the public a great cycle of 38 to 40 "popular lectures" and one of fourteen of a somewhat higher level aimed at the still finer public. In addition, there flourish a number of full courses, secular and religious, etc.—in short, I am convinced that there could be a lecture here every evening in the winter and it would find lots of hearers. The Society of Young Merchants alone (where I also have commitments for two evenings and where I am an honorary member) has an educational program like a respectable institute.

The enthusiasm with which Burckhardt wrote of these activities was in sharp contrast to the sourness of his comments about Basel in his letters in the 1840s, and the evidence of cheerfully accepted social responsibility was undeniable. It was, however, a social responsibility that was entirely bereft of political content and was fastidious, intellectual, and limited in its reach to the educated middle class rather than to the whole community. It is not easy to see in it a truly civic conscience of the kind exemplified by Gottfried Keller.

Keller's future, after his return from Berlin in December 1855, was still uncertain, for he had discouraged his friends from putting his name forward for a professorship in the Polytechnic Institute and had therefore no fixed position or income. Despite the recognition that the publication of his novel had brought him, its four volumes did not find many buyers, and in 1879, when he began the writing of its second and definitive version, Keller is said to have heated his study by burning copies of the first edition. The first series of novellas called *The People of Seldwyla* appeared during the first year after his return, but it sold no more briskly, and the living standard in the house in the Gemeindegasse, where Keller lived with his mother and his sister, could be described as one of genteel poverty. It was not the happiest period in Keller's life, despite the recognition accorded him. He was deeply in debt, drinking too much, and living a life described by Ernst Bächtold, his friend and first biographer, as verging on hopeless dissipation.

Yet, even in this time of frustration, he spent much of his time thinking about the changes that had been taking place in Switzerland and Zürich during the years of his absence, worrying over signs of weakness or retrogression, studying the political issues of the day, and speaking out, both in occasional articles and poems and *Festreden* and in his fictional work, as a preceptor of his people. For this, as he once wrote to his friend Berthold Auerbach, was the duty of the writer. He had "to explain not only the past but the present too, and to strengthen and make more beautiful the seeds of the future, so that the people can still believe, yes, that's the way we are, and that's the way it should be! . . . In the same way that one holds up beautiful pictures before expectant mothers, one must always show the national ground stock, which is pregnant all the time, something better than it already is, and for that purpose one can also criticize it all the more boldly when it needs it."

Keller was particularly interested in the ways in which established folk festivals could be used to promote national integration. He was an enthusiastic participant in the ceremonies attendant upon the *Schützenfesten* and singing competitions, often contributing dedicatory odes or addresses, as he did in the case of the national song festival in Zürich in 1858 and the Schiller Festival of 1859 in Bern, where his prologue was much admired. In his essay "At the Mythenstein," which was written to commemorate the Forest Cantons' dedication of a monument to Friedrich Schiller at Wilhelm Tell's birthplace, he discussed the possibility of combining popular theater with such festivals, folk dramas that might portray, for example, "all kinds of false patriotism, the self-centered, the discontented, the envious, the affected, the crafty, the sentimental, the narrow-minded, the profit-seeking, etc., in recognizable types taken from life . . . presided over by a counterfeit Helvetia enthroned in a colossal franc piece." The spoken text would play upon actual circumstances and events, and in the end the true Helvetia, "a tall, handsome maid in a purple robe, with powerfully blowing Walküre hair and her eyes shaded by the crown of alpine roses on her head," would come to judge the other characters in the drama for their faults and failures and take into her charge their children, a happy throng of boys and girls representing the twenty-two cantons. The choice of theme and treatment for such performances would have to be left to "local popular genius," to the "original fantasy that never dies out in the masses of people," but the result might be an art form, inspired by a "national aesthetics," that would sustain and strengthen the achievement of 1848.

In politics Keller was a stern critic of both private and governmental conduct. He was particularly offended by the tendency of his fellow citizens to assume that, with the passing of the crisis years, they were absolved from any real participation in state affairs and could rely upon the government to protect their interests. Representative government was, in his eyes, a poor substitute for direct democracy, but since modern conditions made the latter impractical, it was essential not only that the individual citizen exercise his franchise but that he do so with care and discrimination. In "Frau Regel Amrain and her Youngster," Fritz is reluctant to waste time and incur the ridicule of his fellow Seldwylers by sitting around in the church waiting for his time to cast his ballot, and he protests that the state is not going to come to a halt simply because one or more of its subjects fails to turn up at the urns. His mother will have none of this argument and, expressing Keller's own stern conviction, says to him:

> What? You want to give the impression of having a free state and are too lazy to sacrifice half a day once in four years to show a little attention and to express your satisfaction or dissatisfaction with the government that you contractually installed? Don't tell me that you would always be there when it was needed! Anyone who is only there when it amuses him and tickles his vanity will be absent one time and have his nose twisted precisely when he least expects it.

How the franchise should be exercised was another question, and in 1860, Keller was the principal drafter of a manifesto calling upon his fellow citizens to show more care in selecting their national representation, making the point that the canton of Zürich could not expect to put a dozen Washingtons and Franklins in the federal assembly but it could at least avoid sending people to Bern who went there as if they were tourists or who were seeking personal profit or whose attitude when decisions were needed would be *"Herr Jesis, was wend er au machen!"*

By the beginning of the 1860s, Keller's politics were becoming increasingly oppositional. In February 1861, in the pages of the *Zürcher Intelligenzblatt*, he attacked Alfred Escher's speech on the Savoy affair at the opening of the session of the Great Council for having, in references to Switzerland's policy of neutrality, dwelt excessively upon the federal state's military weakness, saying that this could only weaken resolution at home and encourage ambitions abroad, and in the months that followed he wrote a series of articles in the same paper in which he found fault with undemocratic attitudes in the Great Council, pointed out deficiencies in existing factory regulations, and criticized other policies of the liberal government. It came then as a considerable surprise to most political observers when the government announced in September 1861 that he had been elected as *Staatsschreiber*, or cantonal clerk.

This at long last resolved the novelist's financial problems, and there is no doubt that this was one of the considerations that led him to put his name forward, although it was probably no stronger than his sense of obligation to the state for its support during his formative years. But, whatever his motives, there is no question of the devotion and efficiency that he brought to the position, which were, indeed, so impressive that the *Zürcherische Freitagszeitung*, which had criticized the appointment vigorously when it was announced, admitted a few weeks later that it had been wrong, and that Keller had made impressive progress in mastering the problems of his job, and that, if he continued as he had begun, he would be one of the most energetic *Staatsschreiber* in Zürich's history.

Energy was certainly a requirement of the position. Keller was *ex officio* secretary of the Governing Council and its office of political affairs and was supervisor of the state chancery and its finances; he was charged with keeping the Council's minutes and drafting communications to the Federal Council and other cantonal governments; after 1862, when he was made second secretary of the Great Council, he had to countersign many of its laws and communications; he was a member of several parliamentary commissions, like the railroad commissions for the Zürich-Zug-Luzern and the Bülach-Regensberg lines, and all requests for passports for domestic and foreign travel, residence certificates, patents, permissions to engage in certain occupations, claims to water rights and the like came to him personally for his approval and signature—all of this, it should be noted, without any provision for the delegation even of the least important tasks to other agencies and without the help of a regular staff. In addition, unless one of the seven Governing Councillors took the task from his shoulders, it was his duty to write the annual "Prayer Day Address" (*Bettagsmandat*), an allocution to the people that called upon them to give thanks for successful harvests or for escape from natural disasters and other dangers, registered the year's successes and failures, and exhorted the citizenry to fulfill their duties and to love God and their country. Keller wrote five of these, for the years 1862, 1863, 1867, 1871, and 1872, all but the first of which were approved and published. The first, which offended by its unusual length and failure to conform in other respects with established practice, is perhaps the most interesting, with its reference to the civil war raging in America and the charge that this dreadful conflict had its origins in the corrosive effects of materialism and greed and with its praise of the Great Council's recent law abolishing the civil disabilities of the Jews, which now, if the Jews were to begin a new life as citizens, must, Keller wrote, be validated by the sympathy and assistance of the Christian population. "What the persecution and condemnation of ages could not bring to pass, love will accomplish."

During the fifteen years in which Keller served as *Staatsschreiber*, his duties left little time for other activities, and even his private correspondence (and he was one of the most prolific and amusing letter writers of the age) was reduced to a trickle. As for literary production, it was limited to the charming *Seven Legends*, which had been drafted in Berlin, the second sequence of Seldwyla stories, and a large number of songs and patriotic verse for public occasions that won him popular acclaim and made him a kind of unofficial national poet laureate but were essentially trivial. For a great artist this was a heavy price to pay for civic conscience. It was not until after Keller's retirement in 1876 that he was able to resume writing in a systematic way, completing the two volumes of his *Züricher Novellen*, the cycle of connected stories called *The Epigram*, the novel *Martin Salander*, and the revision of *Green Henry* before his death in 1890.

V

It is probably true that of all of Keller's works the ones with the greatest popular appeal were the Seldwyla stories and the patriotic "Little Banner of the Seven Upright Ones" from the *Züricher Novellen*. It was *Green Henry*, however, that won him recognition far beyond the confines of his own country and led Nietzsche to call him "the only living German writer." Keller tells us in his autobiographical sketch that he conceived the work in 1842 as "a sad little novel about the wreckage of a young artist's career in which mother and son are destroyed," but in the writing it grew far beyond those modest dimensions, largely because of the very exuberance of Keller's descriptive powers, his incalculable humor, which, as Walter Benjamin once wrote, did not manifest itself as "a golden polish on the surface" but rumbled about in the deep caverns that lay beneath the narrative and expressed itself in the "bulgy arabesques" of Keller's style, and, not least of all, his incomparable gift of creating (to quote one of his poems) "sweet figures of women such as this bitter earth will not sustain." In our present context, however, it must be noted that *Green Henry* is also a novel about the growth of a civic conscience.

Like *Wilhelm Meister's Apprenticeship*, by which it was obviously influenced and with which it has some striking formal similarities, *Green Henry* is a novel of education. It tells the story of how a young man who feels that he was robbed of his youth by misfortune and injustice, and who shirks his responsibilities to family and community in order to indulge his fantasies, is slowly and painfully brought to recognize the duties of citizenship. In the first version of the novel the educational process fails and the young man dies. In the second it succeeds, not least of all because the hero is finally convinced, during his stay in Dortchen Schönfund's castle (which plays the same role in the story as the Turmgesellschaft does in *Wilhelm Meister*), that individual happiness is to be found only in living and working with others, and begins systematically to train himself for the public service. His fortunes and his confidence restored by his stay in the castle, he goes home with love and hope in the future, crossing the border just at the moment when the metamorphosis of a five-hundred-year-old Confederation into a Federal State terminated an organic process that in its energy and diversity caused the smallness of the country to be forgotten, since nothing is in itself small and nothing is large, and a beehive rich in cells, buzzing and well-armed, is often of more significance than an enormous heap of sand.

To the public service of this new state he henceforth devotes his full energies.

Keller has been accused, notably by Adolf Muschg in his remarkable biographical study of the novelist, of having had an idealized view of his fatherland, springing in part from his strong sense of obligation to it and from his unwillingness to admit that the commonwealth was being progressively divided, and the values of its citizens systematically eroded, by the burgeoning power of capitalism. This is undoubtedly true, although, as Muschg also points out, the writer Keller always had a sharper eye than Keller the citizen. He did not share the oversimplified view of Jacob Burckhardt, who, as Kaphahn has pointed out, saw the world as being increasingly dominated by a ruthless, self-seeking, unscrupulous capitalism and an ever more pervasive false democracy, both typified in the influence of the Jews. Nevertheless, the social and political threat posed by capitalism was never far from his mind in his later years. In "The Little Banner of the Seven Upright Ones," one of the characters says, "Luckily there are no terribly rich people among us; wealth is fairly enough divided. But just let fellows with many millions appear, who have political ambitions, and you'll see what mischief they'll get up to!" and, in his nightmares in Munich, Green Henry's mind is troubled by the thought that national identity may really boil down to the question of who has money and who has not. Both "The Lost Laugh," the last of the Seldwyla stories, and *Martin Salander* show a deep pessimism with respect to the ability of democratic values in general, and freedom in particular, to withstand the encroachment of materialism, although the problem does not receive the systematic treatment it deserves.

This was in part due to the waning of Keller's powers, but more perhaps to the persistence of his faith in his people and his country. In his brilliant analysis of the *Züricher Novellen*, Gerhard Kaiser has pointed out that these novellas—which deal successively with the emergence of the *Stadtbürger* in feudal times ("Hadlaub"), the end of the knightly family of the Manesse ("The Fool on Manegg"), the old regime of the eighteenth century in Zürich ("The Landvogt of Greifensee"), the liberal period after 1848 ("The Little Banner of the Seven Upright Ones"), and the time of Zwingli and the Anabaptists ("Ursula")—not only provide a "phenomenology of the citizen" but present a theory of history based upon reformation and renewal, "a sequence of successful bridgings between the ages, in which the old is renewed and the new is tied to the old." But present also in all the stories, although often below the surface of the narrative, is the theme of the people as the prime source of historical vitality, and it was in the endurance and fortitude and common good sense of his fellow countrymen that Keller in the end found the answer to his own nagging doubts about his country's future.

This too was the final message of *Green Henry*, whose hero, now established as the chief administrator of a political district, reflects upon what he has learned from the problems and the people he has encountered in the course of his work and concludes:

> I saw how in my beloved Republic there were people who made this word into an empty phrase and carried it about with them just as wenches going to the fair might carry a small basket on their arm. Others regarded the ideas Republic, Freedom, and Fatherland as three goats which they milked continually, in order to make all kinds of little goats-milk cheeses, while using the words sanctimoniously, exactly like the Pharisees and Tartuffes. Others again, the slaves of their own passions, scented everywhere nothing but servitude and treason, like a poor dog whose nose had been smeared with whey cheese and who consequently thinks that the whole world is made of it. Even this scenting of a state of bondage had a certain small current value, but patriotic self-praise was always above it. The whole thing was a pernicious mildew with the power to destroy a community if it grows too luxuriantly and densely; yet the main body of the people was in a healthy condition, and as soon as it bestirred itself in earnest, the mildew of itself fell away in dust.

Chapter 10

GELD UND GEIST: THE CRISIS OF LIBERALISM

♦

One of the greatest dangers . . . of democracy, as of all other forms of government, lies in the sinister interest of the holders of power: it is the danger of class legislation; of government intended for (whether really affecting it or not) the immediate benefit of the dominant class, to the lasting detriment of the whole. And one of the most important questions demanding consideration, in determining the best constitution of a representative government, is how to provide efficacious securities against this evil.
—JOHN STUART MILL, Representative Government (1861)

Meinen Sie Zürich zum Beispiel
sei eine tiefere Stadt,
wo man Wunder und Weihen
immer als Inhalt hat?
—GOTTFRIED BENN, "Reisen"
(1950)

Alfred Escher

In the last third of the nineteenth century, the great age of liberal ascendancy in European politics came to an end, and in country after country liberal parties began a decline that was to be all but terminal. In England, where William Schenk Gilbert claimed in 1882, in his musical play *Iolanthe*, that Nature had happily contrived that every second child born into the world should be a liberal, all but nine of the century's last twenty-five years were, in fact, years of conservative government, and, although the liberals seemed to recover sharply in the last years before the Great War, they did not survive that conflict as a significant political force. Nor was their plight unique. In 1882 the German National Liberal Party, which had been the strongest in the Reichstag in 1874, with 155 seats, had managed to retain only 47 of them; in Austria the strong liberal parliamentary presence of the seventies had passed never to return; in Belgium the only thing that kept the once dominant Liberal Party from being eclipsed by stronger movements on the right and left was the fact that the constitution provided for proportional representation, and other similar cases might be cited.

The immediate causes of this dramatic change in the fortunes of liberalism varied from case to case, but it is possible to discern general tendencies that contributed to it. Historically, liberalism was the amalgam of beliefs developed by the middle classes as they made their way to a position of political influence in society; it was a philosophy that was determined by the proud individualism of those classes and the intensity of their opposition to all forms of institutional and legal restriction, and, from the period of the French Revolution onward, it was characterized—as Guido De Ruggiero once pointed out in a brilliant but now sadly neglected history of the movement—"by a profound consciousness of the universality of their social and political function." Thus, when Sieyès said that the Third Estate was the nation, what he meant was that its demands were in the interest of all classes and would bring to all of them guarantees of human rights and law and justice and opportunities to improve their material lot. Indeed, when liberalism was at its height, its claim to universality was not only validated by the benefits it brought to society as a whole but was, for the liberal parties, their principal source of vitality, allowing them to attract talents from above and below their social nucleus and to retain the support of significant sections of other classes. This was not a situation that was destined to last. The tumultuous economic development of the second half of the nineteenth century, and the growth on the one hand of trusts, monopolies, and cartels and on the other of a large industrial proletariat, challenged both the coherence of the liberal philosophy and its relevance to the new problems of the age, and the increasing polarization of society eroded the internal homogeneity of liberal organizations. New parties emerged to appeal to the special interests, ambitions, and resentments of groups on the left and right of the political spectrum, using for their purposes arguments based on ideology rather than the reasoned discourse that had been the hallmark of classical liberalism, and in the dawning age of mass politics the precipitous fall of liberal fortunes came remorselessly on.

To this decline Swiss liberalism was not entirely immune. The first signs of what was to be a major crisis of legitimacy came in the early 1860s, and the end of that decade saw the expulsion of the liberals from their principal cantonal strongholds and a sharp curtailment of their strength in the federal government. The constitutional consequences of this were profound and have determined the political and institutional history of Switzerland ever since. On the other hand, the Swiss liberal parties showed considerably more resilience than their sister parties in other lands, and their eclipse was neither final nor protracted. This was one of the principal reasons why the polarization of politics that occurred in other countries, the sharp confrontation of extremist parties of the left and the right with no strong middle parties to blunt and mediate their antagonism, did not take place in Switzerland.

For contemporaries the canton of Zürich provided the most dramatic example of liberalism's crisis of legitimacy, for it was there that the powerful party of Alfred Escher was brought down. This was the result of no single cause, although contemporaries tended to think predominantly in terms of personality and to talk about the price of *hubris*, but of a complex web of circumstances and problems that the liberals proved unable to master.

I

After the rich excitement of the period of the founding of the federal state and the general gratification that attended the rapid industrial development of the decade that followed, a condition of discontent settled over Zürich's life and politics in the 1860s. The economic boom had not benefited all sections of the population equally, and the high profits that were available from investment in railroads and industrial enterprises tended to deprive agriculture of credit, a fact that became more painful in the sixties when grain prices fell precipitously and interest rates and the price of land increased. Zürich farmers had to worry through what were remembered for a long time as the seven bad years. Nor were all sectors of industry in a happier state, for the Civil War in America deprived the overextended silk industry of an important market while denying to the cotton industry its principal source of raw materials. The export of silks, which had increased yearly from 1859 to 1863, fell steeply thereafter and showed no sign of recovery until the beginning of the seventies; the cotton industry was affected by wild fluctuations in the price of raw materials that continued even after the end of the war in America, and there were stoppages and failures that found reflection in unemployment and deprivation.

Not entirely justly, these things were blamed by those who suffered from them upon the wielders of political power and fed a gathering tide of dissatisfaction with the system of representative government that had prevailed since the acceptance of the cantonal constitution of 1848 and with the liberal party that was its beneficiary. There was no doubt that that party had, according to its lights, governed Zürich well. It had scrupulously protected the individual rights of its citizens and the freedom of the cantonal press; it had provided and supported an educational system that was as good as any in Switzerland; it had made Zürich the industrial center of the country and expanded economic opportunity in general. But, as Eduard Fueter once wrote, "this regime had gradually become almost a closed coterie." Because the liberal government possessed powers of cooptation, through the use of indirect elections for some of the seats in the Great Council, and because it appointed most of the officials, including the judges, it effectively excluded the old city aristocracy (the so-called *Zöpfe*) and the great mass of those people in city and countryside who had neither property nor higher education from active participation in the administration of cantonal affairs. During the term of the Great Council the popular electorate was, indeed, not consulted at all, with the result that in quiet times they lost interest in politics, so that their percentage of electoral participation fell below 20 percent.

This situation had not gone without criticism, and, indeed, in the early 1850s it had been targeted for reform by one of the most interesting political personalities of the liberal period. This was Johann Jakob Treichler, the son of a peasant family that had been settled in the highlands at Richterwil for three hundred years, who had come to Zürich to seek fortune and fame in the year 1838. Treichler is a prime example of liberalism's ability to recruit talent from the unprivileged classes, as well as to convert antagonists into friends, for, although he began his political career on the extreme left wing, as a writer for Julius Fröbel's journal, *Das Litterarische Comptoir*, and a friend of Wilhelm Weitling and Mikhail Bakunin in the forties and as a self-styled socialist editor and politician and founder of a remarkably successful consumers cooperative in the fifties, he ended it, not least of all because of the influence of Alfred Escher, as a member of the Governing Council and, by 1867, as President of the Government, or, to use the older terminology, cantonal *Bürgermeister*. As a young radical Treichler had been an incisive critic of the representative system, arguing that it effectively excluded the lower classes from the political process and neglected their interests, and in 1851 his organ, *Das Neue Schweizerische Volksblatt*, issued a nineteen-point program that called for the immediate introduction of such measures of direct democracy as popular referendum and initiative and the people's right to amend the constitution at any time.

It is indicative of the seriousness with which the governing party regarded such proposals that Alfred Escher urged his associate Jakob Dubs to answer them. The son of a publican in

Affoltern, Dubs had studied law in Bern, Heidelberg, and Zürich and had early demonstrated natural gifts of persuasiveness and political intuitiveness that were to bring him to the highest levels of cantonal and federal government, and his dedication to liberal principles and programs was to be enshrined in the educational reform bill of 1859, of which he was the chief author. But Dubs was no believer in direct democracy, and when he responded to Treichler's program in the columns of the Winthertur *Landbote*, his argument was much the same as that used by Robert Lowe in the British House of Commons in 1866 when he rejected the "leap in the dark," the proposed widening of the suffrage to include the unpropertied classes. Dubs argued that to permit people who were not well versed in the law and—more important—did not have the sense of responsibility that came with the possession of property to reject the considered judgments of men with a broad view of the state's interests and to substitute notions of their own would be to invite a flood of legislation motivated by the narrowest and most selfish kind of egoism. "Drink who will out of the magic beaker of the democratic program, we cannot persuade ourselves to do so. That is not, in any case, the democracy in which we believe; that is not the freedom that we revere; that is, least of all, the real, free humanity to which the future belongs." With their right to elect members of the Great Council, to submit petitions, to assemble for political purposes, and to express themselves in a free press, the people had more than enough guarantees of their freedom.

This was persuasive enough in 1851. Ten years later this was no longer true. James Madison once wrote in the fifty-first *Federalist Paper*, "In framing a government which is to be administered by men over men, the great difficulty lies in this: You must first enable the government to control the governed, and in the next place to control itself. A dependence upon the people is no doubt the primary control of government, but experience has taught mankind the necessity of auxiliary precautions." By the sixties many people in Zürich had come to doubt the ability of the government to control itself and to believe that the need for measures to correct its arbitrariness was urgent. This feeling might have been blunted if the government had been more perceptive or more determined, but Alfred Escher's energies were absorbed in the fight to win approval for the Gotthard railway, and Jakob Dubs, elected to the Federal Council after the premature death of Jonas Furrer in 1861, had moved to Bern. The movement for reform, therefore, gathered in strength.

It was fed, as we have seen, by the worsening of economic conditions, although this in itself might have had no political consequence if the general atmosphere had not been conditioned, and the existing dissatisfaction given a sharper edge, by other factors. One was the growing sense that democratic change was the wave of the future, a feeling encouraged by the awareness that in other cantons democratic agitations had already scored some successes. In 1860 the decision of the government of Baselland not to seek reunion with the city from which it had been divided in 1833 led to popular agitations and calls for a new government and a new constitution that were in the end completely successful. In 1862 strong popular protests against the railroad policy of the cantonal government in Bern marked the beginning of a powerful movement for referendum that forced concessions from the council. In the same year a law granting civil rights to Jews in the canton of Aargau touched off a movement of protest that rapidly gathered strength and eventually forced new elections and a change of government. Finally, between 1861 and 1864, a loose coalition of conservatives and self-styled democrats in Geneva revolted against the high-handed methods of the radical-liberal leader James Fazy and demanded a series of constitutional changes, including the use of popular referendum, although these were not immediately achieved. These events received close attention in the national press, and, in his book on the democratic movement of the sixties, Martin Schaffner has cited an article of 1862 by the Aargau correspondent of the Bernese newspaper *Bund* in which he described the burgeoning movement for the extension of popular rights, noting that in addition to its emergence in Basel and Aargau, its influence was notable also in Luzern and was "beginning quietly to stir even in the canton of Zürich." The reporter suggested that the movement had its own natural logic and probably could not be stopped.

The agitations in the other cantons had not left the liberals in Zürich entirely unmoved, and in 1863 the Great Council made some constitutional changes that were intended to appease the desire for change. These, however, left the existing system essentially intact and made no concessions to direct democracy. Indeed, like Alfred Escher's long defense of the liberal record at the opening of the Great Council in January 1864, which Gagliardi compared to the funeral oration of Pericles, they tended to focus the attention of the rapidly increasing number of opponents of the regime not on what had been accomplished but on what had not, and for the next two years, as it became apparent that the government intended to stand pat, dissatisfaction mounted. It was given new energy and made irresistible, however, not by the continued lassitude of the government but by two new factors.

The first of these was what Gottfried Keller in "The Lost Laugh," the last of his Seldwyla stories, called the "demonizing" of the political process, which came about as a result of the emergence of a kind of journalism that was both new to Zürich and alien to liberal standards of political discourse. In 1866, Friedrich Locher, an attorney of dubious reputation with a grievance derived from the loss of a lawsuit, began the publication of a series of pamphlets, the first of which were called "The Barons of Regensberg," that constituted an unrestrained and devastating arraignment, first, of the legal system and its functionaries, then of the bureaucracy as a whole, and finally of—to use Locher's own designation—the "Princeps and His Court." Written in a lively and highly readable prose, and sprinkled with sensational anecdotes, these brochures put the worst possible construction on the policies and actions of the liberal leaders who were its targets, not hesitating, by means of suggestion and innuendo, to impute to them injustice and vindictiveness, sycophantism and lust for power, misuse of public funds and sins of the flesh. Their effect upon the public temper was cumulative and baneful. Greeted at first with consternation and disbelief, they gained in credibility as they became more outrageous, many people being apparently persuaded that such things could not be printed unless there was at least a modicum of truth to them. Locher's formulations were graphic and memorable, and, to give only one example, a passage like "Zürich . . . where the holy figure of Justice wears spectacles instead of a blindfold, through which she puzzles out from the tablets of the law the sacramental words: 'You scratch my back, I'll scratch yours!' " supplied a rich and satisfying stereotype that swiftly became part of the armory of abuse at the opposition's disposal.

Where Locher led, others followed. Commandant Karl Walder, a prominent opposition leader, found it possible, in the pages of the Winterthur *Landbote*, to draw comparisons between the Zürich of Alfred Escher and the Paris of Louis Napoleon and the Duc de Morny, writing, "Our circumstances have gradually won a considerable similarity with those of the French imperial regime: apparent prosperity on the surface, splendor, rouge and golden spangles in the 'higher orders,' and, beside it, much, much inner misery among the people, whose weaknesses are exploited by them. . . . It is as if," he added with a sharp thrust at Alfred Escher, "the curse of unfreedom attaches itself to everything that is touched by this man's hands." Upon credulous minds there is no more effective argument than the false analogy, and to think of Escher as a Napoleon or, worse, as one of the Péreire brothers, whose *Crédit mobilier* was to have a sensational failure in 1867, was as disingenuous as to think of Locher as a Lavater *redivivus*, attacking a regime filled with Grebels. But such comparisons were commonplace in 1866 and 1867 and contributed mightily to the liberal government's loss of credibility.

So did an entirely unexpected outbreak of cholera in the spring of 1867. This highly infectious and deadly disease had been unknown or unidentified in the West before the nineteenth century was well advanced, but, moving outward from India, it fell upon Europe in 1831, infecting 39,000 people in Paris alone, of whom 18,400 died, and penetrating the British Isles through the ports of the northeast and spreading across all of England in the next two years. It struck again in 1848–49, affecting Italy, the coastal areas of Germany, France, where Paris once more was heavily hit, with 19,000 victims, and England, and it came back again in 1865–66, with a similar incidence. Zürich was spared the first two waves of the disease, which appeared only in that part of Switzerland that lay south of the Alps, and, although the city had a brief epidemic in 1854–55, that experience did not prepare it for what happened in the summer of 1867. In June an Italian family, fleeing an epidemic in Rome, came, with a two-year-old son who was already infected, to a small hotel, Zum schwarzen Weggen, in the Niederdorf quarter, which had a bakery attached to it and a busy public house frequented by workers in the Neumühle factory of Escher, Wyss and Company. The child's death was followed almost immediately by reports of cases of cholera in widely separated parts of the city, and in the weeks that followed these multiplied rapidly, so that in one September week alone there were 150 deaths and, by the time the epidemic had run its course, at the end of October, 771 people had been infected, of whom 499 had died. Traugott Koller, who witnessed the worst phase of the epidemic, wrote ten years later, "Anyone who visited Zürich in the autumn of 1867 must have believed that he had been translated to a great death house. Song and pleasure were silenced in the city that was usually filled with the joy of living, the streets were empty and silent, the public houses stood empty, and where earlier magnificent music pleased the ear and the busy activity of the Börse enlivened the chambers of the Tonhalle the eye now saw bed on bed ranged in a lazaret of silent despair."

The incidence of the epidemic was greatest in the place where it started, that densely populated area that was bounded by the west bank of the Limmat, the Rindermarkt, and the Seilergraben, a district of narrow streets and lanes lined with ancient and dilapidated buildings and with slaughterhouses and tanneries and stables and cheap hostelries, all served by the most primitive means of waste disposal and drainage. The new proletarian district on the other side of the Sihl River was also heavily infected. Here the houses were newer than those in the Niederdorf quarter but were badly constructed, often damp and dirty, and dependent upon drains and dunging trenches that were generally clogged. The quality of the drinking water in Außersihl was also unreliable, often coming from suspect wells. The epidemic was, in short, an urban phenomenon, and one centered in those districts where the most deprived and vulnerable classes lived. There were few cases in the Selnau and Stadelhaufen areas, the newest districts in Zürich, or in the highlands surrounding the city, where the more well-to-do citizens lived.

It was this circumstance that made the cholera epidemic of 1867 the crowning blow to the political credibility of the liberal party. As Martin Schaffner has written, their heavy losses made the lower classes more conscious than they had been of their material impoverishment and vulnerability, and more open to the suggestion that their condition was the result of injustice and conscious neglect by the ruling class. One left-wing journal, *La suisse radicale*, wrote, "From political corruption came phys-

ical corruption, and that's why the cholera came first to Zürich."
At the same time the epidemic opened the eyes of many former
supporters of the liberal party to the inequities of the existing
social and economic situation and made them more responsive
to the arguments of the opposition.

By now that opposition was well organized and well posi-
tioned for an assault upon the seats of power. Led by the friend
and benefactor of Richard Wagner, the former cantonal *Staatsschreiber* J. J. Sulzer, and the editor of the Winterthur *Landbote*,
Salomon Bleuler, who had been for six years the parson in Glattfelden before he turned his pronounced literary and political gifts
to journalism, its principal strongholds were in Winterthur and
Uster, which gave it the benefit of historical association with
previous risings of the countryside against the capital city. Bleuler continually underlined this, writing of Zürich's "coalition of
political influence, aristocrats of wealth, railroad matadors, and
intertwining of interests that inflict harm upon the 'provinces'
and vaunt themselves in excess." It was also more heterogeneous
than its usual designation as a democratic movement might
seem to imply because, in its zeal to expel the liberals and change
the mode of government, it appealed to people of widely diverse
political persuasion. Among its leaders were several theologians,
and it had the support of many rural conservatives, while, on
the other hand, it included a lively left wing, the most prominent
members of which were Commandant Karl Walder, an associate
of Gottfried Keller in the days when he was still a *frondeur*, the
burly, tough former militia Captain Karl Bürkli, a self-styled
socialist, and, of greater intellectual force than either of these,
Friedrich Albert Lange. Sometime instructor at Bonn, editor of
a left-wing journal in Duisburg, author of a widely read *History
of Materialism*, and advocate of the views of Ferdinand Lassalle,
Lange had come to Zürich after the victory of his private nemesis
Bismarck in 1866 and become an associate of Salomon Bleuler
and, in the democratic movement, the chief exponent of a kind
of *Kathedersozialismus*, or social policy to be achieved by political, rather than revolutionary, means.

For what it lacked in internal homogeneity, the democratic
movement made up in tactical virtuosity. The liberals had been
in power so long that they were complacent, with slow reflexes
and little imagination. In contrast, the democrats shrewdly

played upon the spirit of Uster of 1830 and argued that it had been betrayed by those who had been its chief beneficiaries in order to protect their privileges from popular criticism. Availing themselves of the classic Swiss means of appealing against the government, they made carefully coordinated plans for popular assemblies to meet on Uster Day, 22 November 1867, in Winterthur, Bülach, Uster, Horgen, Pfäffikon, and other places. In an atmosphere of unrestrained enthusiasm, these *Volksversammlungen* responded to the *Landbote*'s parole, "Forward in closed columns! Fire along the whole line!", approved the general aims of the movement, and elected a cantonal committee of action to draw up a program of specific objectives.

Drafted by Salomon Bleuler, this called for the curtailment of government authority by the introduction of popular initiative and referendum, the shortening of the term of public office, and the abolition of appointments for life; improvement of education, social security for the working classes, and the establishment of a cantonal bank for the benefit of farmers and small borrowers; simplification of the state administration and reduction of the privileges of local communities; improvement and simplification of the legal system by the introduction of civil juries and other reforms; revision of the existing system of penalties for debt, and abolition of existing restrictions on the press and the right of assembly by the lifting of regulations against communists and workers organizations. On 15 December this document was laid before the communities of Zürich, Uster, Winterthur, and Bülach for debate and formal consideration and received unanimous approval, and 27,000 signatures were collected calling upon the Great Council to institute proceedings for a thoroughgoing constitutional revision.

It was with a large package containing these signature sheets that a three-man delegation headed by Karl Bürkli went at the end of December to the office of Government President Johann Jakob Treichler. Bürkli and Treichler had once been fellow socialists, but time and politics had divided them, and Bürkli had long felt that he had been betrayed by his former friend. "We bring the government New Year's greetings!" he said spitefully as he shoved the package across the table. Treichler did not answer, but he was politician enough to realize that great changes impended and that he, the eighty-fifth cantonal *Bür-*

germeister since the time of Rudolf Brun, would probably be the last one to be elected by the Great Council.

II

Having failed to recognize the premonitory signs of the storm that now bore down upon them, the liberals still persisted in believing that it would not break. When the Great Council accepted the petitions directed to it and set 26 January 1868 as the day for the popular referendum on constitutional revision, the *Neue Zürcher Zeitung*, the principal supporter of the liberal government, professed to believe that the people of Zürich would be too sensible to approve any such dangerous attempt to overhaul the charter of their liberties. On 25 January the chief editor, Peter Felber, wrote:

> Can our treasured principles be thrown overboard all of a sudden without disadvantage? It is naturally very inviting for an opposition to step to the leadership of a well-organized business, but in the republic every day must be earned, and progress is as little guaranteed as failure is impossible. . . . Do we want to transform the home of a rich commerce in industry, art, and science into an arena of political boxers, whose ignoble cockfights will attract, instead of the usual envy of the rest of Switzerland, its compassion? We do not regard the situation as critically as that, because we have more confidence in the people.

This could only be considered as whistling to keep one's courage up, and it was belied immediately by the facts. When the polls were closed on 26 January, 59,027 out of 65,534 registered voters had cast their ballots, and of these 47,776 had voted for revision.

These results were discouraging for liberal defenders of the existing form of representative government, but they were still not conclusive, for a constitutional assembly had still to be elected, and much would hang upon its composition. But two events now greatly jeopardized the electoral prospects of the liberals. In the first place, President of the Supreme Court Ullmer, who had been the target of one of Friedrich Locher's most vituperative pamphlets and who had, in consequence, brought legal charges against him for having charged that he had misused his office, suddenly withdrew his case, saying lamely that his action was motivated by a desire to avoid revolution and civil war in Zürich, a statement that angered many people and bewildered more, while at the same time giving a spurious authenticity to Locher's charges. In the second place, Dr. Alfred Escher announced that he would not allow his name to be put forward for election to the constitutional assembly, also a decision that caused bewilderment, since no reasons for it were given, and which discouraged his supporters. Had Escher led the liberal ticket, there seems little doubt that they would have done much better than they did. As it was, when voting took place in March and April, they captured only a third of the assembly's seats, and the democrats were in a position not only to elect its president (J. J. Sulzer) and his deputies but also to dominate the thirty-four-member drafting commission that set about revising the constitution.

As a result, although there were sharp rhetorical duels during the commission's deliberations between (to use Fueter's formulation) partisans of the principle "Everything *for* the people" and those who championed the cause of "Everything *through* the people," the constitution that emerged, and was ratified by the people on 18 April 1869, represented a complete victory for the democratic program. Its first article made this abundantly clear, stating that "the power of the state rests upon the totality of the people. It is exercised unconditionally by the active citizens and conditionally by the agencies and civil servants." The paragraphs that followed showed how seriously the principles of representative government had been watered down, notably by the loosening of any vital connection between the Cantonal (formerly Great) Council and the Governing Council, both of which were henceforth elected by the people, whereas the latter body had previously been elected by the former. In general the people's representatives were put on much tighter leading lines, not only by the shortening of terms of office for both elected and appointed officials, including judges, professors, pastors, and schoolteachers (although both election and appointment were renewable), but by the limitations imposed by the new provisions for referendum and initiative. All laws passed by the Cantonal Council and most decrees issued by the Governing Council had to be submitted to popular referendum at two-year intervals; all single expenditures exceeding 250,000 francs and all recurring expenditures exceeding 20,000 francs were similarly subject to popular approval; the promulgation, abrogation, or amendment of laws could be demanded by citizens, and when such a demand received the support of a third of the members of the Cantonal Council or of 5,000 active citizens, it had to be voted on by the entire electorate.

In addition to these political changes, the new constitution realized other demands made in Salomon Bleuler's program of 1867. Thus, it authorized the establishment of a Cantonal Bank that was intended to facilitate the extension of credit to farmers and small businessmen; it cleared the way for social security legislation for the working class and for the protection of the principle of unionization; it strengthened the progressive nature of the tax system by taxing property as well as income; it reduced some indirect levies, like the tax on salt, and, in the interest of the poorer classes, it took a long step toward abolishing educational fees.

The debates that preceded the acceptance of the new constitution of 1869 had a national resonance, and in the period that followed the Zürich example was imitated, with variations, throughout the whole of the Eidgenossenschaft, not excluding the Catholic cantons. Not all cantonal governments proved willing to allow their hands to be bound by a provision for obligatory referenda on all legislation, and in some there was a tendency to exclude administrative decrees from direct popular surveillance and to retain greater liberty of action in financial affairs. Even so, the wide acceptance of the Zürich model was impressive. By the end of 1869 the obligatory referendum was in place in Bern, Solothurn, and Thurgau, with other cantons soon to follow, and even in those places where it did not apply, appeals to the electorate had been made much easier. Fueter has estimated that in 1870 only 330,000 Swiss were living under the classical form of representative government, as opposed to 1,030,000 in 1860, and that ten years later only one canton, that of Freiburg, still retained unrelieved parliamentary government, that is, the system in which Parliament elects the government and makes the laws.

Direct democracy spread also to the city and federal levels, although in the former case this was more the result of the increase in urban population and the disinclination of new residents to accept government by old elites than it was of the democratic movement. In the city of Zürich, for example, the abolition in 1866 of the last privileges of the *Stadtbürger* by the granting of equal rights in city government to all residents was the logical conclusion of a process set in train by the ending of the right of the guilds to elect the Great City Council in 1857. The constitutional debate in Zürich in 1868 and the changes it wrought had a more perceptible influence upon the revision of the federal constitution, which took place in 1874. It is doubtless true that other pressing concerns counseled this step: the transformation of the international situation as a result of German unification, which necessitated changes in federal military regulations; the need for a codification of constitutional provisions governing commerce and trade, and the desirability of clarifying religious provisions in the light of issues raised by recent papal declarations. Even so those who drafted the new federal constitution could not, given the temper of the times, ignore the victory of direct democracy in Zürich and other cantons, and they made concessions to it while excluding all legislation that could be defined as urgent or of emergency nature from its application. Despite this restriction a demand by 30,000 citizens or eight cantons was sufficient to force the referral of an ordinary federal law or administrative decree to the people for approval or disapproval, provided the issue was raised within three months of the promulgation of the act in question. This provision for referendum in the federal constitution probably improved the position of minorities, and particularly the Catholic minority, in the federal state, while at the same time opening the way to the democratization of the Catholic Party.

In Zürich the changes of 1868–69 marked a decisive defeat for liberalism, but not one that foreshadowed the eclipse of the Liberal Party. The first elections after the acceptance of the new constitution, those for the Governing and Cantonal Councils in May 1869, did, to be sure, confirm the tendency asserted in the elections for the constitutional assembly. The liberals were excluded from the new government and from Zürich's delegation to the federal second chamber (the *Ständerat*, which represented the cantons), but in the Cantonal Council, after great exertions, they were able to hold on to almost two-fifths of the seats, a respectable enough result if one remembered the near demoralization that followed the elections of March 1868. The next ten years were years of democratic supremacy in Zurich's politics, but exclusion from government did not have the wasting effect upon liberal membership and support that occurred in the case of other liberal parties after their political dominance had been broken. For one thing the long-term pattern that was to be observed in countries like Great Britain and Germany and Austria, where liberal parties lost their membership to burgeoning and ideologically inspired mass parties on the extreme left and right, did not apply to Zürich, where the center continued to be stronger than the extremes. After the issue of direct democracy had been settled by the new constitution of 1869, the difference between the liberal and democratic parties was merely one of degree and personality. Both were essentially moderate parties of the middle, a situation enjoined by the popular temper, which—this had been one of the principal reasons for liberal opposition to initiative and referendum—tended to be conservative and opposed to anything that could be described as daring or dangerously innovative.

For the kind of ideological polarization that took place elsewhere, conditions in Zürich were not suitable. The combination of confessional zeal, nationalistic resentment, and economic imperialism that formed the basis of right-wing extremism in other countries did not exist in Switzerland, let alone in Zürich, and the fact that the Democratic Party professed to represent the interest of the working class prevented the development of an independent Socialist Party for a generation. This does not mean that there had been no Swiss working-class movement until that time. At the end of the 1830s artisans and manual workers had formed a national society called the *Grütliverein*, which took as its first objective the promotion of education in the working classes, although in 1848, under the influence of the national enthusiasm of the day, it had revised its statutes and declared that it would henceforth be dedicated to the task of "supporting the progressive aspirations of the fatherland by word and deed." These aims continued to be the guidelines for the society for the next thirty years, during which time it grew to a membership of about 5,000 with sections all over the country. In Zürich the society became closely associated with the democratic movement in the late sixties, and Salomon Bleuler served as editor of its journal, *Der Grütlianer*, which moved its headquarters from Bern to Winterthur. The fact that this association was broken off in 1878, when positions taken by Bleuler's *Landbote* proved incompatible with those advocated by the board of the *Grütli-aner*, was indicative of the increasing politicization of the *Verein* and its growing dissatisfaction with democratic patronage. From that point onward it devoted most of its energies to such specifically workers' causes as free medical care and new factory legislation, and in 1881 it combined with the trade union movement to form a new Social Democratic Party. Its growth was not rapid, however, and it did not become a major factor in Zürich's politics until the years of the First World War.

The defection of their working-class allies doubtless hurt the Democratic Party, but their failure to hold the position that they had won in the elections of 1869 was due much more to the decision of the party leaders to become involved in a grandiose plan for winning for the city of Winterthur the position of political and economic primacy in the canton that had until now belonged to Zürich and to achieve this end by making Winterthur the focal point of a new network of railways that would compete with and supersede Alfred Escher's Northeastern Railway. The subsequent struggle between the Escher system and the projected National Railway of the Winterthur promoters was herculean and provided a last demonstration of Escher's virtuosity as system builder and financier as he fought off the challenge, anticipating his rival's every move and denying it opportunities for expansion by boldly assuming the construction and/or management of a dozen new lines in northeastern Switzerland before relinquishing the presidency of the Northeastern Railway to assume that of the Gotthard line. The fight was continued by his successors and ended with complete victory, caused largely by grave tactical mistakes on the part of the National Railway promoters (indecision on the question whether or not to bypass Zürich, for example) and the consequent drying up of funds, which led to the liquidation of the line by order of the federal courts in 1878. The result was financial catastrophe for the city of Winterthur, as well as an end to its dream of replacing Zürich as the canton's leading city, and a serious weakening of the Democratic Party, whose leadership had made the mistake of identifying themselves with the railway plans. The first signs that their political dominance was on the wane came in 1877 when they lost two seats in the government to liberal (now called Progressive or *Freisinnige*) candidates, and the next years saw a dropping of their popular vote and the loss of their majority in the Cantonal Council.

This offered an opportunity for a revivification of liberalism by way of transformation, or, more precisely, by way of the fusion of the middle parties. This was the work of the Zürich city forester Ulrich Meister, who had been an Escherite liberal since the sixties but who began, in the mid-eighties, to work for a union between his party, minus its more conservative members, and the democrats, who were now free of their socialists. This plan initially made little progress because of the suspicions and lack of imagination of the cantonal leaders of the two parties, and in the early nineties Meister shifted his focus to federal politics and, along with part of the Zürich liberal delegation to the Federal Council, joined together with that body's radical-democratic group. This step led in 1894 to the founding of the Progressive Democratic Party of Switzerland (FDP), which by excluding Catholic conservatives, socialists, and old liberals from its membership, became the true middle party in Swiss politics. It was immediately successful, and in time its Zürich section, which embraced most of the canton's liberals and democrats, became the strongest party in the canton.

III

But it is not enough to view the results of the crisis that affected liberalism in Zürich in the years 1867–69 solely from the standpoint of party politics. What were its more general effects, and particularly its cultural effects, in the period that followed? What became of what Peter Felber had called "the rich commerce of industry, art, and science," the happy combination of *Geld und Geist* that had been characteristic of the Escher era at its height?

Any attempt to answer this question must begin with the observation that the general atmosphere of the last third of the nineteenth century in Europe was more hectic, more nervous, more doubtful than that of the preceding years. Italo Calvino has written that "the nineteenth century from Hegel to Darwin saw the triumph of historical continuity and biological continuity as they healed all the fractures of dialectical antitheses and genetic mutations." It was a time of progress and hope, but it was followed by years of discontinuity and divisibility, in which the goal of history was obscure and biology was used to justify racist ideology. The wars of 1866 and 1870 revolutionized the European balance of power and left a heritage of insecurity and suspicion that soon found expression in a new militarism and a new diplomacy of secret alliances. Simultaneously, the end of the free-trade era ushered in a period of heightened economic competition between nations, of trade wars, of imperialism. It was an age of uncritical nationalism that often degenerated into rabid jingoism and of a new kind of demagoguery whose practitioners eschewed the laws of reason and appealed to the irrational desires and resentments of their fellow men. It was an age of bigness and unabashed materialism. It was an age in which power was sought after, and idealized, and regarded as an end in itself. And because, as Nietzsche once said, "power makes stupid," and because the energy spent in seeking it is denied to other more desirable goals, things of the spirit were less valued than more tangible things, and all of the garish display and vaunting of wealth of the new society could not conceal its cultural impoverishment and lack of wholeness.

These developments did not leave Switzerland untouched. The change in the conditions of international life made the country more vulnerable and emotionally insecure than at any time since the days of Napoleon, and this found curious manifestations. It was not an accident that in the wake of the German victory over France there was an ugly and unprecedented outbreak of xenophobia in Zürich, the so-called Tonhalle riots that were caused by celebrations by the local German population, and that subsequently this persisted in a new and assertive Swiss patriotism that conflicted with the picture of Switzerland as a place of peace and international reconciliation. It was not an accident that the first fruits of the revision of the federal constitution of 1874 was a military reform that created a more centralized army with weakened cantonal restraints upon it. It was not an accident that the son of Francis and Eliza Wille, the friends of Wagner and Herwegh, to whom Conrad Ferdinand Meyer dedicated his long poem *Hutten's Last Days*, should have become a professional soldier and the commander in chief of the Swiss armed forces during the First World War. These were signs of the times, as was the new ostentation that accompanied the booming economic growth of the eighties and nineties and the headlong construction that changed the face of Zürich and led Ricarda Huch to write in her memoirs of her student days in that city, "Hardly any of the new buildings satisfied. They had that somewhat insistent, boastful character with which one sought in that period to express a weight and bigness that conformed to the surging growth of a prosperous community. The reserved and aristocratic nature that was originally common to all the Swiss cities was lost as a result of this, although not to the extent that was true of many German cities after 1870."

Another sign of the times was a pervasive feeling on the part of artists and intellectuals that something had been lost and, because of the change of prevailing values, perhaps irretrievably so. When the poet Heinrich Leuthold returned to Zürich from Munich in the seventies, he was shattered by the change in the intellectual climate and wrote:

> *Wo sind die Enkel jener Gefeierten,*
> *Die dir den Namen, Limmat-Athen, verliehen*
> *Und dir zum Ruhm der freien Heimat*
> *Kronen vertragen im Reich der Schönen?*
>
> *Du fragst umsonst. Setzt' weiter den Wanderstab!*
> *Den Sänger nährt der heimische Boden nicht. . . .*
> *Zugvögel mögen dich geleiten*
> *Über die Berge nach fernen Zonen.*
>
> [Where are the grandchildren of those celebrated ones
> Who bestowed on you the name Athens on the Limmat
> And to the glory of their free homeland
> Wear crowns for you in the realm of the beautiful?
>
> You ask in vain. Go further on your wanderer's staff!
> The native soil does not nurture the singer. . . .
> May birds of passage accompany you
> Over the mountains to the far lands.]

Leuthold may have been thinking of all of those great talents who had made the fifties and sixties such a golden age and who had by now all departed: Theodor Mommsen in 1856, Richard Wagner and Jacob Burckhardt in 1858, Francesco De Sanctis in 1860, Hermann Köchly in 1864, Friedrich Theodor Vischer and Emma and Georg Herwegh in 1866, Jakob Moleschott in 1868, and Gottfried Semper in 1871, followed by many other German intellectuals and members of the two university faculties who felt Zürich uncongenial after the affair in the Tonhalle. This wholesale evacuation had sensibly changed the intellectual temper of the city, but Leuthold was probably thinking less about this palpable loss than about the fact that there were no obvious signs of possible recovery from it. The native soil no longer nurtured the singer.

It was from this time on that Swiss writers began to suffer from that feeling of suffocation, of smothering cant, that they attributed to the materialism of their society and to what they believed to be, in the words of George Steiner, "the self-suppressions of vivid feeling, of anarchic impulse, the shrewd bias toward disciplined mediocrity which [were now] built into Swiss educational and political existence." Out of this grew the anti-Swissness of much of the best Swiss writing in the subsequent period, and, to quote Steiner again, "the perfect appositeness of Dada to its Zürich setting."

Long before Dada, Conrad Ferdinand Meyer had, in his own way, expressed the alienation of the artist from the new Zürich. Swiss by birth, Meyer took no pride in the work of 1848 or in the subsequent triumphs of democracy because, as he viewed the events taking place on the European stage, he could find no signs of greatness in his own country or its political class. "Swissness is repugnant to me," he once wrote to Louise von François. A native of Zürich, he distanced himself from the city, living on an island in the lake like the one on which his hero Ulrich von Hutten died. He disliked Zürich because it was the most bourgeois city in Switzerland, and he hated the bourgeoisie because he believed that they thought only of money and cultivated only those qualities that would enable them to acquire it.

To escape the ignoble materialistic world in which he had been fated to live, Meyer turned to the past for his literary themes, writing brightly colored and violent historical romances in which heroic figures worked out their destinies. In a brilliant study Karl Schmid has pointed out that these stories are also filled with unsympathetic characters intended to represent Zürich's provincialism, Lacadaemonianism, philistinism, and mediocrity, and indeed, once this has been pointed out, it is impossible not to be impressed by the vehemence with which Meyer seizes every opportunity to belabor his compatriots. In

Jürg Jenatsch, a story about confessional strife and foreign intrigue set in the Thirty Years War, Heinrich Waser, *civis turicensis* and sometime diplomat, wanders through embattled Graubünden, infuriating local patriots by refusing to become involved in their quarrels, all of the contestants in which, he is ever eager to point out, are Zürich's allies. At an early point in the story the head of the Catholic Party berates him with the words:

> That's the way you are, you Zürchers! At home you have a reasonable disciplined regime, and you cross yourself against innovation and subversion. If a fellow like our preacher Jenatsch appeared among you, he would soon sit behind locked doors in the Wellenberg, or you would lay his head in front of his feet at once. But from a distance the monster seems remarkable to you, and your guilds applaud his outrages with delight. Your curiosity and your restless spirit enjoy seeing the flames of revolt shoot up brightly, as long as they don't threaten your own roofs.

At the story's end, Jenatsch, described disapprovingly by another Zürcher as a man with "an unsated desire for action," who has "outgrown our narrow circumstances and has been made drunk to the point of madness by his unprecedented triumphs," goes headlong to his fated end, while Waser, now governing *Bürgermeister*, survives by noninvolvement, plump and self-satisfied, "a breath of youthfulness still touching his features, whose earlier sensitive mobility was now overlaid by a placid expression of benevolent cleverness that bordered, however, on slyness."

Meyer's canvases are filled with the unending embroilments of religious confessions and great nations, and his heroes are men of action who ride or struggle against the tides of history —Beckett, Pescara, Hutten, Coligny, Rohan, Gustavus Adolfus. The Swiss among them—with the exception of Jenatsch—are either involved in the actions narrated by accident, like Schadow in *The Amulet*, Armbruster in *The Saint*, and Bläsi Zgraggen of Uri in *The Temptation of Pescara*, or are outsiders by choice, like the Chorherr Burkhard in *The Saint*, perhaps the quintessential Zürcher in Meyer's stories, sitting complacently by his fireside, replete with good food and wine, waiting for someone to tell him a story about the real world.

Not all Zürich intellectuals felt as Meyer did, and there were local writers who found no necessity to look to history or to foreign parts for their themes, finding it perfectly satisfactory to exploit the rich vein opened up by Keller with his Seldwyla stories. None of these, however, had Keller's ability to see his land in Homeric terms, which invested the passions and ultimate tragedy of "A Village Romeo and Juliet" with epic qualities, and their efforts at imitation rarely rose above provincial narrowness and quaintness. The excessive and patently defiant praise that they received from the local press, which was part and parcel of the post-1871 xenophobia, confirmed the worst suspicions of those who aspired to foreign recognition and strengthened the tradition of local cultural pessimism that runs from Meyer and Burckhardt (whose feelings about his native city were almost as hostile as the Zürich novelist's) to Amiel, Wilhelm Schäfer, Friedrich Dürrenmatt, and Max Frisch.

If Meyer complained, with what one sometimes feels was a nagging persistence, about his country's lack of greatness, Frisch has tended to regard the attempt to make a virtue out of not wanting to be great as more damaging to cultural values. His atrabilious invention Stiller, in the novel of that name, poses the question with considerable force. "Is it not true," he asks his exasperated lawyer (exasperated because his client seems to have no trace of patriotic spirit), "that this habitual, and therefore cheap, renunciation of greatness (the whole, the complete, the radical) leads finally to the impotence even of fantasy? The poverty of inspiration, the universal slackness that leaps out at us in this country are certainly plain symptoms of how near they are already to this impotence. . . ." The city of Zürich, he has explained earlier, is not in the least concerned about being called provincial, because its provincialism is prevented from becoming boring by occasional visits from foreign artists and even from "all sorts of native intelligences, who accomplish something in the world outside until their fame gradually flatters their own land, which for its part is in no position to win fame for the very reason that it is provincial, namely without history."

At the same time, cultural judgments are relative. One cannot expect to find an equivalence of standards between nations or classes or occupations. In an interesting entry in his diary, written in Hamburg in November 1948, Frisch reflected on the German fear of being considered a *Spießer* (philistine) and noted that one hardly met a German who didn't bring the word up in his first conversation, as if it were necessary to dispel any suspicion that he was not a bearer and creator of culture. It was clear, Frisch added, that there was a decided difference between German and Swiss ideas of the nature of culture:

> By culture we understand in the first instance civil achievements, the community attitude more than the artistic or scientific masterpiece of a single citizen. Moreover, if it is a rather dry air that surrounds the Swiss artist in his homeland, this evil, no matter how nearly it affects us personally, is merely the disagreeable reverse side of an attitude which, although scorned by most Germans as philistine, on the whole has our complete agreement—precisely because the opposite attitude, the aesthetic idea of culture, has led, and must lead, to a deadly catastrophe.

One feels that the recollection of the horrors of the recent war had impelled Frisch to draw too much from his comparison. On the other hand, to the extent that his definition of the Swiss view of culture was accurate, it helps define one of the consequences of the passing of the liberal age. In the days when the "rich commerce of industry, art, and science" of which Peter Felber spoke was at its height, and *Geld* and *Geist* were mutually supportive and inspiring, there was no such great distinction between individual and community accomplishment as that insisted upon by Frisch. The victory of democracy over liberalism was responsible for the divorce and for the subsequent depreciation of the individualism that lay at the heart of the liberal philosophy. The cultural consequences of this were not long in making themselves evident.

IV

In the summer of 1927, Harry Graf Kessler, diplomat, patron of the arts, friend and biographer of Walther Rathenau, came to Zürich to view an exhibition of Kokoschka's work and then went on to Sils-Maria, where he visited the Nietzsche house, to Chur, where he saw the grave of Jürg Jenatsch and read Meyer's novel for the first time and was much impressed by it ("Jenatsch is . . .

a monster far in advance of his time, whose progeny could be said to rule the world in the nineteenth and twentieth century"), and then went on to San Bernardino. Here he met the Basel painter Alfred Heinrich Pellegrini, the publisher of the *Basler Nachrichten*, Albert Oeri, one of the numerous descendants of Francois and Elisa Wille (whose first name is provided neither by the published diary nor by its index), and the political scientist Emil Dürr, who had just finished a book in which he described what he called "the fatal, materialistically determined, and deeply demoralizing nature" of contemporary Swiss politics. On the second evening of his visit, Kessler recalls:

> ... in an illuminating and fascinating way, Dürr elaborated the view that Conrad Ferdinand Meyer, Jacob Burckhardt, Gottfried Keller, Bachofen, Jeremias Gotthelf, Nietzsche, Gobineau, all the great minds who worked in Switzerland in the middle of the nineteenth century (Gobineau was diplomatic councillor in Bern) were forced by the spectacle afforded by the victory of Swiss democracy into a defensive position against democracy as such and converted to an aristocratic philosophy. In 1831 a leveling process set in that was inimical to culture and lasted until about 1875, which called forth in all of these men, in different mixtures, revulsion, fear, hatred, and contempt. It was the half-educated *petit-bourgeois* who took his half-education to be culture who came to power and, particularly in Basel and Geneva, but also in Zürich and other cantons, shoved aside the old, highly cultivated patrician families. Switzerland in those years anticipated the development of all of Europe. In the different cantons there rose also, democratically based, many petty tyrants, little "Mussolinis," Fazy in Geneva, Escher in Zürich, etc., who imposed a hard, ruthless regime in the interest of the *petit-bourgeoisie*. Since then, Switzerland has been conservative.

If Kessler had believed any of this (by the time he had put it down on paper he seems to have incurred doubts, for he complained about the sympathy that Wille and Pellegrini had for Mussolini and grumbled about "philistine Swiss conservatism"), he would have been an even worse historian than Dürr, who had managed in his slipshod *résumé* to do grave disservice to Keller, Gotthelf, and possibly Nietzsche and had had the effrontery, three years after the murder of Giacomo Matteotti and the establishment of a bloody totalitarianism in Italy, to compare James Fazy and Alfred Escher with the author and beneficiary of those events. It is difficult to decide which was intellectually more offensive in Dürr's discourse, the sentimental assumption that the *ancien régime* in Switzerland was representative of a high culture, a view totally unsupported by the historical realities of the period from 1815 to 1830, or his bland refusal to explain the clear conflict between his putative post-1831 *Nivellierungsprozess* with the well-known record of accomplishment in the years from the Regeneration to the seventies, which was still perceptible in institutional form in Dürr's own time.

It is hardly necessary, at the end of a book that has been largely devoted to describing that record, to rehearse it or to remind the reader of the progress in political and civil liberties and in educational and economic opportunity that the liberals wrought during their ascendancy in Zürich's politics, or of their paramount role in creating the new federal state, or of the refuge they provided for fugitives from tyrannies in other lands, or of their success in making Zürich the cultural and economic center of their country. Perhaps it will be enough merely to say, since it has not been unduly emphasized in the pages above, that, in all of their achievements, the liberals were able to reconcile their responsibility for the well-being of the community with a deep respect for that belief in individuality that lay at the heart of the liberal philosophy, which John Stuart Mill, in his essay "On Liberty" in 1859, expressed by writing:

> It is not by wearing down into uniformity all that is individual in themselves, but by cultivating it and calling it forth, within the limits imposed by the rights and interests of others, that human beings become a noble and beautiful object of contemplation. . . . In proportion to the development of his individuality, each person becomes more valuable to himself, and is therefore capable of being more valuable to others.

To which might be added, as a parting shot in Emil Dürr's direction and in the words of Max Frisch's stern critic of his country's fortunes, Anatol Stiller, that, thanks to the liberals' energy and their high ideals, Zürich and all Switzerland in the middle of the nineteenth century had a sense of purpose and direction. "In those days they had a blueprint. In those days they rejoiced in tomorrow and the day after. In those days they had a historical present."

BIBLIOGRAPHY

♦

Hektor Ammann: "Untersuchungen über die Wirtschaftsstellung Zürich," in: *Zeitschrift für Schweizerische Geschichte*, XXIX (1949), S. 317ff.

Ludovico Ariosto: Orlando Furioso, translated and edited and with an introduction by Barbara Reynolds, 2 vols. London, 1975.

Matthew Arnold: "Schools and Universities on the Continent," in: *Complete Prose Works*, IV. Ann Arbor, Mich. 1964.

F. B. Artz: Reaction and Revolution, 1814–1832. Boston 1934.

Placidus Aversano: Oberst Eduard Ziegler, 1800–1882. Diss., Zürich 1951.

Jakob Baechtold: Gottfried Kellers Leben, 3 vols. Berlin 1894.

Jakob Baechtold: Gottfried Kellers Leben: Seine Briefe und Tagebücher, I. 8th. rev. ed.. Stuttgart 1950.

Emile Bebler: Conrad Ferdinand Meyer und Gottfried Kinkel. Zürich 1949.

Walter Benjamin: "Gottfried Keller," in Benjamin, *Angelus Novus: Ausgewählte Schriften, II*. Frankfurt am Main. 1966.

Jean-François Bergier: Histoire économique de la Suisse. Zürich, Köln 1983.

Urs Berner: "Ein Scheiterhaufen für den Winter: Das Sechseläuten-Fest," in: *Merian*, XXXVI (1983), S. 40ff.

Ernst Bloch: Zur Philosophie der Musik. Frankfurt am Main 1974.

J. K. Bluntschli: Denkwürdigkeiten aus meinem Leben. Nördlingen 1884.

Ernst Böckel: Hermann Köchly. Ein Bild seines Lebens und seiner Persönlichkeit. Heidelberg 1904.

Edgar Bonjour: Geschichte der schweizerischen Neutralität, I. Basel 1965.

Ulrich Bräker: Lebensgeschichte und natürliche Abentheuer des Armen Mannes im Tockenburg. Zürich 1788–89.

Rudolf Braun: Das ausgehende Ancien Régime in der Schweiz. Göttingen, Zürich 1984.

Rudolf Braun: Sozialer und kultureller Wandel in einem ländlichen Industriegebiet im 19. und 20. Jahrhundert. Erlenbach/Zürich 1965.

L. A. Breglio: Francesco De Sanctis. New York 1940.

Asa Briggs: "Robert Lowe and the Fear of Democracy," in Briggs, *Victorian People*. Chicago 1955.

Erwin Bucher: Die Geschichte des Sonderbundkrieges. Zürich 1966.

Erwin Bucher: "Ein sozio-ökonomisches und ein politisches Kapitel aus der Regeneration," in: *Schweizerische Zeitschrift für Geschichte*, XXXII (1982), S. 5ff.

S. Bucher: "Liberalismus und die Krise von 1833," in: *Schweizerische Zeitschrift für Geschichte*, XXXII (1982), 89ff.

H. Büttner: "Die Anfänge der Stadt Zürich," in: *Schweizerische Zeitschrift für Geschichte*, I (1951), 89ff.

Jacob Burckhardt: Briefe, ed. by M. Burckhardt, I. Basel 1949.

Jacob Burckhardt: Briefe, with a biographical introduction, ed. by Fritz Kaphahn. Leipzig n.d.

Jacob Burckhardt: Über das Studium der Geschichte: Weltgeschichtliche Betrachtungen, ed. by Peter Ganz. Munich 1982.

Guido Calgari: L'Arrivo e il Soggiorno del De Sanctis a Zurigo. Zürich 1956.

Italo Calvino: The Literature Machine. Essays. London 1987.

E. H. Carr: Michail Bakunin. London 1937.

E. H. Carr: The Romantic Exiles. A Nineteenth-Century Portrait Gallery. London 1933.

M. E. Compagnon: "Le duel et la mort de Ferdinand Lassalle," in: *Zeitschrift für Schweizerische Geschichte*, XXI (1941), S. 79ff.

Otto von Corvin: Ein Leben voller Abenteuer, ed. by Hermann Wendel. Frankfurt am Main 1924.

Gordon A. Craig: "A Swiss Passion: Green Henry by Gottfried Keller," in: *New York Review of Books*, XXXIV (1987), 25 June 1987.

Gordon A. Craig: Britain and Europe, 1866–1869: A Study in the Application of Non-Intervention. Diss., Princeton 1941.

Gordon A. Craig: "Preußische Offiziere gegen den Militarismus," in: *Demokratie und Diktatur. Geist und Gestalt politischer Herrschaft in Deutschland und Europa*, ed. by Manfred Funke, Hans-Adolf Jacobsen. Düsseldorf 1987.

Benedetto Croce: History of Europe in the Nineteenth Century, trans. from the Italian by Henry Furst. London 1934.

Annemarie Custer: Die Zürcher Untertanen und die Französische Revolution. Zürich 1942.

Karl Dändliker: Geschichte der Stadt und des Kantons Zürich, II: Stadt und Landschaft als Gemeinwesen von 1400 bis 1712, III: Von 1712 bis zur Gegenwart. Zürich 1910, 1912.

Guido De Ruggiero: The History of European Liberalism. Oxford 1927.

Francesco De Sanctis: Lettere da Zurigo a Diomede Marvasi, 1856–1860, ed. by Elisabette Marvasi, with a foreword by Benedetto Croce. Naples 1913.

Jakob Dubs: Die Savoyerfrage rechtlich und politisch beleuchtet. Zürich 1860.

Emil Durr: Neuzeitliche Wandlungen in der schweizerischen Politik. Eine historisch-politische Betrachtung über die Verwirtschaftlichung der politischen Motive und Parteien. Basel 1928.

Friedrich Dürrenmatt: Justiz. Novel. Zürich 1985.

Die Eisenbahn: Gedichte, Prosa, Bilder, ed. by Wolfgang Minaty. Frankfurt am Main 1984.

Emil Ermatinger: Gottfried Kellers Leben, I. Stuttgart, Berlin 1916.

Emil Ermatinger: Gottfried Kellers Leben, 8th. revised ed. Zürich 1950.

Frauen in Aufbruch. Frauenbriefe aus dem Vormärz und der Revolution von 1848, ed. by Fritz Böttger. Darmstadt 1979.

Correspondence de Frederic-Cesar de la Harpe sous la République Helvétique, ed. by Charles Biaudet, Marie-Claude Jacquier, II. Neuchâtel 1985.

Max Frisch: Tagebuch, 1946–1949. Frankfurt am Main 1950.

Max Frisch: Stichworte, ed. by Uwe Johnson. Frankfurt am Main 1985.

Max Frisch: Stiller, Novel. Frankfurt am Main 1953–54.

Eduard Fueter: Die Schweiz seit 1848, Geschichte, Politik, Wirtschaft. Zürich 1928.

"Jonas Furrer," in: *Allgemeine Deutsche Biographie*, VIII, S. 209f. Munich 1887.

Ulrich Gäbler: Huldrych Zwingli: Eine Einführung in sein Leben und sein Werk. Munich 1983.

Ernst Gagliardi: Alfred Escher. Vier Jahrzehnte neuerer Schweizergeschichte, 2 vols. Frauenfeld 1920.

Hermann Giering: Lavater und der junge Pestalozzi. Diss., Berlin 1932.

Johann Wolfgang von Goethe: Dichtung und Wahrheit, Hamburg, ed. by Erich Trunz, Liselotte Blumenthal, IX, X. Munich 1982.

Lionel Gossman: "Basle, Bachofen, and the Critique of Modernity in the Second Half of the Nineteenth Century," in: *Journal of the Warburg and Courtald Institutes*, Jg. 47 (1984), S. 3ff.

Walter Grab: Ein Mann, der Marx Ideen gab. Wilhelm Schulz, eine politische Biographie. Düsseldorf 1979.

Martin Gregor-Dellin: Richard Wagner. Sein Leben, sein Werk, sein Jahrhundert. Munich, Zürich 1980.

Erich Gruner: "Werden und Wachsen der schweizerischen Wirtschaftsverbände im 19. Jahrhundert," in: *Schweizerische Zeitschrift für Geschichte*, VI (1956), S. 33ff.

Ferdinand Gubler: Die Anfänge der schweizerischen Eisenbahnpolitik auf Grundlage der wirtschaftlichen Interessen. Diss., Zürich 1914.

Gottfried Guggenbühl: Paul Usteri, 1768–1831, Lebensbild eines schweizerischen Staatsmannes aus der Zeit der französischen Vorherrschaft und des Frühliberalismus, 2 vols. Zürich 1924.

Gottfried Guggenbühl: Der Landbote, 1836–1936. Winterthur 1936.

Albert Hauser: Schweizerische Wirtschafts-und Sozialgeschichte. Erlenbach/Zürich, Stuttgart 1961.

Albert Hauser: "Über die Lebenshaltung im Alten Zürich," in: *Schweizerische Zeitschrift für Geschichte*, XII (1962), S. 170ff.

Otto Henne: Gottfried Kinkel. Ein Lebensbild. Zürich 1883.

Wolfgang Hermann: Gottfried Semper im Exil. Paris, London, 1849–1855. Zur Entstehung des "Stil," 1840–1877. Basel, Stuttgart 1978.

Emma Herwegh: Briefe von Pietro Cironi, Filippo De Boni, Felice Orsini, Ludwig Schweigert. Manuskript, Herwegh-Archiv, Liesthal.

Emma Herwegh: Tagebücher, 1834–1845, Manuskript, Herwegh-Archiv, Liesthal.

Georg Herwegh: Herweghs Werke in einem Band, ed. by Hans-Georg Werner. Berlin 1967.

Georg Herwegh: 1848: Briefe von und an Georg Herwegh, ed. by Marcel Herwegh. Munich 1896.

Marcel Herwegh: Au soir des dieux. Paris 1933.

Marcel Herwegh: Guillaume Rüstow—un grand soldat, un grand caractère. Paris 1938.

Alexander Herzen: *My Past and Thoughts*, trans. by Constance Garnett, revised by Humphrey Higgens, with an introduction by Isaiah Berlin, 4 vols. London 1968.

Helmut Hirsch: Sophie von Hatzfeldt. Düsseldorf 1981.

E. J. Hobsbawm: The Age of Revolution, 1776–1848. London 1962.

E. J. Hobsbawm: The Age of Capital, 1848–1875. New York 1975.

Hajo Holborn: Ulrich von Hutten and the German Reformation. New Haven 1937.

J. J. Hottinger and G. von Escher: Das alte und das neue Zürich. Zürich 1859.

Ricarda Huch: Frühling in der Schweiz. Jugenderinnerungen. Zürich 1938.

Ricarda Huch: Das Zeitalter der Glaubensspaltung. New edition. Zürich 1987.

Alfred Ibach: Gottfried Keller und Friedrich Theodor Vischer. Diss., Munich 1927.

Meinrad Inglin: Schweizerspiegel. Novel. New ed. Zürich 1955.

Alexander Isler: Bundesrat Dr. Jonas Furrer. Winterthur 1907.

A. Janner: "Jacob Burckhardt und Francesco De Sanctis," in: *Zeitschrift für schweizerische Geschichte*, XII (1932), S. 25ff.

Rudolf Jaun, Georges Rapp et al.: Der schweizerische Generalstab, 3 vols. Basel 1983.

Chr. Jungnickel and Russell McCormach: Intellectual Mastery of Nature: Theoretical Physics from Ohm to Einstein, I: The Torch of Mathematics, 1800–1870. Chicago 1986.

Werner Kaegi: Jacob Burckhardt. Eine Biographie, 4 vols. Basel 1947–77.

Gerhard Kaiser: Gottfried Keller. Eine Einführung. Munich, Zürich 1985.

Gerhard Kaiser: Gottfried Keller. Das gedichtete Leben. Frankfurt am Main 1981.

Gottfried Keller: Ausgewählte Gedichte, ed. by Walter Muschg. Bern 1956.

Gottfried Keller: Gesammelte Briefe, ed. by Carl Helbling, 4 vols. Bern 1950–54.

Gottfried Keller: Sämtliche Werke. Historisch-kritische Ausgabe, ed. by Jonas Fränkel, Carl Helbling, 22 vols. Erlaenbach/Zürich, Munich 1926–48.

Gottfried Keller: Das Tagebuch und das Traumbuch, ed. by Walter Muschg. Basel 1945.

Heinrich Kerler, ed.: Schiller-Reden. Ulm 1905.

Harry Graf Kessler: Tagebücher, 1918–1937. Frankfurt am Main 1961.

Meta Klopstock: Es sind wunderliche Dinger, meine Briefe: Meta Klopstocks Briefwechsel, ed. by Franziska and Hermann Tiemann. Munich 1980.

Jürgen Kocka, ed.: Bürgertum im 19. Jahrhundert: Deutschland im europäischen Vergleich, 3 vols. Munich 1988.

Walter Köhler: Huldrych Zwingli. Stuttgart 1952.

Hans Max Kriesi: Gottfried Keller als Politiker. Frauenfeld, Leipzig 1918.

W. L. Langer: Political and Social Upheaval, 1832–1852. Boston 1969.

Anton Largiader: Geschichte der Stadt und Landschaft Zürich, 2 vols. Erlenbach/Zürich 1945.

Ferdinand Lassalle: Briefe an Georg Herwegh, ed. by Marcel Herwegh. Zürich 1896.

Ferdinand Lassalle: Nachgelassene Briefe und Papiere, ed. by Gustav Mayer, 6 vols. Osnabrück 1967.

J. C. Lavater: Schweizerlieder. Bern n.d.

Mary Sloman-Lavater: Genie des Herzens. Die Lebensgeschichte Johann Caspar Lavaters. Stuttgart, Zürich 1955.

Heinrich Leuthold: Ausgewählte Gedichte, ed. by Adolf Guggenbühl, Karl Hafner. Zürich 1942.

Ernst Lichtenhahn: "Richard Wagners Zürcher Opernaufführungen," in: *Neue Zürcher Zeitung*, CCV, Nr. 281, 1./2. December 1984.

Alfred Liede: Das Herwegh-Archiv im Dichtermuseum Liesthal, mit einem Beitrag von Edgar Schumacher. Liesthal 1960–61.

Friedrich Lipp: Georg Herweghs viertägige Irr-und Wanderfahrt mit der Pariser deutsch-demokratischen Legion in Deutschland. Stuttgart 1850.

James Murray Luck: A History of Switzerland. Palo Alto, Cal. 1985.

Georg Lukács: "Karl Marx und Friedrich Theodor Vischer," in: Lukács, *Beiträge zur Geschichte der Ästhetik*. Berlin 1956.

Alessandro Luzio: Felice Orsini ed. Emma Herwegh. Nuovi Documenti. Florence 1937.

Claus Zoege von Manteuffel: "Ein Meister der glanzvollen Überbauwelt. Die Widersprüche des Gottfried Semper," *Frankfurter Allgemeine Zeitung*, Nr. 34, 9. February 1985.

M. Mauerhofer: "Mazzini et les réfugiés italiens en Suisse," in: *Zeitschrift für Schweizerische Geschichte*, XII (1932), S. 45ff.

Memorabilia Tigurina von 1840 bis 1850, ed. by Fr. Vogel. Zürich 1853.

Memorabilia Tigurina von 1850 bis 1860, ed. by G. von Escher. Zürich 1870.

Bruno Meyer: "Die Entstehung der Eidgenossenschaft. Der Stand der heutigen Anschauungen," in: *Schweizerische Zeitschrift für Geschichte*, II (1952), S. 153ff.

Conrad Ferdinand Meyer: Sämtliche Werke, mit einem Nachwort von Hans Schmeer. Munich, Zürich 1959.

Ludwig Meyer von Knonau: Lebenserinnerungen, 1769–1841, ed. by Gerold Meyer von Knonau. Frauenfeld 1883.

John Stuart Mill: Three Essays: On Liberty. Representative Government. The Subjection of Women. Oxford 1912.

Jakob Moleschott: Für meine Freunde. Lebenserinnerungen. Gießen 1894.

Theodor Mommsen/Otto Jahn: Briefwechsel 1842–1868, ed. by Lothar Wickert. Frankfurt am Main 1962.

Luc Monnier: L'annexion de la Savoie à la France et la politique suisse 1860. Geneva 1932.

Charles Morazé: Les bourgeois conquérants. Paris 1957.

Hans Morf: Zunfverfassung, Obrigkeit und Kirche von Waldmann bis Zwingli. Zürich 1968.

Arnd Morkel: "Hierin kann etwas Beglückendes liegen: Jacob Burckhardts Auffassung von der Universität," *Frankfurter Allgemeine Zeitung*, Nr. 278, 8. December 1984.

Eugen Müller: Eine Glanzzeit des Zürcher Stadttheaters: Charlotte Birch-Pfeiffer, 1837–1843. Zürich 1911.

Kurt Müller: Bürgermeister Conrad Melchior Hirzel, 1793–1843. Zürich 1952.

Conrad von Muralt: Hans von Reinhard. Zürich 1838.

Adolf Muschg: Gottfried Keller. Munich 1977.

Adolf Muschg: "Eine grundanständige Stadt," *Merian*, XXXVI, No. 1 (1983), S. 13ff.

Walter Muschg: "Der Schriftsteller Pestalozzi," S. 105ff., in: Muschg, *Studien zur tragischen Literaturgeschichte*. Bern 1965.

Shlomo Na'aman: Lassalle. Hanover 1970.

Hans Nabholz: "Die Anfänge des Bankwesens in Zürich," in: *Geld- und Kreditsystem der Schweiz. Festgabe für Gottlieb Bachmann*. Zürich n.d.

Werner Naf: Die Schweiz in der deutschen Revolution 1847/49. Frauenfeld 1929.

Werner Naf: Der Schweizerische Sonderbundskrieg als Vorspiel der Revolution 1848. Basel 1919.

Naturforschende Gesellschaft: "Festschrift der Naturforschenden Gesellschaft in Zürich, 1746–1896," in: *Vierteljahrsschrift der Naturforschenden Gesellschaft*, XLI (1896). Zürich 1896.

Michael Naumann: "Bildung und Gehorsam. Zur ästhetischen Ideologie des Bildungsbürgertums," in: Klaus Vondung (ed.), *Das wilhelminische Bildungsbürgertum. Zur Sozialgeschichte seiner Ideen*. Göttingen 1976.

Paul Neitzke: Die deutschen politischen Flüchtlinge in der Schweiz 1848/49. Berlin 1927.

Neuchâtel et la Suisse, par la Conseil d'Etat de la République et du Canton de Neuchâtel. Neuchâtel 1970.

150 Jahre NZZ: Jubiläumsschrift. Zürich 1930.

Ernest Neuman: The Wagner Operas. New York 1983.

Friedrich Nietzsche: "Der Fall Wagner, Nietzsche contra Wagner, Götzendämmerung," in: Nietzsche, *Werke in 6 Bänden*, ed. by Karl Schlechta, III. Munich 1966.
Thomas Nipperdey: Deutsche Geschichte, 1800–1866. Munich 1983.

Michael St. John Packe: Orsini. The Story of a Conspirator. Boston 1957.
Saul K. Padover, ed.: Karl Marx in seinen Briefen. Munich 1981.
R. R. Palmer: The Making of the Democratic Revolution, 2 vols. Princeton 1959, 1964.
Johann Heinrich Pestalozzi: Lienhard und Gertrud, 4 vols. Zürich 1781.
Johann Heinrich Pestalozzi: Wie Gertrud lehrt ihre Kinder. Zürich 1801.
Johann Heinrich Pestalozzi: Gesammelte Werke in zehn Bänden, ed. by Emilie Bosshart, Emanuel DeJung et al., V: Politische Schriften bis 1798. Zürich 1946.
Johann Heinrich Pestalozzi, in: Allgemeine Deutsche Biographie, XXV 432ff. Munich 1887.
Hans Conrad Peyer: Von Handel und Bank im alten Zürich. Zürich 1968.
G. R. Potter: Zwingli. Cambridge 1976.
S. S. Prawer: Karl Marx und die Weltliteratur. Munich 1983.

Heinz Quitzsch: Gottfried Semper: Praktische Ästhetik und politischer Kampf. Braunschweig 1981.

J. R. Rahn: Zürcher Taschenbuch. Zürich 1920.
J. H. Randall: The Making of the Modern Mind. New York 1940.
William E. Rappard: Die Bundesverfassung der Schweizerischen Eidgenosschenschaft, 1848–1948: Vorgeschichte, Ausarbeitung, Weiterentwicklung. Zürich 1948.
Willy Real: Die Revolution in Baden 1848/49. Stuttgart 1983.
Elisa von der Recke: Tagebücher und Selbstzeugnisse, ed. by Christine Träger. Munich 1984.
Albrecht Rengger: Kleine, meist ungedruckte Schriften, ed. by Friedrich Kortüm. Bern 1838.
Fritz Rieter: Der Sonderbundkrieg: Eine Skizze. Zürich 1948.
Fred Rihner: Illustrierte Geschichte der Zürcher Altstadt. Aarau 1975.
Paul Rilla: Gottfried Keller. Sein Leben in Selbstzeugnissen, Briefen und Berichten. Berlin 1943.
J. J. Rüttiman: Dr. Jonas Furrer. Zürich 1861.

Gert Sautermeister: "Gottfried Keller: Der grüne Heinrich," in: *Romane und Erzählungen des bürgerlichen Realismus*, ed. by Horst Denkler. Stuttgart 1980.

Martin Schaffner: Die Demokratischen Bewegungen der 1860er Jahre: Beschreibung und Erklärung der Zürcher Volksbewegung von 1867. Basel, Frankfurt am Main 1962.

Schiller-Reden, ed. by Heinrich Kerler. Ulm 1905.

Wolfgang Schivelbuch: Geschichte der Eisenbahnreise: Zur Industrialisierung von Raum und Zeit im 19. Jahrhundert. Frankfurt am Main 1979.

Fritz Schlawe: Friedrich Theodor Vischer. Stuttgart 1959.

Hans Rudolf Schmid: Schweizerische Pioniere der Wirtschaft und Politik, IV. Alfred Escher. Zürich 1956.

Karl Schmid: Aufsätze und Reden. Stuttgart, Zürich 1957.

Karl Schmid: Unbehagen im Kleinstaat. Stuttgart, Zürich 1963.

Heinrich Schmidt: Die deutschen Flüchtlinge in der Schweiz 1833–1836. Zürich 1899.

Robert Schneebeli, ed: Zurich. Geschichte einer Stadt. Zürich 1986.

Boris Schneider: Der Kanton Zürich 1987.

Hans Schneider: Geschichte des Schweizerischen Bundesstaates 1948–1918. Stuttgart, Zürich 1931.

Albert Schoop: Johann Konrad Kern, 2 vols. Frauenfeld, Stuttgart 1968, 1976.

Karl Schurz: Lebenserinnerungen, I. Berlin 1911.

An die Schweiz. Gedichte von Haller bis Nietzsche, ed. by Walter Muschg. Basel 1945.

Gottfried Semper: Gottfried Semper und die Mitte des 19. Jahrhunderts: Symposion vom 2. bis 6. December 1974, Eidgenössische Technische Hochschule, Zürich. Basel, Stuttgart 1976.

Gottfried Semper, 1803–1879: Baumeister zwischen Revolution und Historismus. Katalog zur Ausstellung "Gottfried Semper zum 100. Geburtstag" im Albertinum in Dresden. Munich 1980.

George Bernard Shaw: The Perfect Wagnerite. New ed. New York 1967.

James J. Sheehan: German Liberalism in the Nineteenth Century. Chicago 1978.

Franz Sigel: Denkwürdigkeiten des Generals Franz Sigel aus den Jahren 1848 und 1849, ed. by Wilhelm Blos. Mannheim 1902.

Ludwig Snell: Beherzigungen bei der Einführung der Pressefreiheit in der Schweiz und über gesetzliche Bestimmungen über die Presse. Zürich 1829.

"Ludwig Snell," in: *Allgemeine Deutsche Biographie*, XXXIV, 508ff. Munich 1892.

Lewis W. Spitz: The Protestant Reformation, 1517–1559. New York 1985.

Peter Stadler: Die Universität Zürich 1833–1983. Zürich 1983.

Peter Stadler: "Zürcher Geist und schweizerische Identität," in: *Neue Zürcher Zeitung*, CCVI, Nr. 109, 13. May 1985.

Peter Stadler: "Wirtschaftsführer und Politiker: Zum hundersten Todestag Alfred Eschers," in: *Neue Zürcher Zeitung*, CCIII, Nr. 283, 4./5. December 1982.

Peter Stadler: "Die Hauptstadtfrage in der Schweiz 1798–1848," in: *Zeitschrift für Schweizerische Geschichte*, XXI (1971), S. 526ff.

"Philipp Albrecht Stapfer," in: *Allgemeine Deutsche Biographie* XXXV, 451ff. Munich 1893.

A. Steiner: "Richard Wagner in Zürich," in: *Neujahrsblätter der Allgemeinen Musik-Gesellschaft in Zürich*. Zürich 1901, 1902, 1903.

Georg Steiner: "What Is 'Swiss'?" in: *The Times, Literary Supplement*, 7. December 1984.

Gerhard Storz: Der Dichter Friedrich Schiller. Stuttgart 1959.

Klaus Sulzer: "Zürichs Entwicklung zum Wirtschaftszentrum der Schweiz," in: *Zürich einst und jetzt*, ed. by Römerhof-Verlag. Zürich 1951.

Hans Peter Treichler: Gründung der Gegenwart. Portraits aus der Schweiz, 1850–1880. Zürich 1985.

Paul Usteri: Rede über den Entwurf eines Tagsatzungsbeschlusses wegen Mißbrauch der Publizität in Inneran Angelegenheiten. Zürich 1828.

P. de Vallière: Treue und Ehre. New ed. Lausanne 1940.

Friedrich Theodor Vischer: "Mein Lebensgang," in: Vischer, *Ausgewählte Werke*, III. Berlin, Stuttgart 1921.

"Friedrich Theodor Vischer" in: *Allgemeine Deutsche Biographie*, XL, 31ff. Munich, 1896.

Cosima Wagner: Die Tagebücher, ed. and with commentary by Martin Gregor-Dellin, Dietrich Mack. Munich 1976.

Richard Wagner: Ausgewählte Schriften und Briefe, ed. by Alfred Lorenz, 2 vols. Berlin 1938.

Richard Wagner: Mein Leben, ed. by Martin Gregor-Dellin, 2 vols. Munich 1963.

Richard Wagner: Die Musikdramen. Hamburg 1971.

"Richard Wagners Teilnahme am Dresdener Maiaufstand und seine

Flucht nach Zürich," in: *Neue Zürcher Zeitung,* CXVIII, Nr. 34, 19. November 1898.

Richard Wagner-Handbuch, ed. by Ulrich Müller, Peter Wapnewski. Stuttgart 1986.

Dokumente zur Geschichte des Bürgermeisters Hans Waldmann, ed. by Ernst Gagliardi, 2 vols. Basel 1911.

Robert C. Walton: Zwingli's Theocracy. Toronto 1967.

Peter Wapnewski: Der traurige Gott: Richard Wagner in seinen Helden. Munich 1978.

Peter Wapnewski: Tristan, der Held Richard Wagners. Berlin 1981.

Wolfgang von Wartburg: Zürich und die Französische Revolution. Basel 1956.

Wolfgang von Wartburg: "Zur Weltanschauung und Staatslehre des frühen schweizerischen Liberalismus," in: *Schweizerische Zeitschrift für Geschichte,* VIII (1959), 1ff.

Frank Wedekind: Gesammelte Briefe, ed. by Fritz Strich, I. Munich 1924.

Leo Weisz: Persönlichkeit und Zeitung. I: Die Redaktoren der Neuen Zürcher Zeitung. Zürich 1961.

Leo Weisz: Persönlichkeit und Zeitung. II: Die Neue Zürcher Zeitung im Kampfe der Liberalen mit den Radikalen, 1849–1872. Zürich 1962.

Oskar Weltli: Zürich-Baden, die Wiege der schweizerischen Eisenbahnen. Zürich 1946.

Walter Wettstein: Die Regeneration des Kantons Zürich. Die liberale Umwälzung der dreißiger Jahre, 1830–1839. Zürich 1907.

Lothar Wickert: Theodor Mommsen. Eine Biographie, III: Wanderjahre. Frankfurt am Main 1969.

Lothar Wickert, ed.: Theodor Mommsen and Otto Jahn. Briefwechsel 1842–1868. Frankfurt am Main 1962.

Sigmund Widmer: Zürich. Eine Kulturgeschichte, IX: Aufschwung mit dem Liberalismus. Zürich 1982.

Sigmund Widmer: Illustrierte Geschichte der Schweiz. Zürich 1973–77.

Peter Weide: Wilhelm Rüstow, 1821 bis 1878. Diss. Munich 1957.

Eliza Wille: Fünfzehn Briefe Richard Wagners mit Erinnerungen und Erläuterungen. Munich 1935.

Wydler, Leben und Briefwechsel von Albrecht Rengger, 2 vols. ed. by Ferdinand Wydler. Zürich 1847.

Zürich: Geschichte einer Stadt, ed. by Robert Schneebeli. Zürich 1986.

—Antiquarische Gesellschaft in Zürich, 1832–1952, Festgabe zum

150jährigen Bestehen, Mitteilungen der Antiquarischen Gesellschaft, XLI. Zürich 1982.

—Vom Variété zum neuen Schauspielhaus. Die Geschichte des Schauspiels in Zürich, ed. by Neues Schauspiel AG. Zürich 1978.

—Die Universität Zürich 1833–1933 und ihre Vorlaufer, ed. by Ernst Gagliardi, Hans Nabholz et al. Zürich 1938.

S. Zurlinden: Hundert Jahre. Bilder aus der Geschichte der Stadt Zürich in der Zeit von 1814 bis 1914, 2 vols. Zürich 1914.

INDEX

♦

Zürich 1850